MACMILLAN MSM SECONDARY MATHEMATICS

BOOK 1

Graham Newman
Head of Mathematics, Prestwich High School, Bury,
and Chief Examiner in GCSE Mathematics

Ken Taylor
Head of Mathematics, The Grange School,
Shrewsbury

Macmillan Secondary Mathematics Series Editor:
Dr Charles Plumpton

MACMILLAN

First edition 1990

Published by
MACMILLAN EDUCATION LTD
Houndmills, Basingstoke, Hampshire RG21 2XS
and London
Companies and representatives
throughout the world

Cover design by Plum Books, Southampton

Printed in Hong Kong

British Library Cataloguing in Publication Data
Newman Graham
Macmillan secondary mathematics.
Bk. 1.
1. Mathematics
I. Title   II. Taylor, Ken
510
ISBN 0–333–34606–8

10   9   8   7   6   5   4
00   99 98 97 96 95 94 93 92 91

The authors and publishers wish to thank the following for
permission to use copyright material:

The Automobile Association for the reproduction of maps from
AA Handbook 1986/7. Copyright © The Automobile
Association; British Railways Board for the reproduction of a
timetable with Intercity logo; The Controller of Her Majesty's
Stationery Office for the Ordnance Survey Outdoor Leisure Map,
1:25000. Crown Copyright reserved; Geographers' A–Z Map
Company Ltd and Ordnance Survey for material from *A–Z Atlas
of Manchester*. Crown Copyright reserved; Greater Manchester
Passenger Transport Executive for timetable information;
Guinness Publishing Ltd for ten facts from *The Guinness Book of
Records 1989*. Copyright © 1988 by Guinness Publishing Ltd;
Independent Television Publications Ltd for a timetable from
T.V. Times.

Every effort has been made to trace all the copyright holders, but
if any have been inadvertently overlooked the publishers will be
pleased to make the necessary arrangement at the first
opportunity.

Cover picture copyright The Photo Source

Contents

Preface; v

1. Numbers; 1
Number patterns; Factors and multiples; Programmes; Prime numbers; Digits; Problems; Fibonacci sequence

2. Angles; 11
Turns; Degrees; Angle classification; Measuring angles; Calculations with angles; Angles and direction

3. Number work; 27
Money; Digits; Fractions; Sale time; Place value; Decimals; Calculators; Fraction solids

4. Sets; 39
Sets; Sorting sets; Set notation; Elements; Overlapping sets

5. Measure: length; 55
Measures of length; Mixing units

6. Operations; 65
Flow diagrams; Operations; Bodmas

7. Shape; 75
Looking at triangles; Angles in triangles; Angles in quadrilaterals; Looking at quadrilaterals

8. Algebra; 87
Function machines; Letters for numbers; Flow charts; Substitution; Simplifying expressions; Simple expressions

9. Area and perimeter; 99
Area; Perimeter; Tiling; Using formulas

10. Directed numbers; 111
Starting points; Temperatures; Temperature changes; Temperature differences; Equalities; Inequalities; Missing numbers; Limits

11. Coordinates; 123
Maps; Road maps; Drawing maps; Ordnance Survey maps; Positive coordinates; Move and draw; Positive and negative coordinates; Lines; Using letters

12. Measure: capacity and mass; 141
Capacity; Mass; Scales and dials

13. Symmetry; 149
Line symmetry; Coordinates; Rotational symmetry; Plane symmetry; Rotating solids

14. Statistics; 159

Collecting data; Grouped data; Bar charts; A data base; Pictograms; Bar charts and grouped data; Interpretation of graphs and charts

15. Maps and bearings; 177

Mapwork; Bearings; Maps; Scales; Bearings and scales; Planning journeys; Mileage charts

16. Time and timetables; 191

Time; 24-hour clocks; Using time

17. Volumes and nets; 201

Volumes; Formulas; Packing; Nets; Packaging

18. Equations; 213

Finding the unknown; Balancing equations; Solving equations; Rearranging equations; Brackets; Getting the order right; Harder equations

19. Tiles and tessellations; 227

Tiles and tessellations

Preface

This book forms part of the Macmillan Secondary Mathematics Series, which has been written to correspond to the National Criteria for GCSE Mathematics examinations, and to the Mathematics National Curriculum assessment and testing framework. Books 1 and 2 have been written to provide work for pupils of all abilities, and in preparation for either the X or Y stream of books in the series.

Book 1 contains some revision of topics covered at Key Stages 1 and 2, which should help consolidate this work, and further extend the skills which have already been used. Each chapter has been broken down into a number of concise sections to ease pupils' progress through a topic. The sections contain worked examples and sets of graded exercises. In addition there are many mathematics investigations which can be used to supplement skills learnt, and offer extensions to the exercises. Each chapter ends with a revision exercise which will provide additional practice if needed.

In terms of the National Curriculum, the work covered in Book 1 corresponds with levels 3–5, including some work at levels 1 and 2, and covers both the profile components, attributing weight corresponding to the weightings given in the attainment targets. This book has been written specifically for students in Year 7. Examples used are in the context of 'using and applying mathematics', and are in realistic contexts of everyday life at home and at work, within today's multicultural society.

1. NUMBERS

B.C.

300
200
100
0
100
200
300
400
500
600
700
800
900
1000
1100
1200
1300
1400
1500
1600
1700
1800
1900
2000

A.D.

ERATOSTHENES of ALEXANDRIA (c. 276-194 B.C.)

A brilliant mathematician, a poet and a geographer. He was a friend of Archimedes. He used mathematics and shadows cast by the sun to prove that the earth is curved. He developed his 'sieve' for finding **Prime Numbers** (SEE PRIME NUMBERS, INVESTIGATION B

LEONARDO FIBONACCI (SON OF BONACCI) OR LEONARDO DA PISA (1170 – 1250)

Wrote the book 'Liber Abaci' in 1202 A.D. He adopted the HINDU-ARABIC system of mathematical notation. His work covered arithmetic and algebra- a standard text of the time. Other books covered geometry and trigonometry. He is more widely known for his **Fibonacci Sequence** of numbers. (SEE THE FIBONACCI INVESTIGATIONS ON P. 9)

KARL FRIEDERICH GAUSS from Brunswick · Germany (1777 – 1855)

One of the three greatest mathematicians of all time, along with Archimedes and Newton. He mastered many languages and was an astronomer. At the age of ten he discovered a quick method of finding the sum of the digits from 1 to 1000. (SEE INVESTIGATION B ON THE PROBLEMS PAGE)

$$1+2+3+...+999+1000 ?$$

Number patterns

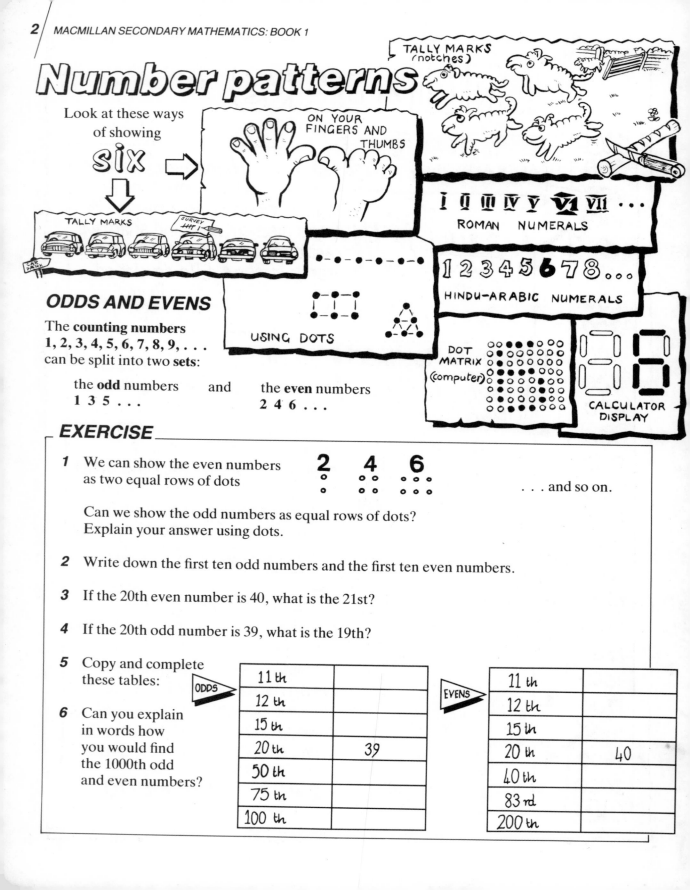

Look at these ways
of showing

six ⟹

ON YOUR
FINGERS AND
THUMBS

TALLY MARKS
(notches)

I II III IV V VI VII ...
ROMAN NUMERALS

TALLY MARKS

SURVEY

1 2 3 4 5 6 7 8 ...
HINDU-ARABIC NUMERALS

USING DOTS

ODDS AND EVENS

The **counting numbers**
1, 2, 3, 4, 5, 6, 7, 8, 9, . . .
can be split into two **sets**:

DOT
MATRIX
(computer)

CALCULATOR
DISPLAY

the **odd** numbers   and   the **even** numbers
1 3 5 . . .   2 4 6 . . .

EXERCISE

1 We can show the even numbers   **2**   **4**   **6**
    as two equal rows of dots   ° ° °   ° ° °

    . . . and so on.

Can we show the odd numbers as equal rows of dots?
Explain your answer using dots.

2 Write down the first ten odd numbers and the first ten even numbers.

3 If the 20th even number is 40, what is the 21st?

4 If the 20th odd number is 39, what is the 19th?

5 Copy and complete
    these tables:

6 Can you explain
    in words how
    you would find
    the 1000th odd
    and even numbers?

ODDS ▷

11 th	
12 th	
15 th	
20 th	39
50 th	
75 th	
100 th	

EVENS ▷

11 th	
12 th	
15 th	
20 th	40
40 th	
83 rd	
200 th	

Investigation A

DOT PATTERNS

Look at these dot patterns:

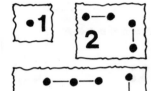

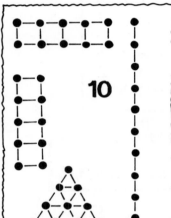

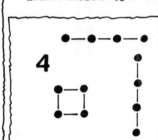

We can see from these patterns that:

all numbers can be shown as a **line**
4 and 10 can be **rectangles**
3 and 10 can be **triangles**
4 can be a **square**

(*a*) Draw dot patterns for all counting numbers from 1 to 16.

(*b*) Record your results in a table like this . . .

Number	Rectangle	Triangle	Square
1			
2	✗	✗	✗
3	✗	✓	✗
4	✓	✗	✓
. . .			
10	✓	✓	✗
. . .			
16			

Complete the table for all the counting numbers 1 to 16.

(*c*) Write down the first ten square numbers.

(*d*) Write down how you can work out the 20th square number.

(*e*) Write down the first ten triangle numbers.

(*f*) Explain how you found each triangle number.

Investigation B

ODD SQUARES

$16 = 4 \times 4 = 4^2$ or '4-squared'

16 ⟹ [dot pattern] ⟹ $16 = 1 + 3 + 5 + 7$

Using dots
(*a*) Represent the first ten square numbers in a similar way.

(*b*) How many consecutive odd numbers (starting with 1) need to be added to make these square numbers?

400   900   1600

Factors and multiples

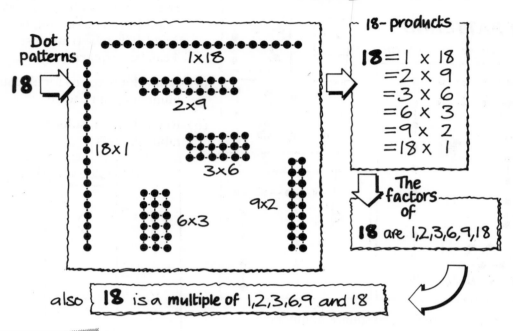

The factors of **18** are 1,2,3,6,9,18

also **18** is a multiple of 1,2,3,6,9 and 18

Investigation

Here is a dot pattern for 24.

So   the 24-**product** is $3 \times 8 = 24$
      two **factors** of 24 are 3 and 8
and   24 is a **multiple** of 3 and of 8.

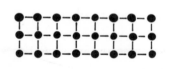

(a) Use dot patterns to find other products equal to 24.

(b) Use your products to find other factors of 24.

(c) Of which numbers is 24 a multiple?

(d) Using dot patterns, find the factors of 12, 15, and 28.

EXERCISE

1 Using products, find the factors of

8, 10, 16, 17, 20, 22, 30, 32, 56, 64

2 What name do we use for the multiples of 2?

3 Which number is a factor of all whole numbers?

4 Of which numbers is 12 a multiple?

5 Find the factors of all the numbers from 1 to 30.

Programs

1

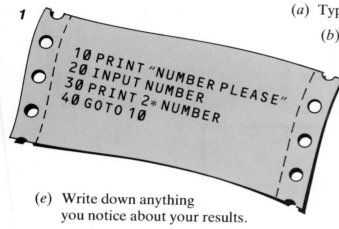

```
10 PRINT "NUMBER PLEASE"
20 INPUT NUMBER
30 PRINT 2 * NUMBER
40 GOTO 10
```

(a) Type this program into a computer.

(b) RUN the program.

(c) Type in a different number each time you are asked for one.

(d) Make a list or a table of your results:

Input	Output
6	12
20	. . .
.	.
.	.
.	.

(e) Write down anything you notice about your results.

2 Write down what happens when you change line 30 of the program to
(a) 30 PRINT 3 * NUMBER
(b) 30 PRINT 4 * NUMBER
Write down your results in each case.

3 Change the program so that it will print out multiples of
(a) 10   (b) 7   (c) 12   (d) 33   (e) 337

4 Investigate the output of this program:

As you RUN the program, record your results.

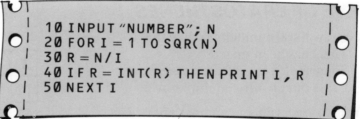

```
10 INPUT "NUMBER"; N
20 FOR I = 1 TO SQR(N)
30 R = N / I
40 IF R = INT(R) THEN PRINT I , R
50 NEXT I
```

5 Decide what type of numbers these programs generate:

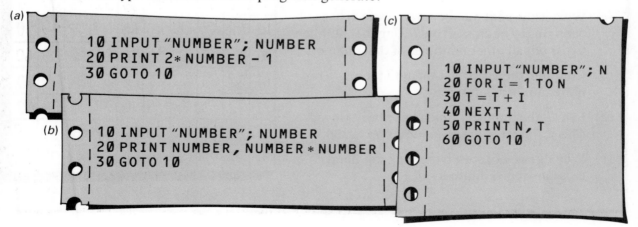

(a)
```
10 INPUT "NUMBER"; NUMBER
20 PRINT 2 * NUMBER – 1
30 GOTO 10
```

(b)
```
10 INPUT "NUMBER"; NUMBER
20 PRINT NUMBER , NUMBER * NUMBER
30 GOTO 10
```

(c)
```
10 INPUT "NUMBER"; N
20 FOR I = 1 TO N
30 T = T + I
40 NEXT I
50 PRINT N , T
60 GOTO 10
```

Prime numbers

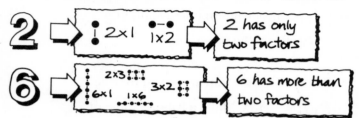

Investigation A

(a) Look at the work you have completed so far and list the numbers from 1 to 30 which are prime numbers.

(b) Say why these are *not* prime numbers
4 12 30 18 27

(c) One of these numbers is not a prime number: 333, 337. Explain your answer.

2 is a **prime** number

6 is not a **prime** number

Investigation B

SIEVE OF ERATOSTHENES

(a) Draw a 100 number grid like this:
The 2 has been ringed.
Some multiples of 2 are crossed out.
Cross out all other multiples of 2.

(b) The next available number after 2 is 3.
Ring the 3. Cross out all other multiples of 3.

(c) What is the next number after 3 which has not been ringed or crossed out? Ring that number. Cross out all other multiples of that number.

(d) Continue the investigation until there are no more numbers left to ring.

(e) List all the numbers which have been ringed. This is the **set of prime numbers up to 100**.

(f) Why did we not start by ringing the 1 and crossing out all multiples of 1?

1	2	3	4	5	6	7	8	9	10
11	12	13	14	15	16	17	18	19	20
21	22	23	24	25	26	27	28	29	30
31	32	33	34	35	36	37	38	39	40
41	42	43	44	45	46	47	48	49	50
51	52	53	54	55	56	57	58	59	60
61	62	63	64	65	66	67	68	69	70
71	72	73	74	75	76	77	78	79	80
81	82	83	84	85	86	87	88	89	90
91	92	93	94	95	96	97	98	99	100

Digits

Investigation A

Use a calculator if you need to

LAST DIGIT CHECK

(a) Choose any whole number.
Multiply the number by 2.
Is your number odd or even?
Try as many odd or even numbers
as you need to.
Comment on your results.

(b) Choose any even number.
Multiply it by 5.
Choose four other even
numbers and multiply each
one by 5.
What do you notice about
the *last digit* in each answer?
Choose any five odd
numbers and repeat the
activity.

(c) Choose any whole number.
Multiply the number by 10. Try at
least five other numbers. What do
you notice about the *last digit* of
each answer? Without a calculator,
write down the answers to
(i) 6 × 10
(ii) 9 × 10
(iii) 10 × 10
(iv) 15 × 10
(v) 23 × 10
(vi) 65 × 10
(vii) 371 × 10
(viii) 10 × 1061
(ix) 10 × 9099
(x) 641 372 × 10

EXERCISE 1

Say which of these numbers
are divisible by 2, 5 or 10

65, 32, 64, 70, 1300, 1302,
632, 835, 1915, 1000.

EXERCISE 2

1 Investigate the digit sums of multiples of 3.

2 How could you check for a multiple of 6?

·3 What can you say about these numbers

15, 64, 17, 60, 38, 83, 121, 47, 33, 95,
1062, 4440, 9113, 6666

Investigation B

DIGIT SUMS

(a) Use a calculator to show
that 2889 is a multiple of 9.

(b) Then, follow this flow chart

2889

Add the digits
2 + 8 + 8 + 9 = 27

Add the digits
2 + 7 = 9

The *digit sum* of 2889 is 9.

(c) Try other multiples of 9.

(d) Try numbers which are *not* multiples of 9.

(e) Which of these numbers are multiples of 9?

1999   22041   3037   59321   681093

Problems

Investigation A

GRID FACTORS

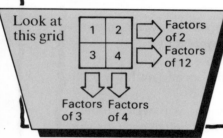

Look at this grid

1	2
3	4

→ Factors of 2
→ Factors of 12

↓ ↓
Factors of 3   Factors of 4

Each row and column can be factors of other numbers. We are choosing the *lowest* possible number.

Describe each row and column of these grids in the same way.

(a)
1	2
4	3

(b)
1	3
4	2

(c)
1	2	3
4	5	6
7	8	9

(d)
1	2	3
8	9	4
7	6	5

(e)
1	2	4
3	5	7
6	8	9

(f)
1	6	3
9	5	7
4	8	2

Investigation B

Karl Friederich Gauss (1777–1855)

When he was aged 10 years, he was asked by his teacher to add together a sequence of consecutive whole numbers starting at 1. His teacher was surprised when he gave the correct answer very quickly.

His quick method enabled him to find the sum of the consecutive whole numbers from 1 to 10, 1 to 100, 1 to 1000, and so on, in a short time.

Can you find a quick method?

Gauss – a triangle number problem

(a)   Add together $1 + 2 + 3 + 4 + 5 + 6$.

(b)   Add $(1 + 6), (2 + 5), (3 + 4)$.

(c)   Comment on your answers to (a) and (b).

(d)   Pair off these numbers to find the sum of
$$1 + 2 + 3 + 4 + 5 + 6 + 7 + 8 + 9 + 10$$

(e)   Use 'pairing off' to work out the sums of integers from
1 to 20   1 to 30   1 to 100   1 to 1000

Investigation C

HIDDEN SCORE

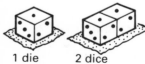

1 die
6 hidden

2 dice
3 + 6 + 4 + 6 hidden

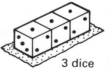

3 dice

Identical dice are set out as shown. They are all the same way around. Some faces are hidden on the bottom or between the dice.

Investigate the total scores *not visible* on the dice.
Note: the 5 *is* visible on each of the dice.
Copy and complete the table:

Number of dice	Hidden score
1	6
2	19
3	
4	
5	
10	
20	
50	
	2606

Fibonacci sequence

Investigation A

RECTANGLES

Look at the sequence of diagrams right.
The next diagram is drawn by adding a square.
Look at the pattern of squares.
What size square do we add next?
Where do we draw the next square?

The dot in a circle on the new square is
diagonally opposite the previous dot in a circle.

(a) The squares have sides 1, 1, 2, 3, 5, ...
Continue this sequence.

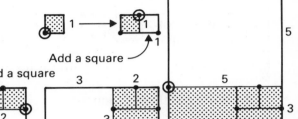

(b) Continue the diagrams and the
sequence of dots on the corners.

(c) Join the 1st dot to the 2nd dot to the
3rd . . . with a smooth, curved line.

Investigation B

TREES

A particular tree only
produces new branches on
'old wood'.

Look at the tree diagrams and
see if you can continue the
growth of the trees.

Write down how many
branches there are at each
stage.

Stage	1	2	3	4	5	6

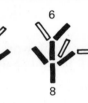

| Branches | 1 | 1 | 2 | 3 | 5 | 8 |

─Key─
The new wood is
shown as
The old wood is
shown as

Stage 7

How many branches?

PROGRAMS

```
10 A = 1
20 B = 1
30 PRINT A , B
40 C = A + B
50 PRINT C
60 A = B
70 B = C
80 GOTO 40
```

1 Type and RUN this program on a computer.

2 Record the print out.

3 Record the print out when you change these
lines:
(a) 20 B = 3 (b) 10 A = 3 (c) 10 A = 2
20 B = 4   20 B = 5

Revision exercise

1 Say whether each of these numbers is odd or even: 15, 37, 624, 1006, 2939.

2 This is a dot pattern of 36.   Is 36 (*a*) a square number, (*b*) a triangle number?

(*c*) Draw as many dot patterns for 36 as you can.

3 Work out these products:

(*a*) 5×12 (*b*) 4×15 (*c*) 20×3 (*d*) 1×60

What do you notice? Which products are missing?

4 Use products to find the factors of:
(*a*) 36   (*b*) 60   (*c*) 100   (*d*) 39   (*e*) 40

5 Write down which of the numbers:

16, 37, 40, 55, 59, 79, 81, 105, 116, 3000

are divisible by (*a*) 2   (*b*) 5   (*c*) 10.

6 Try to work out what each of these programs does to the number 15.

Explain in words what you think each program does.

(a)
```
10 INPUT NUMBER
20 PRINT 5*NUMBER
30 END
```

(b)
```
10 INPUT NUMBER
20 PRINT NUMBER ÷ NUMBER
30 END
```

7 Find the next three numbers in each sequence:

(*a*) 1, 2, 3, 4, . . . , . . . , . . . ,   (*b*) 1, 2, 3, 5, . . . , . . . , . . . ,

(*c*) 1, 2, 4, 7, . . . , . . . , . . . ,   (*d*) 1, 2, 4, 8, . . . , . . . , . . . ,

(*e*) 1, 2, 5, 10, . . . , . . . , . . . ,   (*f*) 1, 3, 7, 13, . . . , . . . , . . . ,

(*g*) 1, 4, 9, 16, . . . , . . . , . . . ,   (*h*) 1, 3, 6, 10, . . . , . . . , . . . ,

Explain in words how you continue each sequence.

8 Continue this pattern by looking at the *differences* between adjacent numbers.

Can you now extend the original sequence?

1		4		10		20		35		56		84		120
	3		6		10	...	...	...	...	...	...	...	...	
		3		4	...	...	...	...	...	...	...	...		
			1	...	...	...	...	...	...	...				

2. Angles

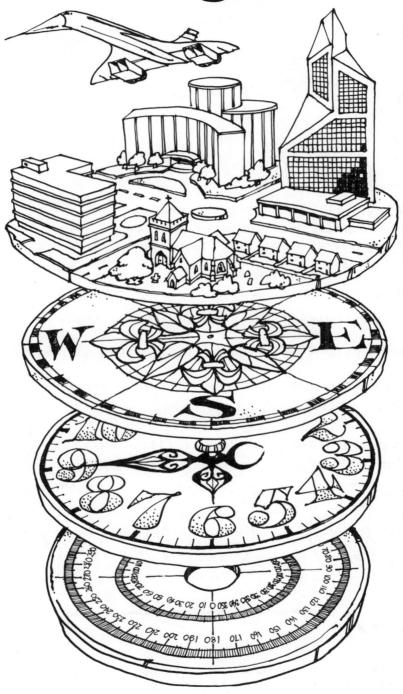

Turns

Tom and his friends are on an amusement ride.
Every few seconds they are turned around and their
positions are changed:

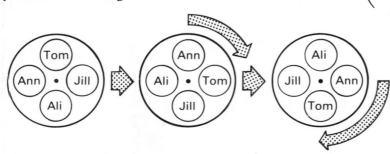

The point at the centre of the ride is the **centre of rotation**.
They are turning through $\frac{1}{4}$ turns or **right angles**. After two
$\frac{1}{4}$ turns Tom is facing the opposite way. Two $\frac{1}{4}$ turns make
a $\frac{1}{2}$ turn.

EXERCISE 1

1 After how many $\frac{1}{4}$ turns will Tom be back at his starting position?

2 After how many $\frac{1}{4}$ turns will Tom have moved around the ride twice?

3 Draw the positions of Tom and his friends after this number of $\frac{1}{4}$ turns:

(*a*) 3 (*b*) 6 (*c*) 8 (*d*) 11 (*e*) 17 (*f*) 20

4 Give three possible answers for the number of $\frac{1}{4}$ turns needed to reach
each of these positions:

(*a*)
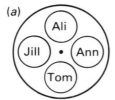

(*b*)
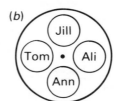

(*c*)
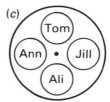

Investigation A

In how many different positions could Tom and his friends sit?
In how many different positions could 5 people sit in the ride?

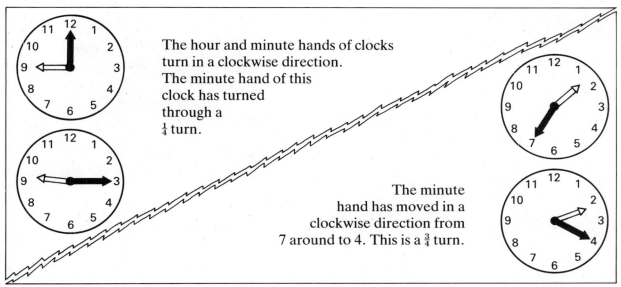

The hour and minute hands of clocks turn in a clockwise direction. The minute hand of this clock has turned through a ¼ turn.

The minute hand has moved in a clockwise direction from 7 around to 4. This is a ¾ turn.

EXERCISE 2

1 Describe the turn in moving the minute hand from:
(*a*) 3 to 6   (*b*) 8 to 2   (*c*) 1 to 10   (*d*) 2 to 11   (*e*) 9 to 3   (*f*) 5 to 5   (*g*) 7 to 4

2 What is the turn made by the minute hand after:
(*a*) 1 hour   (*b*) 15 minutes   (*c*) 3 hours   (*d*) 1 day   (*e*) 20 minutes?

3 How many minutes have elapsed after:
(*a*) ¾ turn   (*b*) 1½ turns   (*c*) $\frac{1}{60}$ turn   (*d*) ⅓ turn   (*e*) $\frac{1}{12}$ turn   (*f*) ⅙ turn?

4 Write down where the minute hand stops if:

Investigation B

When a minute hand has made one complete turn, by what fraction has the hour hand turned? During a day, how many turns are made by

(*a*) the hour hand
(*b*) the minute hand
(*c*) the second hand?

(*a*)   it starts at 3 and makes ½ turn

(*b*)   it starts at 7 and makes ¼ turn

(*c*)   it starts at 10 and makes ¾ turn

(*d*)   it starts at 1 and makes ¼ turn

(*e*)   it starts at 5 and makes ⅓ turn

(*f*)   it starts at 4 and makes 1½ turns

(*g*)   it starts at 3 and makes ⅔ turn

(*h*)   it starts at 12 and makes ½ turn

(*i*)   it starts at 1 and makes ⅙ turn

(*j*)   it starts at 6 and makes $\frac{5}{12}$ turn.

Degrees

A complete turn is divided into 360 degrees
(written as 360°).
This is a compass rose used by sailors
to navigate the world's oceans.

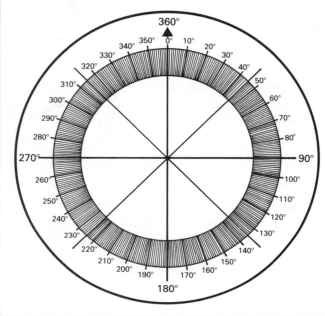

Directions can also be given
in terms of compass points.

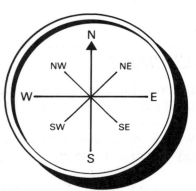

EXERCISE 1

How many degrees are there in each of the following?

1 $\frac{1}{4}$ turn	**2** $\frac{3}{4}$ turn	**3** $\frac{1}{2}$ turn	**4** $\frac{1}{8}$ turn	**5** $\frac{1}{10}$ turn
6 $\frac{3}{8}$ turn	**7** $\frac{3}{10}$ turn	**8** $\frac{7}{8}$ turn	**9** $\frac{9}{10}$ turn	**10** $\frac{7}{10}$ turn
11 $\frac{5}{8}$ turn	**12** $\frac{1}{16}$ turn	**13** $\frac{3}{16}$ turn	**14** $\frac{1}{12}$ turn	**15** $\frac{11}{12}$ turn

Compare the two types of compass, and find how many
degrees there are between these compass points
(give two answers for each question):

16 N and E	**17** W and S	**18** NE and SE	**19** SW and N	**20** W and SE
21 NE and E	**22** N and NE	**23** NW and SE	**24** W and E	**25** W and SW

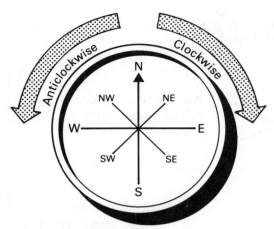

Turns are described as being in the **clockwise** direction, or the **anticlockwise** direction.

EXERCISE 2

In which direction will you be facing if you start at:

1 North and move $\frac{1}{4}$ turn clockwise

2 East and move $\frac{1}{2}$ turn anticlockwise

3 SW and move $\frac{3}{4}$ turn anticlockwise

4 NW and move 90° clockwise

5 SE and move 270° clockwise

6 SW and move 135° anticlockwise

7 N and move $\frac{3}{8}$ turn anticlockwise

8 South and move 45° clockwise

9 SW and move $\frac{1}{4}$ turn anticlockwise

10 East and move $\frac{1}{8}$ turn clockwise

Angle classification

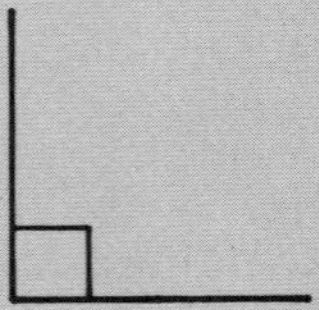

A $\frac{1}{4}$ turn is exactly 90°

and is shown in a diagram by

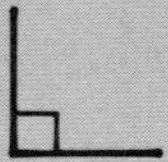

A 90° angle we call a right-angle. If you look around you will see many right-angles, as they are the angles most commonly met.

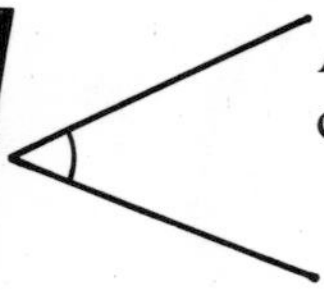

Any angle less than 90° we call an **acute** angle.

Any angle more than 90° we call an **obtuse** angle. This type of angle is less than 180°.

EXERCISE

Without measuring, write down the name you would give to each of the following angles:

1   2 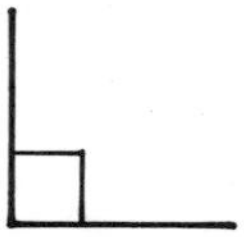   3 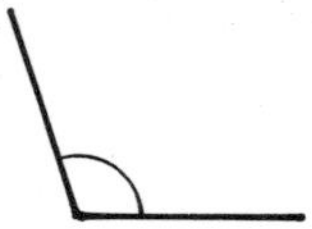   4

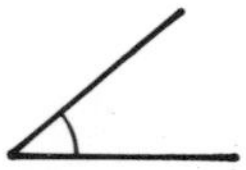

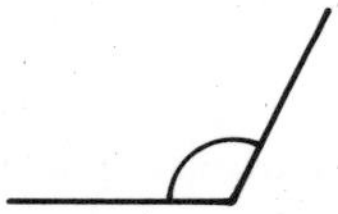

5    6 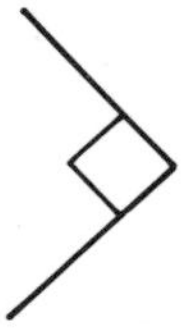   7 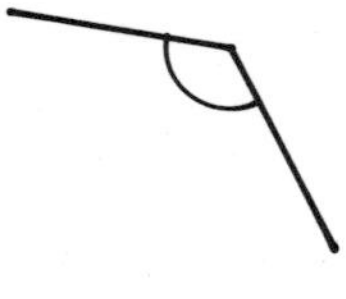   8

9 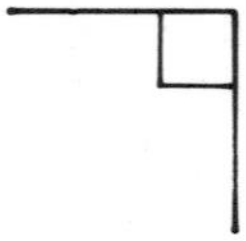   10 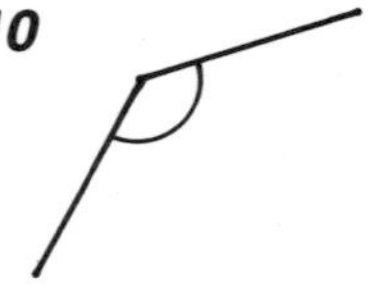   11    12

What type of angle is each of the following?

| **13** | 45° | **14** | 120° | **15** | 90° | **16** | 20° | **17** | 5° | **18** | 155° | **19** | 85° |
| **20** | 100° | **21** | 105° | **22** | 32° | **23** | 172° | **24** | 98° | **25** | 178° | | |

Measuring angles

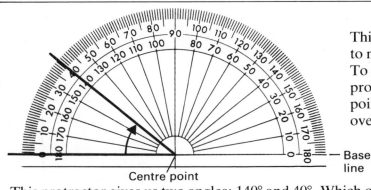

This is a 180° protractor which we use to measure angles.
To measure an angle we place the protractor with the centre point on the point of the angle, and the base line over one of the lines of the angle.

This protractor gives us two angles: 140° and 40°. Which one is correct?
The angle we are measuring is clearly an acute angle as it is less than 90°.
If the protractor gives us 140° and 40°, the angle cannot be 140°. It is therefore 40°.

EXERCISE 1

Copy and complete the table for each angle. Begin by making an estimate of the angle size before measuring the angle.

1

2

3

4

5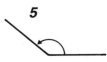

6

7

8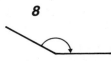

9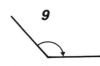

10

	Estimate	Measurement	Type of angle
1			
2			
3			
4			
5			
6			
7			
8			
9			
10			

EXERCISE 2

Draw the angles:

1	45°	**2**	90°	**3**	135°	**4**	105°	**5**	35°	**6**	60°
7	120°	**8**	170°	**9**	52°	**10**	73°	**11**	103°	**12**	15°
13	162°	**14**	88°	**15**	128°						

16 Using your protractor accurately draw this compass rose.

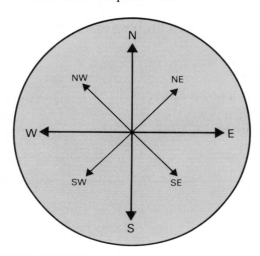

17 Draw these regular polygons.

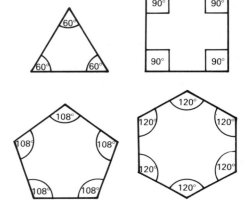

Keep all the sides equal.

How accurately can you draw an angle? In groups, choose and draw the same angle, then measure each other's angles. How accurately have the angles been drawn? How accurate are the protractors you are using? How do they compare?

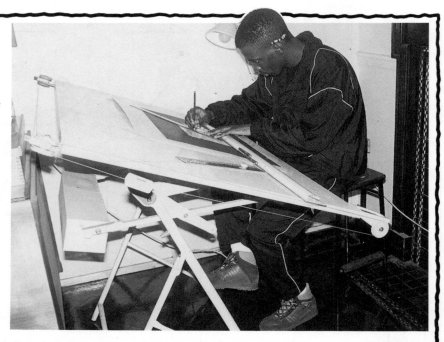

A **reflex** angle is more than 180°, but less than 360°.

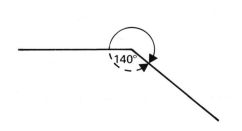

How do we measure a reflex angle with a protractor? *We don't!*

The angles at a point add up to 360°. If we measure the obtuse angle we can calculate the reflex angle.

The obtuse angle is 140°. So the reflex angle we want will be 360° − 140° = 220°.

EXERCISE 3

Measure these reflex angles.

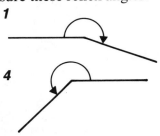

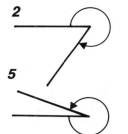

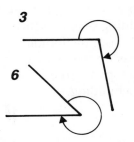

EXERCISE 4

Measure these angles.

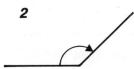

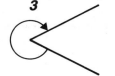

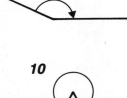

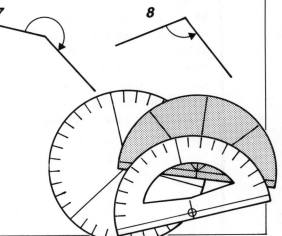

EXERCISE 5

Draw these angles:

1	200°	**2**	310°	**3**	285°	**4**	190°	**5**	365°
6	265°	**7**	330°	**8**	198°	**9**	237°	**10**	302°

Investigation B

Inclination is the angle measured to a horizontal level.
Can you use your protractor to make an inclinometer
to measure angles to the horizontal?
How can you tell when you are
holding your protractor horizontally?
Use your inclinometer to
measure the inclination of
the top of a tree,
or a building.

Investigation C

Measure the inclination of an
object as in Investigation B.
Move closer to the object and
measure the inclination again.
What has happened to the
angle? What happens to the
angle if you move further
away from the object? Can
you explain what you have
discovered?

Calculations with angles

ANGLE FACTS

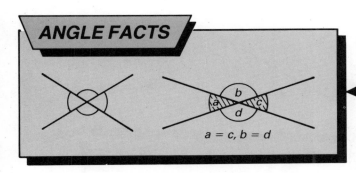

$a = c, b = d$

Draw two lines that cross, and measure all four angles.
Repeat the exercise with a different pair of lines.
You should find that the angles which are opposite each other are the same size.

Draw a 90° angle. Draw a line through the angle, and measure the angles formed. These two angles should add up to 90°. Any two angles which add up to 90° are called **complementary**.

$$a + b = 90°$$

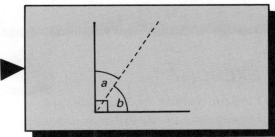

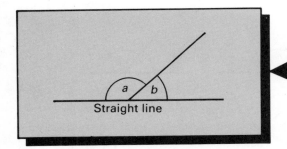

Straight line

Starting with a straight line, measure any pair of angles as shown. These two angles should add up to 180°. Any two angles which add up to 180° are called **supplementary**.

$$a + b = 180°$$

Any angles drawn on a straight line should add up to 180°

$$a + b + c = 180°$$

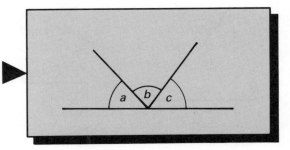

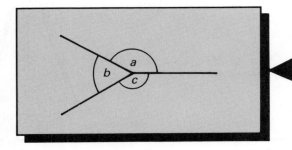

Any angles drawn to a point should add up to 360°.

$$a + b + c = 360°$$

Calculations

It is not always necessary to draw accurate diagrams in order to find missing angles. We can use the angle facts to help us.

The missing angle is 120°. (Vertically opposite angles are equal.)

The missing angle is 360° − 80° = 280° (Angles at a point add up to 360°.)

The missing angle is 180° − 30° = 150° (Angles on a straight line add up to 180°.)

EXERCISE 1

Find the missing angle in each case.
Do not use a protractor.

1
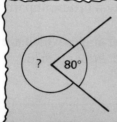
140°
?

2

50°
?

3
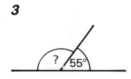
? 55°

4
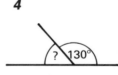
? 130°

5
65°
?

6

?
310°

7

?
30°

8
?
15°

9

65° ?

10
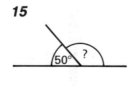
?
38°

11
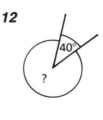
165°
?

12
40°
?

13
199°
?

14
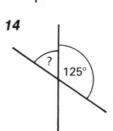
?
125°

15
50° ?

Inclinometer

EXERCISE 2

Find the missing angle in each case.

1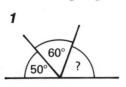

2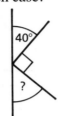

3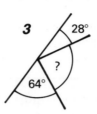

4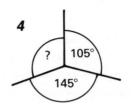

5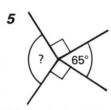

6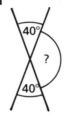

7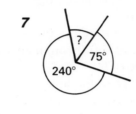

8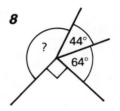

9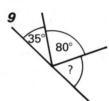

10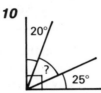

Use a calculator if you need to

EXERCISE 3

Find the value of *x* in each of the following.

1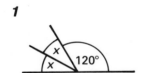

2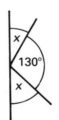

3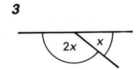

4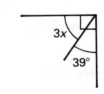

5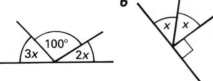

6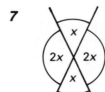

7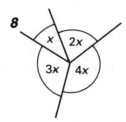

8

9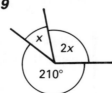

10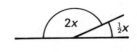

Angles and direction *EXTENSION*

We have already seen how angles can be used to indicate direction. A remote control pen is controlled by the following instructions:

FORWARD 100		To go forward 100 units, which is equivalent to 10 cm
RIGHT	90	To turn to the right (clockwise) through an angle of 90°
LEFT	90	To turn to the left (anticlockwise) through an angle of 90°

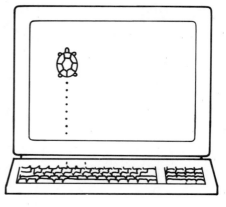

A square is drawn using the following instructions:

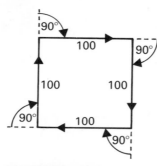

FORWARD 100
RIGHT 90
FORWARD 100
RIGHT 90
FORWARD 100
RIGHT 90
FORWARD 100
RIGHT 90

Since the same pair of instructions are repeated four times we have a shorter way of writing this:

REPEAT 4 [FORWARD 100 RIGHT 90]

EXERCISE

Follow these instructions, and draw the shape created by the remote control pen:

1 FORWARD 100
　　RIGHT 60
　　FORWARD 50

2 REPEAT 4 [FORWARD 50 RIGHT 90]
3 REPEAT 3 [FORWARD 100 RIGHT 120]
4 REPEAT 4 [FORWARD 50 RIGHT 60]

Investigation *A*

Can you write out a series of instructions to draw the regular polygons: pentagon (5 sides); octagon (8 sides); decagon (10 sides); dodecagon (12 sides)?

Investigation *B*

Make up some of your own pictures using these instructions.

Revision exercise

1 What fraction of a complete turn does the minute hand move through from
   (*a*) 5 to 8   (*b*) 6 to 12   (*c*) 1 to 10   (*d*) 4 to 6   (*e*) 9 to 10?

2 Write down where the minute hand stops if it

   (*a*)   starts at 2 and makes $\frac{1}{4}$ turn   (*b*)   starts at 5 and makes $\frac{3}{4}$ turn

   (*c*)   starts at 4 and makes $\frac{2}{3}$ turn   (*d*)   starts at 7 and makes $\frac{5}{6}$ turn.

3 How many degrees are there in (*a*) $\frac{1}{4}$ turn? (*b*) $\frac{1}{2}$ turn (*c*) $\frac{2}{3}$ turn (*d*) $\frac{1}{12}$ turn?

4 How many degrees are there between these compass points
   (give two answers for each)?

   (*a*) N and W   (*b*) NW and NE   (*c*) SE and S   (*d*) SW and E

5 Write down the name you would give to the following angles,
   which you should also draw:

   (*a*) 60°   (*b*) 205°   (*c*) 115°   (*d*) 80°   (*e*) 300°   (*f*) 155°

Find the missing angle in each case.

6 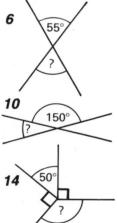   **7** 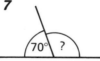   **8**   **9**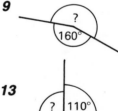

10 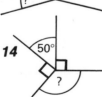   **11** 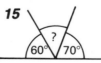   **12** 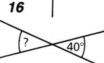   **13**

14   **15**   **16** 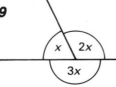   **17**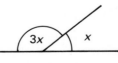

Find the value of *x* in each case.

18   **19**   **20**

3. Number work

A HALF OF A HALF OF A HALF OF A HALF = ONE SIXTEENTH

£2.15 HALF PRICE?

¼ of ⅓ of ½ of 'one whole' equals ¹/₂₄ of 'one whole'

Money

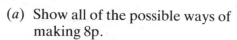

Investigation A

CHANGE

How many ways can you receive 7p in change from a shop assistant?

$$7p = \boxed{5p} + \boxed{2p} = \boxed{5p} + \boxed{1p} + \boxed{1p}$$

There are six ways altogether.

(a) Show all of the possible ways of making 8p.

(b) Find the *three* ways of making 17p in change using: 7 coins   8 coins   9 coins

(c) How many ways are there of making 17p?

Investigation B

MONEY PROBLEM

Anne has 8 pence. What can she buy so that she uses all her money?

4 × 2p raffle tickets	= 8p
1 × 5p bun + 1 × 3p biscuit	= 8p
2 × 3p biscuits + 1 × 2p raffle ticket	= 8p

(a) Anil has 11p and arrives when there are only 7p cakes and 3p biscuits left. Can he spend all his money?

(b) Sanya arrived when there were only drinks and biscuits. She had 19p. Could she spend all her money?

(c) Derek arrived with Sanya. Could he spend all his 25 pence?

(d) Show that 11p is the largest amount you cannot spend buying 7p cakes and 3p biscuits.

(e) Find the largest amount it is *not* possible to spend completely when the only items on sale are:

2p tickets	+	5p buns		
3p biscuits	+	5p buns		
3p biscuits	+	11p drinks		
2p tickets	+	11p drinks		

2p tickets	+	7p buns
7p buns	+	11p drinks
5p buns	+	7p cakes
5p buns	+	11p drinks

(f) Is there a quick way of working out the results to part (e)?

Digits

Investigation A

4–DIGITS   Using the digits **7, 5, 2, 0**, we can form these 4–digit numbers

7520   5027   2705   5702   2507   and others.

(*a*) Which of the numbers are
   (i) odd   (ii) even or   (iii) multiples of 5?

(*b*) Using the same digits write down
   (i) the smallest multiple of 10
   (ii) the smallest multiple of 2.

(*c*) Write down all the possible multiples of 5 using the same digits.

(*d*) How many 4-digit numbers are possible altogether not starting with zero?

Investigation B

SUMS AND DIFFERENCES

Using the digits 1, 2, 3, 4, we can write down

a sum of 2-digit numbers

$$\begin{array}{r} 1\,2\,+ \\ 3\,4 \\ \hline 4\,6 \end{array}$$

a difference of 2-digit numbers

$$\begin{array}{r} 3\,4\,- \\ 1\,2 \\ \hline 2\,2 \end{array}$$

(*a*) Use the same digits to make
   the *largest* possible sum
   the *smallest* possible sum
   the *largest* possible difference
   the *smallest* possible difference.

(*b*) Choose your own four digits and repeat (*a*).

(*c*) Using the digits 1, 2, 3, 4, 5, 6, write down the largest and smallest possible differences and sums of 3-digit numbers.

Investigation C

PRODUCTS

Using the digits 1, 2, 3, 4, we can write the products

$$\begin{array}{r} 123\times \\ 4 \\ \hline 492 \end{array} \quad \text{and} \quad \begin{array}{r} 12\times \\ 34 \\ \hline 408 \end{array}$$

(*a*) Use the same digits to find the
   largest product
   largest *odd* product
   smallest *even* product
   smallest product.

(*b*) Investigate the products using the digits

   1, 2, 3, 4, 5
   1, 2, 3, 4, 5, 6

Use a calculator if you need to

Fractions

Investigation A

SHAPES

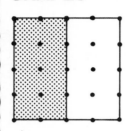

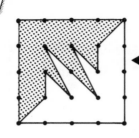

We write this as $\frac{1}{2}$ (one part out of two parts).

◀ Here are two more halves.

(a) Draw some grids of your own. Find some other ways of dividing the grids into two identical halves.

(b) The shaded sections below represent different fractions:

▲
This grid has been divided into two equal parts. Each section is called a **half**.

EXERCISE 1

1 Looking at the work you have done so far, write down how many $\frac{1}{4}$'s, $\frac{1}{8}$'s, $\frac{1}{16}$'s equal $\frac{1}{2}$ and $\frac{1}{4}$.

2 Copy and complete these:

(a) $\frac{1}{8} = \frac{}{16}$

(b) $1 = \frac{}{2} = \frac{}{4} = \frac{}{8} = \frac{}{16}$

3 By looking at the patterns of numbers, see if you can complete these:

(a) $\frac{1}{2} = \frac{}{4} = \frac{}{8} = \frac{}{16} = - = -$

(b) $\frac{1}{4} = \frac{}{8} = \frac{}{16} = -$

(c) $\frac{1}{2} = \frac{}{4} = \frac{}{6} = \frac{}{8} = - = - = - = \frac{}{16}$

4 The following are sets of marks in some tests. Write down which ones are *exactly* half marks, *more* than half marks or *less* than half marks.

$$\frac{10}{20}, \quad \frac{11}{20}, \quad \frac{4}{10}, \quad \frac{12}{30}, \quad \frac{37}{60}, \quad \frac{13}{25}, \quad \frac{49}{80}, \quad \frac{162}{300}$$

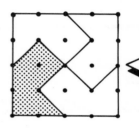

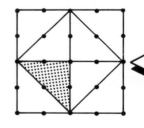

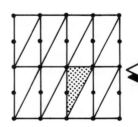

Find other $\frac{1}{4}$'s, $\frac{1}{8}$'s, and $\frac{1}{16}$'s of your own.

EXERCISE 2

1 Use the small shape to fill each larger shape.

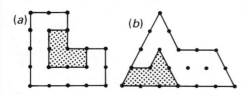 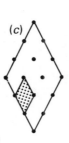 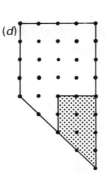 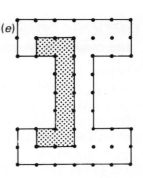

What fraction is the small shape of
the larger shape in each?
What fraction is not shaded in each?

2

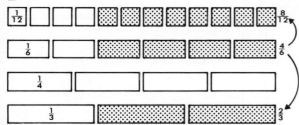

The 'fraction block' shows

$$\frac{4}{6} = \frac{8}{12} = \frac{2}{3}$$

Use the block to complete these:

(a) $\dfrac{1}{2} = \dfrac{}{4} = \dfrac{3}{} = \dfrac{}{12}$

(b) $\dfrac{9}{12} = \dfrac{}{4}$ (c) $\dfrac{2}{6} = \dfrac{1}{}$

(d) $\dfrac{1}{4} = \dfrac{}{}$ (e) $\dfrac{}{6} = \dfrac{1}{}$

3 Draw your own '24-fraction block' to help
you complete these:

(a) $\dfrac{4}{8} = \dfrac{}{24} = \dfrac{1}{} = \dfrac{}{6} = \dfrac{6}{} = \dfrac{}{4}$ (b) $\dfrac{2}{3} = \dfrac{}{12} = \dfrac{4}{}$

Investigation **B**

FRACTION DOMINOES – HARDER FRACTIONS

The 12 dominoes shown on the
right will all link together like this.

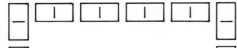

Match up the equivalent fractions.

$\frac{1}{2}$	$\frac{2}{5}$	$\frac{3}{8}$	$\frac{1}{4}$	$\frac{5}{8}$	$\frac{30}{50}$
$\frac{4}{12}$	$\frac{8}{12}$	$\frac{10}{16}$	$\frac{40}{100}$	$\frac{10}{80}$	$\frac{2}{3}$

$\frac{4}{5}$	$\frac{3}{4}$	$\frac{15}{20}$	$\frac{9}{24}$	$\frac{3}{5}$	$\frac{3}{12}$
$\frac{4}{20}$	$\frac{8}{10}$	$\frac{1}{8}$	$\frac{1}{3}$	$\frac{4}{8}$	$\frac{1}{5}$

It may help to look at these and complete them.

$$\frac{1}{5} = \frac{2}{10} = \frac{}{20} = \frac{}{40} = \frac{}{80} = \frac{20}{}$$

Sale time

GROCERY DEPARTMENT

The grocery section in a supermarket has reduced to half price some items which are close to their 'sell by' dates.

How much would you pay for them now? (All reduced items are on the list.)

GROCERY DEPT.

JUICE 60p
LEMONADE 30p
CRISPS 16p
CREAM 50p
CHOC BAR 20p
CAKES 18p
MILK 28p
SQUASH 36p
YOGURT 36p
PIZZA 56p
BREAD 80p
BREAD 48p

ELECTRICAL SHOP

SALE ½ MARKED PRICES

P.C. SYSTEM £520

1 ONLY MICROWAVE £180

WASHING MACHINE £400

HI·FI £390

½ PRICE
T.V. WAS £500 NOW £250

FRIDGE/FREEZER £250

Example
In this sale a TV is reduced to half of its price.

Was £500

$$\frac{1}{2} \text{ of } £500 = \frac{£500}{2} = £250$$

So to find *half* of something we *divide by 2*.

(*a*) Find the sale prices of the items in the shop window.

(*b*) In a previous sale the sign on the shop window was

'¼ OFF MARKED PRICES'.

What were the sale prices in the previous sale?

¼ OFF MARKED PRICES

EXAMPLE
The £500 TV
is reduced by ¼.
¼ of £500
= £500 ÷ 4
= £125
Sale price = £500 − £125 £375

FURNITURE STORE

⅓ OFF FURNITURE

PINE FURNITURE

DRESSER £240
MIRROR £60
WARDROBE £270
TABLE £90
BED £330

(*a*) Work out how much you would save on each item of furniture.

(*b*) Work out the sale prices of the furniture above.

Place value

ADDITION

François has to add together
432 and 747.
In words four-hundred and thirty-two
seven-hundred and forty-seven
He does it in his head in a strange way:

he adds the *hundreds* first and gets
400 + 700 = 1100
he then adds on the *tens*
1100 + 30 = 1130
1130 + 40 = 1170
then the *units*
1170 + 2 = 1172
1172 + 7 = 1179

This is how he would summarise his
addition:
400 + 700 → 1100 + 30 → 1130 + 40 →
1170 + 2 → 1172 + 7 → 1179

(a) Add the two numbers in as many
different ways as you can.
(b) Write down how you performed
each addition.

SUBTRACTION

François uses a similar method to
subtract the numbers 747 and 154.

He subtracts the *hundreds* first
700 − 100 = 600
then the *tens*
40 − 50 is awkward, so he
has to *owe* 10
The *units* give 7 − 4 = 3

He then has   600 + (he owes 10) + 3
= 603 less 10, which is 593.

(a) Subtract the two numbers in a
different way.

(b) Write down how you would do it in
your head.

EXERCISE 1

1   Either use François's method of adding or
your own to work out these in your head:

(a) 369+   (b) 632+   (c) 444+   (d) 629+
830   381   637   472

(e) 846+   (f) 345+   (g) 555+   (h) 789+
345   262   438   823
810   212   445

2   Write down how you added each set of
numbers together.

3   Write down the value of the highest digit in
each of the additions in question 1?

EXERCISE 2

1   Either use François's method or your own to
subtract these numbers in your head:

(a) 627 − 314   (b) 518 − 306   (c) 917 − 717

(d) 903 − 818   (e) 492 − 384   (f) 617 − 418

(g) 837 − 627   (h) 178 − 149   (i) 643 − 178

(j) 333 − 268
Write down how you subtracted each pair of
numbers.

2   Find the total weight of strawberries in boxes
(a) A + B   (b) B + C   (c) A + C
(d) A + B + C

3   For the strawberries in question 2, how much
heavier is
(a) box B than box A   (b) box C than box A
(c) box B than box C?

Decimals ×10

Investigation A

We can write 32p in different ways:

as 30p + 2p or 3 × 10p + 2p

as 3 × 10 = 30, which you should know.

(a) How many pence are there in
   (i) 5 × 10p   (ii) 7 × 10p   (iii) 4 × 10p
   (iv) 9 × 10p   (v) 10 × 10p   (vi) 12 × 10p
   (vii) 30 × 10p (viii) 24 × 10p (ix) 80 × 10p?

(b) Write down a *rule* for
   'multiplying a whole number by 10'.

Investigation B

How many 10p's are there in £5?

In £1 there are 10 × 10p, so in £5 there are

5 × (10 × 10p) = (5 × 10) × 10p = 50 × 10p

(a) How many 10p's are there in
   (i) £2   (ii) £3   (iii) £8   (iv) £15
   (v) £10   (vi) £20   (vii) £16   (viii) £81?

(b) Work out how many 20p's there are in
   (i) £1   (ii) £2   (iii) £5   (iv) £8
   (v) £10   (vi) £3   (vii) £7   (viii) £12

(c) Explain how you could use some answers
   in (a) to find some answers in (b).

 ÷10

How many 10p's are there in 60p?
60p = 6 × 10p, so 60p ÷ 10p = 6

(a) How many 10p's are there in
   (i) 30p   (ii) 50p (iii) 70p   (iv) 90p
   (v) 110p   (vi) 40p (vii) 150p (viii) 200p
   (ix) 360p?

(b) Write down a *rule* for
   'dividing a multiple of 10 by 10'.

Investigation C ×100

How many pence are there in £4?
In £1 there are 100p, so in £4 there are
   4 × 100p = 400p   so 4 × 100 = 400

(a) How many pence are there in
   (i) £5 (ii) £2 (iii) £7 (iv) £8 (v) £3
   (vi) £10 (vii) £9 (viii) £11 (ix) £20
   (x) £15 (xi) £30 (xii) £64?

(b) Write down a *rule* for
   'multiplying a whole number by 100'.

Investigation D

How many pence are there in £5.37?
In £5 there are 500p
We say £5.37 as five pounds and thirty-seven
pence, so we have

   500p + 37p = 537p

Note: £5.37 and 537p have the same digits.

(a) How many pence are there in
   (i) £2.40   (ii) £3.65   (iii) £6.82
   (iv) £7.77   (v) £8.43   (vi) £9.16
   (vii) £6.03 (viii) £4.01 (ix) £5.76?

CALCULATORS

(b) Multiply each amount by 100

   (a) £3.72 (b) £6.15   (c) £9.05
   (d) £6.72 (e) £8.44   (f) £10.71
   (g) £13.06 (h) £90.70

(c) Write down a *rule* for what happens to
   the decimal point when
   'a decimal number is multiplied by 100'.

(d) Multiply these decimals by 10

   (i) 6.35 (ii) 9.07 (iii) 11.46 (iv) 6.021

(e) Write down a *rule* for
   'multiplying a decimal number by 10'.

Investigation **E**

How many £s in 500p?

$$100p = £1$$
so $500p = £5$
so $500 ÷ 100 = 5$

$÷ 100$

(*a*) How many £s are there in
  (i) 600p (ii) 200p (iii) 700p
  (iv) 300p (v) 1000p (vi) 900p
  (vii) 1200p (viii) 400p (ix) 4300p?

(*b*) Write down a *rule* for
  'dividing a multiple of 100 by 100'.

Investigation **F**

How many £s in 537p?
We know that

$$500p = £5$$
and $537p = 500p + 37p = £5 + 37p = £5.37$

(*a*) Use a calculator to change these to £s
  (i) 537p (ii) 682p (iii) 126p (iv) 407p
  (v) 360p (vi) 977p (vii) 1003p (viii) 817p
  (ix) 293p (x) 36p (xi) 803p (xii) 540p

(*b*) Write down a *rule* for
  'dividing a whole number by 100'.

EXERCISE 1

Without using a calculator, work out
1 the number of pence in
  (*a*) £5.16 (*b*) £7.35 (*c*) £13 (*d*) £8.61 (*e*) £23 (*f*) £3.70 (*g*) £0.53 (*h*) £0.03

2 the number of £s in
  (*a*) 602p (*b*) 742p (*c*) 1600p (*d*) 819p (*e*) 1800p (*f*) 820p (*g*) 67p (*h*) 7p

3 (*a*) £7 × 10 (*b*) £12 × 100 (*c*) £60 × 100 (*d*) £36 × 10 (*e*) £25 × 10 (*f*) £17 × 100

4 (*a*) £8.35 × 10 (*b*) £19.30 × 100 (*c*) £24.33 × 10 (*d*) £4.26 × 100

5 (*a*) £835 ÷ 10 (*b*) £1930 ÷ 100 (*c*) £115 ÷ 100 (*d*) £45 ÷ 100

6 (*a*) 65 × 10 (*b*) 65 ÷ 10 (*c*) 65 × 100 (*d*) 6.5 ÷ 100 (*e*) 6.5 × 10
  (*f*) 0.65 × 100 (*g*) 6.5 × 100 (*h*) 0.65 × 10 (*i*) 6.5 ÷ 10 (*j*) 6.5 ÷ 100

ORDER

Write these amounts in order (highest first):
  38p, £3.6, £3.06, £0.36, £3.16

$£3.6 = 3.6 × 100p = 360p$
$£3.06 = 3.06 × 100p = 306p$
$£0.36 = 0.36 × 100p = 36p$
$£3.16 = 3.16 × 100p = 316p$

So, in order, the amounts are:
  £3.6, £3.16, £3.06, 38p, £0.36

EXERCISE 2

Order these

1 £4.07, £0.47, 36p, £4.70, £47, £3.06, 51p
2 315p, £3, £0.75, £4.6, £4.08, 303p, £0.07
3 0.32, 0.3, 6.7, 6.07, 6.17, 9.03, 9.2, 0.17
4 4.6, 5.7, 6.01, 6.1, 5.07, 4.66, 4.05, 6.74
5 £100.7, £103, £100.08, £130, £100.35

Calculators

GAMES

GAME 1   **Rules** ....2 Players
1   One of you type in a number less than 100.
2   Take turns to *add* a number to the total.
3   If your addition makes the total go over 100, then you lose.

GAME 2   **Rules** ....2 players
1   One of you type in a number less than 100.
2   Take turns to *multiply* the total by a number of your choice.
3   If you make the total go over 100, then you lose.

EXERCISE

1   See if you can write down a number smaller than

   (*a*) 0.1   (*b*) 0.01
   (*c*) 0.0001

2   Which of these is the smallest?

       0.00001, 0.000007,
       0.0000011

PROGRAM

What does this program do?

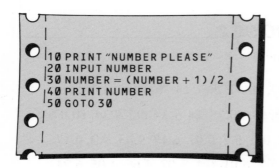

```
10 PRINT "NUMBER PLEASE"
20 INPUT NUMBER
30 NUMBER = (NUMBER + 1)/2
40 PRINT NUMBER
50 GOTO 30
```

RUN this program until you reach a conclusion.

FLOW CHART

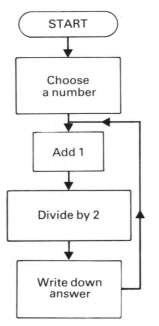

Use a calculator if you need to

Follow the flow chart, using any number to start with.
Stop when you think you have written down enough answers.
Repeat with different starting numbers.
What do you notice?

What happens if you start with a number less than 1 (say 0.5)?
Which 'start' number gives the same answer each time?

Fraction solids

CUBE SLICES

This cube has been sliced, but the two parts are not equal. So it has not been halved.

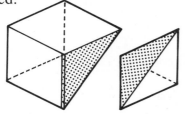

1 Which of these slices cut the cube in half?

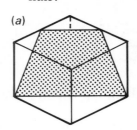

(*a*)

(*b*)

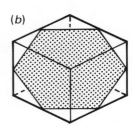

(*c*)

(*d*)

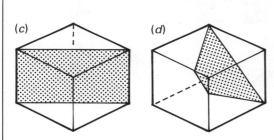

(*e*)

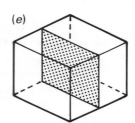

(*f*)

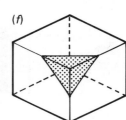

2 Draw other slices of cubes which *do* and *do not* cut the cube in half.

HALF-FULL

(*a*)

(*b*)

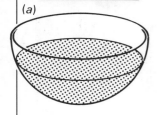

Only one of these containers is half full.

1 Which one is half-full?

2 Which are *over* half-full?

3 Which are *under* half-full?

4 Draw the containers without the 'liquid' and show how each could be sliced in half.

(*c*)

(*d*)

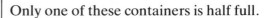

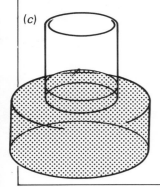

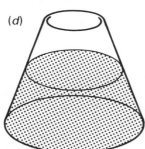

(*e*)

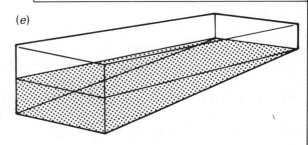

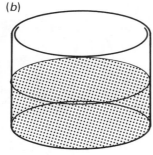

Revision exercise

1  A certain post office has only 3p and 8p stamps.

(*a*) What values of stamps can it *not* make using 3p and 8p combinations?

(*b*) What is the highest value the post office cannot make up?

2 Find the *two* ways of making 15p with (*a*) 6 coins　(*b*) 7 coins　(*c*) 8 coins

3 In each of these, say what fraction is (*a*) black　(*b*) shaded　(*c*) blank

4 Complete these 'equivalent' fractions

(*a*) $\dfrac{3}{10} = \dfrac{}{20} = \dfrac{}{40}$　　(*b*) $\dfrac{48}{64} = \dfrac{24}{} = \dfrac{}{16} = \dfrac{6}{} = \dfrac{}{4}$

5 Work out the '$\dfrac{1}{2}$ price' sale prices of these items which cost

(*a*) £4.60　(*b*) £9.80　(*c*) £24.50　(*d*) £11.30　(*e*) £16.20

6 What is the total mass of (*a*) 635 g and 857 g　(*b*) 731 kg and 129 kg?

7 How much longer is (*a*) 63 cm than 47 cm　(*b*) 437 mm than 285 mm?

8 Work out (*a*) 36×10　(*b*) 41×100　(*c*) £3.34 × 10
(*d*) £3.34 × 100　(*e*) £342 ÷ 10　(*f*) £342 ÷ 100

9 How many pence in (*a*) £6.07　(*b*) £4.4?

10 Place in order (highest first) 0.33, 0.4, 0.09, 0.11, 0.30, 0.86, 0.9

4. Sets

THE SET OF **LEGO** TECHNIC

Sets

A set is a collection of things which have something in common.

The set of numbers on a calculator

A set of mathematical instruments

The set of people in a family

We use the brackets { } to show a set.

{0, 1, 2, 3, 4, 5, 6, 7, 8, 9} = {numbers on a calculator}

The things which make up the set are called **elements**.

EXERCISE 1

1　What possible sets can we get from a calendar?

2　What sets could we get from within your school?

3　What sets are there connected with the pop music industry?

4　How is football divided into sets?

EXERCISE 2

Write out the elements of each set:

1　{colours of the rainbow}　　　　**2**　{daily national morning newspapers}

3　{continents of the world}　　　　**4**　{suits of cards}

5　{TV channels}　　　　　　　　**6**　{meals of the day}

7　{days in a week}　　　　　　　**8**　{vowels}

9　{British coins}　　　　　　　**10**　{points of the compass}

Investigation A

How many sets can you name? List the members of each set you write down. You might like to consider sets from people and objects around you, in your class, or at home.

EXERCISE 3

Describe each of the following sets:

1 { ITV, *BBC*1, TWO, 4 }

2 { BSB, SKY }

3 {+, −, ×, ÷}

4 { ☁, ☁, ☼, ⚡ }

5 { A41, B5142, M4 }

6 {mistletoe, holly, pudding, turkey}

7 {coffee, tea, chocolate}

8 {BBC, Amstrad, Sinclair, Nimbus, Apple}

9 {Rover, Metro, Maestro}

10 { M27, SE4, LA2, WA7, NW1, SK14 }

11 {Frosties, Toppers, Shreddies}

12 {Irish, North, Adriatic, Caspian}

13 {Sharp, Texas, Casio, Dixons}

14 {cod, haddock, plaice, whiting}

15 {Forties, Biscay, Dogger, Irish}

EXERCISE 4

List the members of the following sets:

1 {even numbers less than 10}

2 {odd numbers less than 10}

3 {multiples of 5 less than 30}

4 {multiples of 4 less than 30}

5 {divisors of 15}

6 {divisors of 12}

7 {all numbers between 14 and 20}

8 {all numbers between 45 and 50}

9 {multiples of 6 between 50 and 100}

10 {even numbers between 70 and 80}

Write down a description of each set:

11 {12, 14, 16, 18}

12 {51, 53, 55, 57, 59}

13 {7, 14, 21, 28, 35, 42, 49}

14 {54, 63, 72, 90, 99}

Investigation B

How many elements of a set can you find? This game is played in pairs. One player starts by picking a thing and saying the name of it; the other player then has to say the name of something which is in the same set. The game continues, each player taking it in turn to say the name of something in this same set. When a player cannot think of anything, or says the name of something which is not in the set, then that player loses the round. The winner starts the next round.

Sorting sets

On many occasions we have to sort things into groups or sets.
Decision trees help us organise this process into a short series
of questions. To classify any object, we could use the
following decision tree:

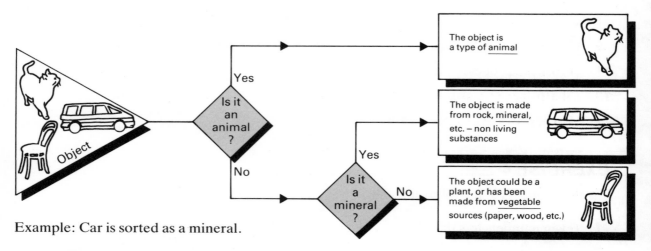

Example: Car is sorted as a mineral.

EXERCISE 1

Use the decision tree above to classify the following objects as either
animal, mineral, or vegetable.

1 elephant	**2** exercise book	**3** chalk	**4** carrot
5 fly	**6** calculator	**7** fish	**8** apple
9 road	**10** mouse	**11** tea cup	**12** daisy

EXERCISE 2

For each problem draw a decision tree with questions requiring yes/no answers.

1 Animals need to be sorted into:

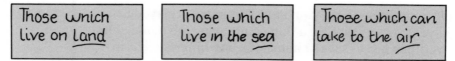

Use your decision tree to sort the following:
(*a*) blackbird (*b*) lobster (*c*) tiger (*d*) fly (*e*) whale (*f*) dog.
(*g*) How would you sort a frog, or a duck? Can you suggest how you might change
your decision tree?

2 To draw a state pension you need to be male and over 65, or female and over 60.
Make a decision tree to sort people with a series of yes/no questions, and decide whether they can receive a pension.
Use your decision tree to decide if the following will receive a pension:
(*a*) Mark, aged 58   (*b*) Vera, aged 70   (*c*) Bill, aged 63   (*d*) Jane, aged 66
(*e*) Sadiah, aged 59   (*f*) John, aged 65   (*g*) Ali, aged 68.

3 People can be accepted on to a training programme for retail managers if they have five good GCSE grades, *or* if they have three good GCSE grades *and* have worked in a large store, *or* if they have had a full-time job in a store for more than two years.
Draw a decision tree for this situation.

4 A group of children is to be divided into four smaller sets: boys and girls 11 years and under in age, boys and girls over 11 years in age. Draw a decision tree to help sort them.

5 As eggs are collected from a farm they have to be graded according to the table. Draw a decision tree to help the farm assistant sort the eggs.

Egg grading	
Size 1	70g or over
Size 2	65g to 69g
Size 3	60g to 64g
Size 4	55g to 59g
Size 5	50g to 54g
Size 6	45g to 49g
Size 7	less than 45g

6 Automatic washing machines are programmed to run a number of washing cycles.

All clothes should be sorted and washed on the correct cycle.

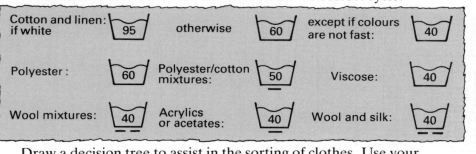

Cotton and linen: if white 95   otherwise 60   except if colours are not fast: 40

Polyester: 60   Polyester/cotton mixtures: 50   Viscose: 40

Wool mixtures: 40   Acrylics or acetates: 40   Wool and silk: 40

Draw a decision tree to assist in the sorting of clothes. Use your decision tree diagram to decide the washing cycle most suitable for the clothes with these washing labels:

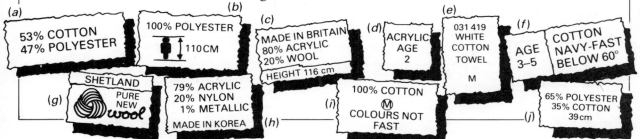

(*a*) 53% COTTON 47% POLYESTER

(*b*) 100% POLYESTER 110 CM

(*c*) MADE IN BRITAIN 80% ACRYLIC 20% WOOL HEIGHT 116 cm

(*d*) ACRYLIC AGE 2

(*e*) 031 419 WHITE COTTON TOWEL M

(*f*) AGE 3–5   COTTON NAVY-FAST BELOW 60°

(*g*) SHETLAND PURE NEW wool

(*h*) 79% ACRYLIC 20% NYLON 1% METALLIC MADE IN KOREA

(*i*) 100% COTTON Ⓜ COLOURS NOT FAST

(*j*) 65% POLYESTER 35% COTTON 39cm

EXERCISE 3

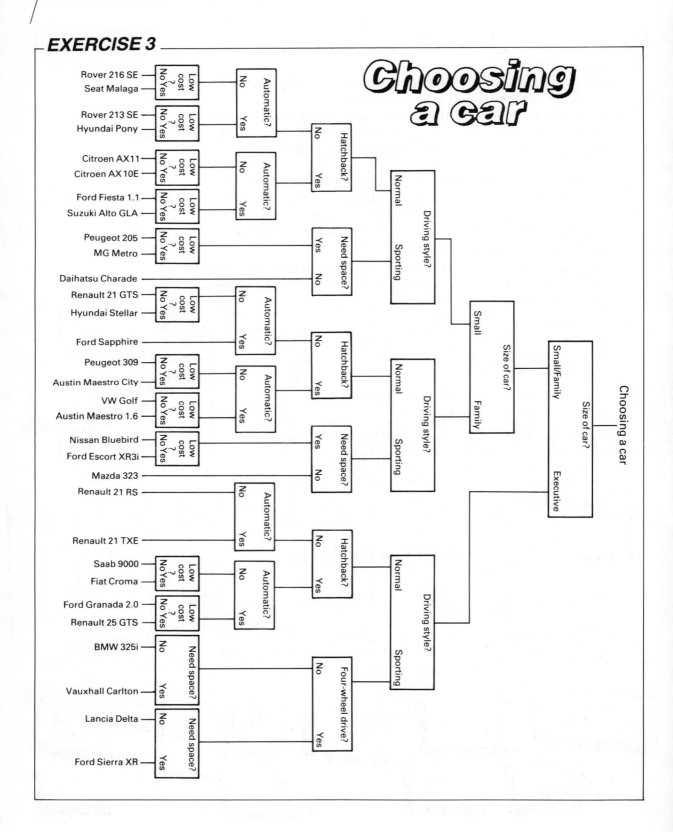

Choosing a car

In using the decision tree opposite, most people would want a low-cost, non-automatic car unless they say otherwise. Use the decision tree to find the recommended car in each of these cases.

1   A small car, normal style, with hatchback.

2   A sporty executive car, four-wheel drive, with a lot of space.

3   A small sporty car, with little space needed.

4   A normal family car, with hatchback, automatic, but not necessarily low-cost.

5   A small car, low-cost, automatic, without hatchback.

6   A sporty family car, with plenty of space, and low-cost.

7   A normal style executive car, hatchback and automatic.

8   A family car of normal style, neither hatchback nor automatic, and low-cost.

9   A small, normal-styled car, without hatchback, with automatic, but not necessarily low-cost.

10   An executive car with a normal style and a hatchback, not automatic, but cheap.

Write a full description of each of these cars:

11   Ford Fiesta 1.1

12   Mazda 323

13   Ford Granada 2.0

14   Renault 21 GTS

15   Austin Maestro 1.6

These game pieces are of two colours, and two sizes. How many are there of each? We can use a table to show the information:

	Red	Blue
Rectangle	3	5
Circle	3	3

The table will help us gather information about the pieces, and compare the information.

EXERCISE 4

1 Use the information above to answer these questions.
How many pieces are there which are
(*a*) rectangular   (*b*) circular   (*c*) red   (*d*) blue?

2 Draw a table to compare black/white shapes with those shapes which have all straight edges and some straight edges.
How many shapes are there with
(*a*) just straight edges
(*b*) some straight and some curved edges?
How many shapes are   (*c*) white   (*d*) black?

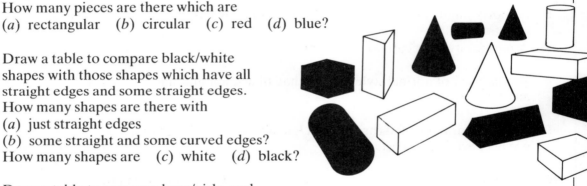

3 Draw a table to compare boys/girls, and divide the information into those who are: less than 5, between 5 and 12, between 12 and 16 years of age.
How many are there who are (*a*) boys
(*b*) girls   (*c*) boys 5 or more years of age
(*d*) children over 11 years of age
(*e*) girls under 5 years of age?

David	4	Bill	6	Brendan	7
Susan	10	Trisha	13	Steven	8
Jeff	13	Rozina	5	John	14
Alan	16	Adam	13	Mark	8
Ali	6	Beatrice	14	James	13
Paul	15	Tina	12	Peter	15
Jane	7	Anna	4	Liz	8
Helen	12	Lucy	3	Gemma	7

4 A survey of householders was conducted to find out how many had gas or electric cookers, and central heating boilers. This information is shown on the bar chart.
Transfer this information to a table to make comparisons easier.
(*a*) How many appliances were
    (i) gas   (ii) electric?
(*b*) How many cookers were in use?
(*c*) How many houses had central heating?

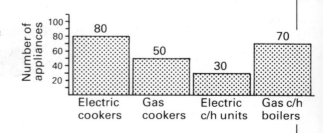

5 Draw a table to compare black/white shapes, and how many there are of each of the three types of shape.

How many shapes are there which are
(*a*) circles   (*b*) triangles
(*c*) black squares   (*d*) white
(*e*) white circles   (*f*) black?

Draw a table to compare glasses/mugs, and those which are patterned or plain.
(*a*) How many mugs are there?
(*b*) How many glasses are there?
(*c*) How many are plain?
(*d*) How many are patterned?

7 Transfer the information on the sheet to a simpler table to compare boys/girls and history/geography.
(*a*) How many boys took history?
(*b*) How many students took
      (i) geography   (ii) history?
(*c*) How many girls took geography?

8 Draw a table to compare the information for the four types of vehicles, with that concerning the direction in which the vehicles were travelling on this particular road.

How many of the vehicles recorded were
(*a*) cars and vans going North
(*b*) vehicles going South   (*c*) lorries
(*d*) cars   (*e*) vehicles going North?
(*f*) What was the total number of vehicles recorded?

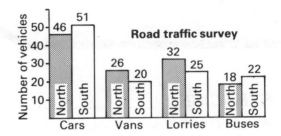

Road traffic survey

	History	Geography
Alan	✓	
James		✓
Tony	✓	✓
Ann	✓	✓
Bill	✓	
Ahmed		✓
Tina	✓	
Kelly	✓	✓
Joe		✓
Margaret	✓	

	History	Geography
Ali	✓	
Julie	✓	✓
Martin		✓
Rozana	✓	✓
Mark		✓
Paul	✓	
Lisa	✓	✓
Louise	✓	✓
Harry		✓
Samantha	✓	

Set notation

Can you write down the elements of the set

{names of living persons without heads}?

This would be quite difficult, as clearly there are no elements to the set.

> A set with no elements we write as { }.
> We say the set is **empty** and can give it the symbol ∅

EXERCISE

Which of the following sets are empty?

A = {red roses} B = {black roses} C = {numbers less than 0} D = {British cars}

E = {names of people who have swum the Atlantic Ocean}

F = {children in your class} G = {people who have climbed Mount Everest}

H = {orange seals} I = {men over 3 m in height} J = {numbers more than 5}

K = {vacuum cleaners which wash clothes} L = {animals with an 8 foot nose}

Investigation

List as many sets as you can which are empty.

> An empty set { }
> or ∅ we also call the
> **null** set.

Elements

A fork is an **element** of the set {kitchen utensils}.
We write this as

      fork ∈ {kitchen utensils}
         ↑

means 'is an element of'

We also write

      dog ∉ {kitchen utensils}
        ↑

means 'is not an element of'

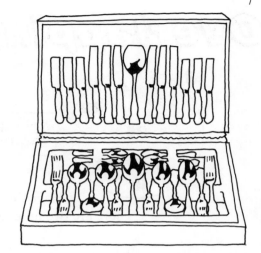

EXERCISE

Write down whether each of the following statements is true or false.

1 Aberdeen ∈ {sunny holiday resorts}   **2** tape deck ∈ {hi-fi system}

3 Blackpool ∉ {British cities}   **4** guitar ∈ {orchestral instruments}

5 Nigeria ∉ {EEC}   **6** 24 ∉ {factors of 48}

7 cats ∈ {pets which can be trained}   **8** Michael Jackson ∉ {pop stars}

9 cheetah ∈ {animals which live in Africa}

10 Coronation Street ∉ {soap programmes on television}

Copy the following and include ∈ or ∉ for each question.

11 99   {prime numbers}   **12** BOEING 747   {fighter aircraft}

13 tea cup   {kitchen crockery}   **14** toast   {breakfast cereals}

15 goat   {farm animals}   **16** Snowdon   {British mountain peaks}

17 potato   {vegetables}   **18** 3   {divisors of 111}

19 Swansea   {towns in North Wales}   **20** seaweed   {edible seafood}

Write down whether each of these statements is true or false.

21 $21 \in \{1, 1, 2, 3, 5, 8, \ldots\}$

22 $\frac{1}{100} \in \left\{ \frac{1}{2}, \frac{1}{4}, \frac{1}{8}, \frac{1}{16}, \ldots \right\}$

23 $1000 \notin \{1, 5, 25, 125, \ldots\}$

24 $100 \in \{1, 4, 9, 16, 25, \ldots\}$

25 $65 \notin \{10, 11, 13, 16, 20, \ldots\}$

Overlapping sets

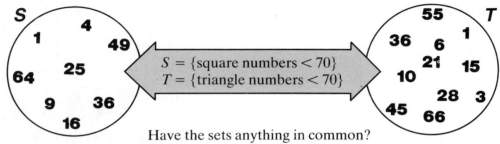

$S = \{$square numbers $< 70\}$
$T = \{$triangle numbers $< 70\}$

Have the sets anything in common?
There are two numbers which occur in both sets: 1 and 36.

We say the **intersection** of S and T is
$\{1, 36\}$, and write:

$$S \cap T = \{1, 36\}$$
$\uparrow$
means 'intersection'

We can show the intersection where the two sets cross
over as a diagram:

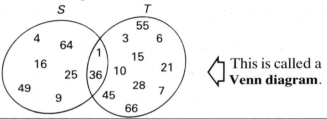

This is called a
Venn diagram.

EXERCISE 1

Find the intersection of each pair of sets, drawing a Venn diagram in each case.

1 $O = \{1, 3, 5, 7, 9, 11\}$; $P = \{2, 3, 5, 7, 11\}$

2 $E = \{2, 4, 6, 8, 10\}$; $T = \{1, 3, 6, 10\}$

3 $F = \{$factors of 30$\}$; $S = \{$factors of 75$\}$

4 $A = \{$factors of 24$\}$; $B = \{$factors of 32$\}$

5 $M = \{$multiples of 2 $< 20\}$;
$N = \{$multiples of 3 $< 20\}$

6 The diagram shows who, out of a group of
friends, likes CDT or science at school.

   (*a*) Who likes both CDT and science?

   (*b*) Who likes CDT?

   (*c*) Who likes science?

   (*d*) Who does *not* like science?

7 (*a*) Which creatures would you normally
find in a house and on a farm?

   (*b*) Which creatures would be found only
on a farm?

   (*c*) Write the set of creatures you might
find in a house.

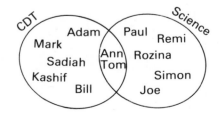

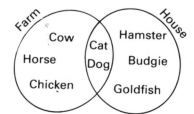

8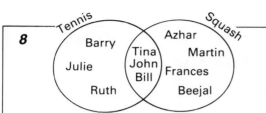

(a) Who likes to play squash?

(b) Who does *not* like to play squash?

(c) Who likes both tennis and squash?

9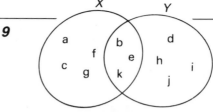

Write down the set of letters which are
(a) in set X (b) in set Y
(c) in both set X and set Y
(d) not in set X.

10 The set of children who deliver morning newspapers is {Paul, Martin, Jane, Ali, Mark}. The set of children who deliver evening newspapers is {Julie, Ali, Chris, Paul, John}. Draw a Venn diagram to represent this situation.

11 The factors of 12 are {1, 2, 3, 4, 6, 12}. The factors of 16 are {1, 2, 4, 8, 16}. Draw a Venn diagram in which you can place these numbers.

12 Draw a Venn diagram for these two sets:
{Blackpool, Morecambe, Fleetwood, Liverpool},
{Cleveleys, Preston, Blackpool, Lytham, Fleetwood}.

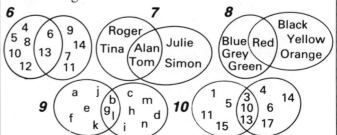

The **union** of two sets is the set formed when the two sets are joined together.

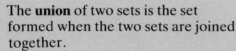

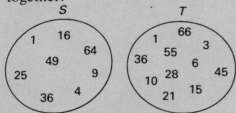

$S = \{\text{square numbers} < 70\}$
$T = \{\text{triangle numbers} < 70\}$

The union of S and T is {1, 3, 4, 6, 9, 10, 15, 16, 21, 25, 28, 36, 45, 49, 55, 64, 66}.
The union of S and T we write as $S \cup T$. Notice all the elements of both S and T are included, but the numbers which occur in both sets, 1 and 36, need only be written once.

EXERCISE 2

Write down the union of each pair of sets.

1 $A = \{a, b, c, d, e\}$; $B = \{f, g, h, i, j\}$

2 $X = \{1, 3, 5, 7, 9\}$; $Y = \{6, 7, 8, 9, 10\}$

3 $M = \{\text{whole numbers between 0 and 10}\}$
$N = \{\text{even numbers between 3 and 15}\}$

4 $A = \{m, a, t, h, s\}$; $B = \{m, a, c\}$

5 $P = \{\text{factors of 12}\}$; $Q = \{\text{factors of 16}\}$

Write out the union of the sets given in the Venn diagrams.

6 (4, 5, 8, 10, 12) (6, 13) (9, 14, 7, 11)

7 Roger, Tina, Alan, Tom, Julie, Simon

8 Blue, Grey, Green, Red, Black, Yellow, Orange

9 a, j, e, f, k, b, g, l, c, m, h, n, i, d

10 (1, 11, 15, 5, 3, 10, 13, 4, 6, 17, 14)

A **subset** is a set which is contained by another set.

$A = \{1, 2, 3, 4, 5\}; B = \{2, 3\}$

We write
$B \subset A$

↑

'is a subset of' or 'is contained within'

EXERCISE 3

Are these statements true or false?

1 $\{a, b, c, d\} \subset \{a, b, c, d, e, f\}$

2 $\{3, 5, 7\} \subset \{1, 2, 3, 4, 5, 6, 7, 8\}$

3 $\{red\} \subset \{colours of the rainbow\}$

4 $\{black\} \subset \{colours of the rainbow\}$

5 $\{kangaroo\} \subset \{animals from Africa\}$

6 $\{Monday, Tuesday\} \subset \{days of the week\}$

7 $\{oak, ash\} \subset \{British trees\}$

8 $\{washing machine\} \subset \{kitchen cutlery\}$

9 $\{dog, cat\} \subset \{domestic pets\}$

10 $\{darts, football\} \subset \{sporting games\}$

11 $\{1, 2, 3, 4\} \subset \{1, 2, 3, 4\}$

12 $\{alphabet\} \subset \{vowels\}$

EXERCISE 4

1 Write down
(a) set A
(b) set B
(c) set $A \cap B$
(d) set $A \cup B$.

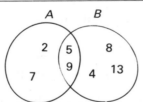

2 Write down
(a) set P
(b) set Q
(c) set $P \cap Q$
(d) set $P \cup Q$.

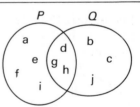

For each of the following, draw a Venn diagram, and write out the sets $A \cup B$ and $A \cap B$.

3 $A = \{1, 4, 6, 7, 9, 11, 15\}$;
$B = \{3, 6, 9, 12, 15\}$

4 $A = \{c, h, a, x, y\}$;
$B = \{s, e, c, t, a, x\}$

5 $A = \{numbers less than 10\}$;
$B = \{odd numbers between 4 and 16\}$

6 $A = \{3, 4, 5, 6, 9, 12, 13\}$;
$B = \{6, 7, 8, 9, 10, 11, 12\}$

7 Write down (a) set A (b) set B
(c) set C (d) set $A \cup B$
(e) $B \cap C$ (f) set $A \cap B \cap C$.

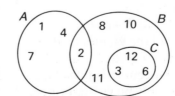

Revision exercise

1 Write out the elements of each set:
    (*a*) {metric units of length}   (*b*) {days in the week}
    (*c*) {odd numbers between 20 and 30} (*d*) {prime numbers less than 20}.

2 Describe these sets:
    (*a*) {a, e, i, o, u}   (*b*) {11, 13, 15, 17, 19}
    (*c*) {Saturday, Sunday}   (*d*) {England, Wales, Scotland, N. Ireland}.

3 Use the decision tree to classify the following vegetables
    as either pod/bulb/stem, roots, or greens

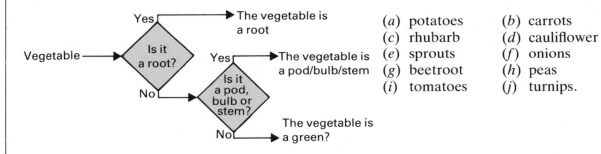

    (*a*) potatoes   (*b*) carrots
    (*c*) rhubarb   (*d*) cauliflower
    (*e*) sprouts   (*f*) onions
    (*g*) beetroot   (*h*) peas
    (*i*) tomatoes   (*j*) turnips.

4 Draw a decision tree with yes/no questions to classify lights into:

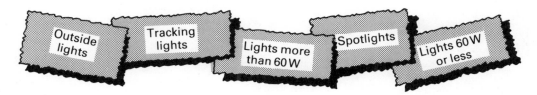

5 Use the information given to
    produce a table to help you answer
    the questions below.

Apples preferred		
French red	✓ ✓ ✓ ✓ ✓	
English red	✓ ✓ ✓ ✓ ✓ ✓	
French green	✓ ✓ ✓ ✓ ✓ ✓ ✓ ✓ ✓ ✓	
English green	✓ ✓ ✓ ✓ ✓ ✓ ✓ ✓ ✓ ✓ ✓ ✓	

How many people preferred (*a*) English apples   (*b*) French apples
(*c*) green apples   (*d*) red apples?

Questions 6 and 7 overleaf

Revision exercise

6 Draw a Venn diagram and write out the sets $A \cup B$ and $A \cap B$.

(a) $A = \{3, 5, 7, 9, 11, 13, 15\}$; $B = \{9, 10, 11, 14, 17\}$.

(b) $A = \{a, b, c, d, e, f, g\}$; $B = \{e, g, h, i, j\}$.

7 Write down (a) set A (b) set B (c) set C
(d) $A \cap B$ (e) $A \cup B$ (f) $A \cap C$ (g) $B \cap C$
(h) $A \cup B \cup C$ (i) $B \cup C$ (j) $A \cap B \cap C$.
Are the following true or false?
(k) $A \subset B$ (l) $B \subset C$ (m) $B \subset A$ (n) $C \subset B$

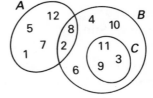

5. MEASURE: LENGTH

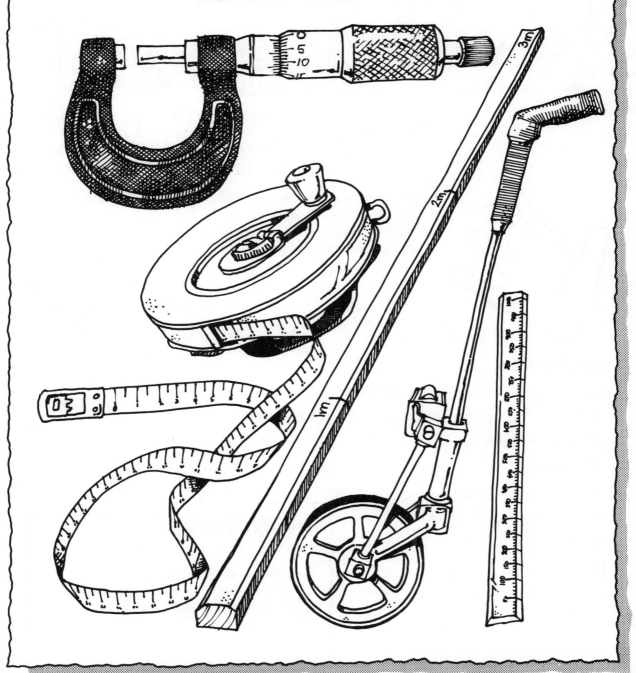

Measures of length

Martin and Susan each have a horse. They want to know which horse is taller, and use a handspan to measure the height of each horse. Martin measures his horse as 10 handspans, Susan measures her horse as 13 handspans. Does this mean Susan's horse is the taller?

When handspans were first used to measure the height of horses, a standard length of handspan was agreed on, so everyone would then use the same handspan. The scale at the edge of this page is a **standard handspan**.

One handspan

1 handspan

EXERCISE 1

Which of the following is a standard length:

1 The width of your exercise book.

2 The length of a pen.

3 A piece of string.

4 A ruler.

5 The widths of the desks or tables.

6 The length of your stride.

7 The length of your thumb.

8 The length of a sheet of A4 paper.

9 The board rubber.

10 A stone.

Investigation A

Use the handspan to make your own 'handspan ruler'. Write down the names of some common objects, and their lengths, measured in handspans.

Investigation B

Bill needs to order some shelves for a wall. He can only find a piece of string with which to measure, and sends off this order for his wood.

Write out a reply to Bill, explaining what he has done wrong. What would you advise him to do? We could have used a piece of string with which to measure, provided we all understood exactly how long the string was.

Shelving: 6 sections
Width: ¼ piece string
Length: 2½ pieces of String

EXERCISE 2

Copy and complete the table, making measurements as indicated.

Measure to use	Width of your desk/table	Your height	Height of your desk/table
Width of your exercise book			
Length of your text book			
The conker shown right			
Your handspan			
Length of your ruler			

Investigation C

Make a list of all the types of measurements you frequently make, and the units you use to make these measurements (e.g. weight in . . . ?).

Clearly to have different measurements throughout the world would make measurement confusing. The most common measure used internationally is the **metre**. The metre is divided into 100 centimetres, with which we are familiar on a ruler. Each centimetre is divided into 10 millimetres.

EXERCISE 3

1

(a) What is the length of the nail in centimetres?

(b) What is the length of the nail in millimetres?

(c) How wide is the head of the nail?

2 (a) How high is the bottle in centimetres?

(b) How high is the bottle in millimetres?

(c) How high is the liquid in the bottle?

3 (a) How long is the pencil rubber?

(b) How long is the pencil?

(c) How long is the pencil lead at the end of the pencil?

4 Estimate, in centimetres *without* measuring, the lengths of the following lines:

(a) _____

(b) _____

(c) _____

(d) _____

(e) _____ (f) _____

Write down your estimates for all six lines, then go back and measure them with a ruler. How near were your estimates?

5 Estimate, in millimetres *without* measuring, the lengths of the following lines:

(a) _____ (d) ____

(b) _____ (e) _____

(c) _____ (f) _____

Write down your estimates for all six lines, then go back and measure them with a ruler. How near were your estimates?

6 Estimate, in metres, the height of (a) a man (b) the door (c) the classroom ceiling.

7 Estimate, in metres, the width and the length of the classroom.

Mixing units

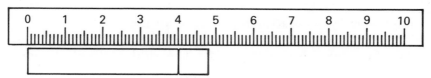

The first piece of wood is of length 4 cm. The second piece of wood is of length 8 mm. The total length is therefore 4 cm 8 mm. Can we write this measurement as a single figure?

4 cm 8 mm = 40 mm + 8 mm = 48 mm

We could also write 48 mm as 4.8 cm. So

4 cm 8 mm = 48 mm or 4.8 cm.

EXERCISE 1

Copy and complete the table.

	Mixed units	Millimetres	Centimetres			Mixed units	Millimetres	Centimetres
1	3 cm 6 mm				11		20 mm	
2	5 cm 3 mm				12		45 mm	
3	2 cm 2 mm				13		32 mm	
4	8 cm 1 mm				14		76 mm	
5	7 cm 4 mm				15			4 cm
6	12 cm 2 mm				16			6·6 cm
7	10 cm 0 mm				17		135 mm	
8	13 cm 7 mm				18		142 mm	
9	8 cm 4 mm				19			8·7 cm
10	9 cm 9 mm				20			10·4 cm

The tallest human being was Robert Pershing Wadlow (1918–40) whose height was 2.72 m. The smallest human being was Pauline Musters (1876–95) whose greatest height was 61 cm. The largest chest measurement belonged to Robert Hughes (1926–58); it was 2.64 m. Queen Catherine De Medici (1519–89) of France was reputed to have a waist of 33 cm. The longest finger nails are those of Shridhar Chillal of India: 413.5 cm for five nails. Swarmi Pandarasannadhi had the longest hair, of 7.92 m in length. The longest beard was grown by Hans Landseth at 5.33 m.

We use a variety of units for measuring length:
$10\,mm = 1\,cm$ $100\,cm = 1\,m$ $1000\,m = 1\,km$

EXERCISE 2

Which metric units would you use to measure the following?

1 The thickness of your exercise book.

2 The width of the blackboard.

3 Your height.

4 The distance from school to home.

5 The length of a page in this book.

6 The height of Mount Everest.

7 The length of an ant.

8 The distance you could run.

9 The width of a pencil.

10 The length of a pencil.

Investigation

A scuba diver is preparing to have a wet-suit made for him. He has to have ten measurements taken, in centimetres. Working with a friend, copy and complete the table for yourself.

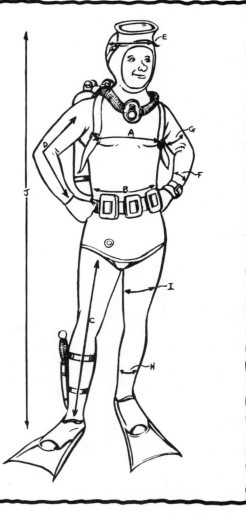

	Measurement statistics	
A	Chest	
B	Waist	
C	Inside leg	
D	Inside arm	
E	Crown of head	
F	Wrist	
G	Upper arm	
H	Ankle	
I	Upper leg	
J	Height	

EXERCISE 3

Draw lines of the following lengths:

1	25 mm	**2**	2.5 cm	**3**	32 mm
4	3.2 cm	**5**	48 mm	**6**	4.8 cm
7	16 mm	**8**	1.6 cm	**9**	60 mm
10	6 cm				

What did you find out from completing the exercise? You should now have a good understanding of both millimetres and centimetres. Complete the table.

Length in millimetres	Length in Centimetres	Length in Millimetres	Length in Centimetres
20			3
40			7
33			2.1
27			5.5
53			9.2
120			10.5
183			12.3
5			0.07

```
0    10   20   30   40   50   60   70   80   90   100
|ılılılılı|ılılılılı|ılılılılı|ılılılılı|ılılılılı|ılılılılı|ılılılılı|ılılılılı|ılılılılı|ılılılılı|
```
```
|ılılılılılılılılılılılılılı|
```
30 cm school ruler

1 metre ruler

A one metre ruler is considerably longer than a school ruler. Remember 2 metres is slightly more than the average height of an adult male.

    100 centimetres = 1 metre

So 2 m 45 cm = 200 cm + 45 cm = 245 cm
we could also write 245 cm as 2.45 m
so 2 m 45 cm = 245 cm or 2.45 m.

XERCISE 4

Copy and complete the table.

	Mixed units	Centimetres	Metres
1	4 m 23 cm		
2	6 m 18 cm		
3	2 m 93 cm		
4	1 m 3 cm		
5	0 m 83 cm		
6	2 m 5 cm		
7	4 m 7 cm		
8	1 m 10 cm		
9	3 m 85 cm		
10	2 m 1 cm		
11		125 cm	
12		433 cm	
13		105 cm	
14			3.05 m
15			1.11 m
16		95 cm	
17		320 cm	
18			2.40 m
19			1.97 m
20		514 cm	

For each question write the lengths in order of size, starting with the smallest:

21 3 cm 3 mm, 68 mm, 3 m, 1 m 15 cm, 2.5 m, 4 cm, 380 mm, 103 cm

22 70 mm, 230 cm, 2 cm 5 mm, 180 cm, 2 m 30 cm, 5 cm, 12 cm 7 mm, 400 mm

23 1 m 42 cm, 1.7 m, 6.5 cm, 1 m 97 cm, 120 mm, 4 cm 3 mm, 540 cm, 620 mm

24 23 cm 5 mm, 3.24 m, 280 mm, 168 cm, 1040 mm, 4.5 cm, 5 cm, 325 cm

25 1200 mm, 4 cm, 40 cm 7 mm, 5 m 28 cm, 205 mm, 180 cm, 3.7 cm, 950 mm

26 2 cm 3 mm, 400 cm, 2 m, 2.3 cm, 4 m 10 cm, 300 mm, 2 m 35 cm, 2050 mm

Revision exercise

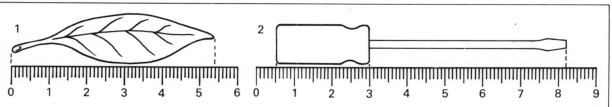

1 What is the length of the leaf
    (*a*) in cm   (*b*) in mm?

2 What is the length of the handle
    (*a*) in cm   (*b*) in mm?
    What is the total length of the screwdriver
    (*c*) in cm   (*d*) in mm?

Write down the lengths of each of these lines in (*a*) cm   (*b*) mm:

3 —————————   **4** ————————————————   **5** ——————————————————————————

6 ——

7 —————————————————————————   **8** ——————————————————————————————

Copy and complete the tables.

	Mixed units	millimetres	Centimetres
9	3cm 5mm		
10	4cm 6mm		
11	7cm 9mm		
12	12cm 5mm	125mm	
13			10cm
14			1.5cm
15		84mm	
16	10cm 1mm		
17		3mm	
18			0.2cm

	Mixed units	Centimetres	Metres
19	1m 32cm		
20	3m 5cm		
21		85cm	
22			2.35m
23	9m 40cm		
24		70cm	
25	2m 1cm		
26			2.4m
27		3cm	
28			4m

29 How many centimetres are there in a metre?

30 How many millimetres are there in a metre?

31 How many metres are there in a kilometre?

32 How many centimetres are there in a kilometre?

33 How many millimetres are there in a kilometre?

6. Operations

$15 - 7 \times 2 = 16?$

Use an ALGEBRAIC calculator. Which is the correct answer?

We use the BODMAS CONVENTION

$15 - 7 \times 2 = 1?$

Flow diagrams

FOLLOWING INSTRUCTIONS

Use whole numbers only on this page.
Follow the operations in each of these flow diagrams:

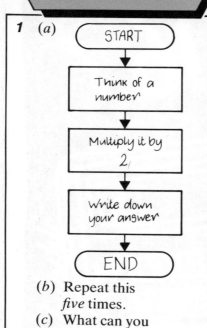

1 (a)

START

Think of a number

Multiply it by 2

Write down your answer

END

(b) Repeat this *five* times.
(c) What can you say about your answers?

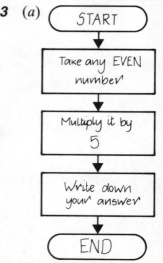

2 (a)

START

Think of any EVEN number

Multiply it by 2

Write down your answer

END

(b) Repeat this *five* times.
(c) Describe your set of answers.

3 (a)

START

Take any EVEN number

Multiply it by 5

Write down your answer

END

(b) Repeat this *five* times.
(c) What do you notice about your answers?

PROBLEM

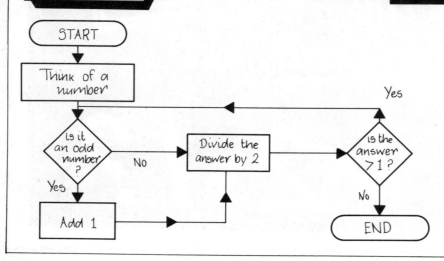

START

Think of a number

Is it an odd number?

Add 1

Divide the answer by 2

Is the answer 71?

Yes

No

No

Yes

END

(a) Choose a number greater than 10.

(b) Which number greater than 10 gets through the flow chart in the shortest time?

(c) Which number less than 10 gets through the flow chart in the shortest time?

NUMBER SEQUENCES

1 (a) Start with the number 1.

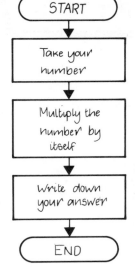

START
↓
Take your number
↓
Multiply the number by itself
↓
Write down your answer
↓
END

(b) Repeat for the numbers 2, 3, . . . , 9, 10.

(c) Look at your answers. What name do we give to this sequence of numbers?

(d) Starting with *integers* only, is it possible to get these answers
(i) 400 (ii) 2
(iii) 144
(iv) 40?
Explain your answers.

2 (a) Start with the number 1.

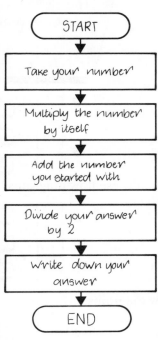

START
↓
Take your number
↓
Multiply the number by itself
↓
Add the number you started with
↓
Divide your answer by 2
↓
Write down your answer
↓
END

(b) Repeat for the numbers 2, 3, 4, . . . , 10.

(c) Look at your answers. What name do we give to this sequence?

(d) What number did you start with if your answer is 5050?

3 Fibonacci sequence

START
↓
Write down the number 1 twice
↓
Add together the last two numbers you wrote down
↓
Write down your answer
↓
Have you written 10 numbers? — No (loop back)
↓ Yes
END

(a) Check that your sequence commences 1, 1, 2, . . .

(b) What number do you finish with if you start with 4 and 5 instead of 1 and 1 in the sequence above?

Operations

OTHER FLOW DIAGRAMS

Example: $\boxed{4}$ —$\boxed{x5}$— $\boxed{}$ means:

Start with 4, then multiply by 5.
The answer is 20.
So we can complete the flow chart

$\boxed{4}$ —$\boxed{x5}$— $\boxed{20}$

EXERCISE 1

Copy out *all* these flow diagrams.
Work out the answer in each case.

1 $\boxed{7}$ —$\boxed{+13}$— $\boxed{}$ **2** $\boxed{20}$ —$\boxed{-11}$— $\boxed{}$

3 $\boxed{10}$ —$\boxed{x3}$— $\boxed{}$ **4** $\boxed{16}$ —$\boxed{\div2}$— $\boxed{}$

5 $\boxed{100}$ —$\boxed{x3}$— $\boxed{}$ **6** $\boxed{16}$ —$\boxed{\div10}$— $\boxed{}$

Work out the start number in each of these flow diagrams.

7 $\boxed{}$ —$\boxed{x3}$— $\boxed{21}$ **8** $\boxed{}$ —$\boxed{-9}$— $\boxed{12}$

9 $\boxed{}$ —$\boxed{\div3}$— $\boxed{10}$ **10** $\boxed{}$ —$\boxed{+15}$— $\boxed{31}$

11 $\boxed{}$ —$\boxed{+1\frac{1}{2}}$— $\boxed{4}$ **12** $\boxed{}$ —$\boxed{x5}$— $\boxed{100}$

Work out the answers in these flow diagrams.

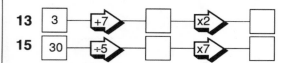

13 $\boxed{3}$ —$\boxed{+7}$— $\boxed{}$ —$\boxed{x2}$— $\boxed{}$

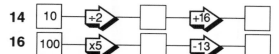

14 $\boxed{10}$ —$\boxed{\div2}$— $\boxed{}$ —$\boxed{+16}$— $\boxed{}$

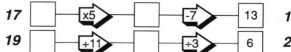

15 $\boxed{30}$ —$\boxed{\div5}$— $\boxed{}$ —$\boxed{x7}$— $\boxed{}$

16 $\boxed{100}$ —$\boxed{x5}$— $\boxed{}$ —$\boxed{-13}$— $\boxed{}$

Work out the start numbers in each of these.

17 $\boxed{}$ —$\boxed{x5}$— $\boxed{}$ —$\boxed{-7}$— $\boxed{13}$ **18** $\boxed{}$ —$\boxed{-6}$— $\boxed{}$ —$\boxed{\div2}$— $\boxed{10}$

19 $\boxed{}$ —$\boxed{+11}$— $\boxed{}$ —$\boxed{\div3}$— $\boxed{6}$ **20** $\boxed{}$ —$\boxed{+3}$— $\boxed{}$ —$\boxed{x10}$— $\boxed{30}$

Work out the missing operations in these. Find *two* solutions where possible.

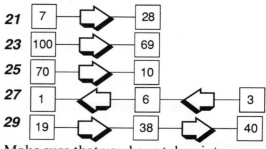

21 $\boxed{7}$ —$\Rightarrow$— $\boxed{28}$

23 $\boxed{100}$ —$\Rightarrow$— $\boxed{69}$

25 $\boxed{70}$ —$\Rightarrow$— $\boxed{10}$

27 $\boxed{1}$ —$\Leftarrow$— $\boxed{6}$ —$\Leftarrow$— $\boxed{3}$

29 $\boxed{19}$ —$\Rightarrow$— $\boxed{38}$ —$\Rightarrow$— $\boxed{40}$

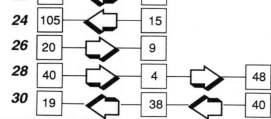

22 $\boxed{7}$ —$\Leftarrow$— $\boxed{14}$

24 $\boxed{105}$ —$\Leftarrow$— $\boxed{15}$

26 $\boxed{20}$ —$\Rightarrow$— $\boxed{9}$

28 $\boxed{40}$ —$\Rightarrow$— $\boxed{4}$ —$\Rightarrow$— $\boxed{48}$

30 $\boxed{19}$ —$\Leftarrow$— $\boxed{38}$ —$\Leftarrow$— $\boxed{40}$

Make sure that you have taken into account the direction of the arrow.

EXERCISE 2

Use +, −, × or ÷ in each arrow to make these correct.

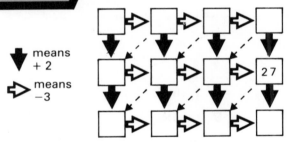

1 4 ⟹ 3 ⟹ 2 ⟹ 10

2 4 ⟹ 3 ⟹ 2 ⟹ 24

3 4 ⟹ 3 ⟹ 2 ⟹ 3

4 4 ⟹ 3 ⟹ 2 ⟹ 6

5 4 ⟹ 3 ⟹ 2 ⟹ 5

6 235 ⟹ 107 ⟹ 342

7 201 ⟹ 5 ⟹ 1005

8 16 ⟹ 8 ⟹ 2

9 25 ⟹ 25 ⟹ 1

10 482 ⟹ 379 ⟹ 341 ⟹ 520

11 172 ⟹ 8 ⟹ 18 ⟹ 10

12 5 ⟹ 2 ⟹ 1 ⟹ 7

13 9 ⟹ 6 ⟹ 3 ⟹ 18

14 3 ⟹ 2 ⟹ 1 ⟹ 7

15 4 ⟹ 3 ⟹ 2 ⟹ 1 ⟹ 8

16 5 ⟹ 4 ⟹ 3 ⟹ 2 ⟹ 1 ⟹ 9

17 6 ⟹ 5 ⟹ 4 ⟹ 3 ⟹ 2 ⟹ 1 ⟹ 21

18 184 ⟹ 85 ⟹ 129 ⟹ 3 ⟹ 76

19 125 ⟹ 25 ⟹ 4 ⟹ 20

20 4 ⟹ 3 ⟹ 2 ⟹ 14

> Use a calculator if you need to

PROBLEM

1 Copy out this table and work out the missing numbers if

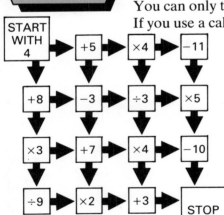

means + 2

means − 3

2 Find the missing numbers when the 27 is changed to 8.

3 Find the missing numbers
if ▼ means 'divide by 2'
and ⟹ means 'multiply by 3'.

4 Make up a table of your own.

5 What operation does the diagonal dotted line represent in each case?

ROUTES

You can only travel down ▼ or right ➡
If you use a calculator press the = button after each operation.

START WITH 4 → +5 → ×4 → −11
+8 → −3 → ÷3 → ×5
×3 → +7 → ×4 → −10
÷9 → ×2 → +3 → STOP

(*a*) How many routes are there?

(*b*) Which is the *highest* scoring route?

(*c*) Which route gives a score of 0?

(*d*) How many routes give a score of 11?

(*e*) Which route gives an answer of −2?

Bodmas

ORDER OF OPERATIONS

So far the order of operations has been decided for you in flow charts. But $3 + 4 \times 5$ could be

$$\underbrace{3 + 4} \times 5 \quad \text{or} \quad 3 + \underbrace{4 \times 5}$$

$$= \quad 7 \quad \times 5 \qquad = 3 + 20$$
$$= 35 \qquad\qquad = 23$$

Mathematicians will say that the second answer is correct. This is because they work with a set of rules or conventions.

Look at this: (a) $15 - 6 + 2$
and (b) $15 - 6 \times 2$

(a) ➤ do '15 − 6' then '+ 2' ➤ 11.
(b) ➤ do '6 × 2' then 'take from 15' ➤ 3.
Even your calculator may have given an answer of 18 to (b)!

CONVENTIONS

In order that we obtain only *one* answer, we perform operations in a particular order.

All × or ÷ *first*, from left to right
then + or − from left to right.

EXERCISE 1

Work out these calculations.

1 $20+7-5$ **2** $6\times3-2$ **3** $8-6-2$

4 $13-2\times3$ **5** $8-6+2$ **6** $8-6\div2$

7 $8\div2+6$ **8** $8\times3\div6$ **9** $6\div3\times8$

10 $3\times2\times5$ **11** $16-8\div2$ **12** $16\div8-2$

13 $12+9\div3$ **14** $18-9-9$ **15** $18\div9+9$

16 $18+9\div9$ **17** $18-9\div9$ **18** $27\div9\div3$

19 $27-9\div3$ **20** $27-9\times3$ **21** $27\div9\times3$

22 $27+33\div3$ **23** $33-27\div3$ **24** $100\div25\times4$

25 $6\times3-2\times7$ **26** $15-2\times3+5$

27 $18\div3+3\times2$ **28** $27+3-7-9$

29 $20-11-9\div3$ **30** $16-7+8-9-3$

31 $6\div3\times4\div2\times5$ **32** $10+7\times3-2\times8\div4$

33 $7\times3-2\times5-4\times2$ **34** $7-3\times2+5\times4\div2$

35 $16\div2+6\times3-8-6\div3+15\times2-7+3+2\times5$

BRACKETS

Look at this flow chart:
But if we write this out we get:

(using *conventions*) $3 + 4 \times 5 = 23$ *not* 35.

So how can we write out this expression to get an answer of 35?
We need to perform $3 + 4$ first and we use **brackets** to indicate this.
Our expression for the flow chart now becomes $(3+4) \times 5 = 35$.
(**Note:** that $3 + 4 \times 5 = 23$ does *not* require brackets.)

EXERCISE 2

Complete these flow charts then write down each one as an expression,
using brackets where necessary.

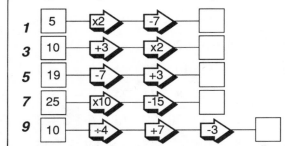

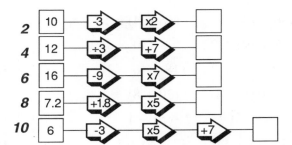

CONVENTION

We always perform the operation(s)
within the brackets first.

Examples

(*a*) $\quad 15 - (6 - 4)$
$= 15 - 2$
$= 13$

(*b*) $\quad 12 \div (6 \div 2) \div 2$
$= 12 \div 3 \div 2$
$= \ 4 \div 2 = 2$

EXERCISE 3

Work out each of the following and state which did not need brackets.

1 $\quad 12 - (4 + 3)$ *2* $\quad 20 - (9 + 3)$ *3* $\quad (5 + 3) - 2$ *4* $\quad (5 - 2) + 3 - 4$

5 $\quad (6 \times 4) + 7$ *6* $\quad 6 \times (4 + 7)$ *7* $\quad (5 \times 6) \div 3$ *8* $\quad 5 \times (6 \div 3)$

9 $\quad (18 - 10) + 2$ *10* $\quad (2 + 3) \times 5$ *11* $\quad 2 + (3 \times 5)$ *12* $\quad (3 \times 5) + 4$

13 $\quad 28 - (5 - 2 + 1)$ *14* $\quad (28 - 5) - (2 + 1)$ *15* $\quad (12 + 5) \times 2 - 15$

16 $\quad 12 + (5 \times 2) - 15$ *17* $\quad (12 + 5 \times 2) - 15$ *18* $\quad (2 \times 3) + (4 \times 5)$

19 $\quad 2 \times (3 + 4) \times 5$ *20* $\quad (20 \div 4) + (5 \times 2)$ *21* $\quad 20 - (4 + 5 \times 2)$

EXERCISE 4

Work out each pair of calculations below.
If they are *equal* use the '=' symbol.
If they are *not equal* use the '≠' symbol.

1 $(8 + 2) + 3 \ldots 8 + (2 + 3)$

2 $(8 - 3) - 2 \ldots 8 - (3 - 2)$

3 $(2 \times 3) \times 4 \ldots 2 \times 3 \times 4$

4 $12 \div 3 \div 2 \ldots 12 \div (3 \div 2)$

5 $4 \times (2 \times 5) \ldots (4 \times 2) \times 5$

6 $(12 + 8) - 3 \ldots 12 + (8 - 3)$

7 $6 - 3 + 2 \ldots 6 - (3 + 2)$

8 $36 \div (4 + 5) \ldots (36 \div 4) + 5$

9 $(5 \times 10) \div 2 \ldots 5 \times (10 \div 2)$

10 $(18 \div 6) \div 3 \ldots 18 \div (6 \div 3)$

11 $20 + (8 \div 4) \ldots (20 + 8) \div 4$

12 $7 - 5 - 1 \ldots (7 - 5) - 1$

13 $7 - (5 + 1) \ldots (7 - 5) + 1$

14 $12 - 4 \times 2 \ldots 12 - (4 \times 2)$

15 $(12 + 4) \times 2 \ldots 12 + 4 \times 2$

16 $12 - 8 \div 2 \ldots (12 - 8) \div 2$

17 $(30 + 10) \div 5 \ldots 30 + (10 \div 5)$

18 $21 - 3 + 4 - 1 \ldots 21 - (3 + 4 - 1)$

19 $18 \div (9 - 3) \div 2 \ldots (18 \div 9) - (3 \div 2)$

20 $(10 + 3) \times (5 + 2) \ldots 10 + (3 \times 5) + 2$

EXERCISE 5

Put brackets into each of these calculations,
where necessary, to make them correct.

1 $4 + 3 + 2 = 9$

2 $13 - 4 + 2 = 11$

3 $13 - 4 + 2 = 7$

4 $12 - 7 + 1 = 4$

5 $8 - 2 \times 2 = 4$

6 $8 \div 4 \times 2 = 4$

7 $9 - 2 - 1 = 6$

8 $6 + 3 \times 2 = 12$

9 $28 - 5 + 3 = 20$

10 $5 \times 6 \div 3 = 10$

11 $20 \div 5 + 4 = 8$

12 $5 \times 12 \div 3 = 20$

13 $4 + 8 \div 2 = 6$

14 $12 \div 3 \times 2 = 2$

15 $3 \times 7 + 4 = 25$

16 $6 \times 5 - 4 = 26$

17 $6 \times 5 - 4 = 6$

18 $6 - 5 - 4 = 5$

19 $6 - 5 + 1 = 0$

20 $16 \div 4 \times 2 = 2$

21 $16 \div 4 \times 2 = 8$

22 $15 - 6 \div 3 = 13$

23 $1 + 4 \times 5 = 25$

24 $12 - 10 \div 2 = 7$

25 $5 - 2 - 1 = 4$

26 $9 \times 2 + 7 = 81$

27 $9 \times 2 + 7 = 25$

28 $9 - 2 \times 7 = 49$

29 $4 + 5 \div 3 = 3$

30 $24 \div 8 - 2 = 4$

31 $24 \div 8 - 2 = 1$

32 $15 - 6 \div 3 = 3$

33 $4 \times 4 + 5 = 36$

34 $12 - 10 \div 2 = 1$

35 $36 \div 9 \div 3 = 12$

36 $13 - 12 \div 3 = 9$

37 $14 + 3 \times 2 = 34$

38 $12 \div 3 + 7 = 11$

39 $5 \times 2 + 5 - 9 = 6$

40 $6 \times 8 - 7 = 6$

Investigation A

Sometimes calculators can give 'wrong' answers.

(*a*) Try the problems in the previous two exercises using a calculator.
Which calculations did the calculator get right?

(*b*) Does the calculator use the same conventions as you do?

SUMMARY

Examples

1 $60 - 3 \times (\underline{4 + 5}) = 60 - \underline{3 \times 9} = 33$

2 $7 - \frac{1}{4}$ of $(\underline{20 \times 3} - 48) + \underline{1 \div 2}$
  $= 7 - \frac{1}{4}$ of $(\underline{60 - 48}) + 0.5$
  $= 7 - \underline{\frac{1}{4} \text{ of } 12} + 0.5$
  $= \underline{7 - 3} + 0.5 = \underline{4 + 0.5} = 4.5$

Check the examples carefully.
Check that the order of operations has
been followed. (The operation
performed has been underlined at each
stage.)

You have seen that the *order of operations* is
important in calculations.
The order in which we perform operations is
known as BODMAS.

B Brackets
O of
D Division
M Multiplication
A Addition
S Subtraction

We also work from left to right.

EXERCISE 6

Work out:

1 $20 - 3 \times 5 + 6 \div 3 - 4 + 16 \div 8$

2 $6 \times 3 - 2 \times 4 + 9 \div 3 - 2 \times 1 + 5 \times 2 - 24 \div 8 + 4 \times 6$

3 $6 \times (3 - 2) \times 4 + 9 \div (3 - 2) \times (1 + 5) \times 2 - 24 \div (8 + 4) \times 6$

4 $(6 \times 3 - 2) \times 4 + 9 \div 3 - 2 \times 1 + (5 \times 2 - 24 \div 8) + 4 \times 6$

5 $6 \times (3 - 2) \times (4 + 9) \div 3 - 2 \times (1 + 5 \times 2) - 24 \div (8 + 4 \times 6)$

6 $(\frac{1}{2}$ of $12 - 4) \times 2 + \frac{1}{4}$ of $(80 - 16) \times 3 - \frac{1}{3}$ of 9

7 $\frac{1}{2}$ of $(12 - 4) \times 2 + (\frac{1}{4}$ of $80 - 16) \times 3 - \frac{1}{3}$ of 9

8 $\frac{1}{2}$ of $(12 - 4 \times 2) + \frac{1}{4}$ of $(80 - 16 \times 3) - \frac{1}{3}$ of 9

9 $\frac{1}{2}$ of $(12 - 4) \times 2 + \frac{1}{4}$ of $80 - 16 \times (3 - \frac{1}{3}$ of $9)$

10 $(\frac{1}{9}$ of $(6 \times (((80 - \frac{1}{2}$ of $60) + 5) \div 11) - 12)) - 2$

Investigation B 1234

We can use all the digits 1, 2, 3, 4 like this:

$1 \times (2 + 3) - 4 = 1$ $1 + 2 + 3 - 4 = 2$ $1 \times 2 \times 3 \times 4 = 24$

and so on, keeping the digits in the same order.

(a) Is 24 the highest number we can make using the digits 1, 2, 3, 4?

(b) How many of the numbers from 1 to 24 can you make this way?
Write down all your answers.

Revision exercise

1 Follow this flow chart:

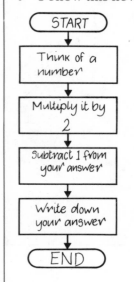

(a) Try *five* different numbers.

(b) Do you notice anything about your answers?

(c) Which number goes through the flow chart unchanged?

(d) How can you change the flow chart so that it only produces *even* numbers?

2

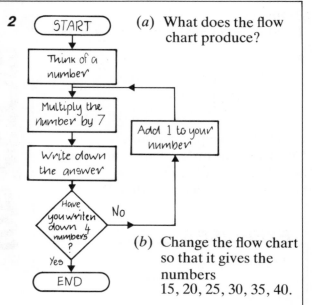

(a) What does the flow chart produce?

(b) Change the flow chart so that it gives the numbers 15, 20, 25, 30, 35, 40.

3 Complete these flow diagrams:

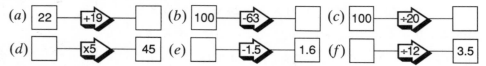

(a) 22 — +19 — ☐ (b) 100 — -63 — ☐ (c) 100 — ÷20 — ☐

(d) ☐ — x5 — 45 (e) ☐ — -1.5 — 1.6 (f) ☐ — ÷12 — 3.5

4 Complete these flow diagrams:

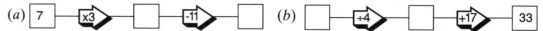

(a) 7 — x3 — ☐ — -11 — ☐   (b) ☐ — ÷4 — ☐ — +17 — 33

5 Place the correct operation symbol in each arrow:

(a) 6 ⇨ 3 ⇨ 4 ⮕ 12   (b) 12 ⇨ 4 ⇨ 5 ⇨ 7 ⮕ 8

6 Work out these calculations:

(a) $16 + 7 - 3$ (b) $16 + 7 \times 3$ (c) $3 \times 4 \div 2$ (d) $6 \times 4 - 18 \div 3$

(e) $4 + 25 \div 5 - 3 \times 2 + 1 \times 7 - 30 \div 15 + 12 - 8 + 4 - 24 \div 3$

7 Place brackets in these to make each statement correct:

(a) $4 + 3 \times 2 - 1 = 7$ (b) $4 + 3 \times 2 - 1 = 13$ (c) $4 + 3 \times 2 - 1 = 9$

8 Work out:

(a) $7 \times 5 - 6 \div 2 + 10 \times 5 + 30 \div 5 - 7 - 11$ (b) $\frac{1}{2}$ of $(3 \times 10 - 2 \times 9) - 36 \div 18$

7. SHAPE

25 shapes have been used to make the 'M'. 24 of them are DIFFERENT in some way. Which one has been used twice?

Use some or all of the shapes to make some TANGRAMS of your own.

Looking at triangles

ANGLE CHECK

The four corners of a sheet of A4 size paper are all **right-angles (90°)**.

SHEET SIZE A4

Tear off one corner of a sheet of paper. One angle should be 90°.

We can use the corner to show that the angle below is greater than 90°.

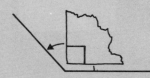

EXERCISE 1

Use your torn off corner to say whether each angle in the triangles below is less than 90°, equal to 90°, greater than 90°.

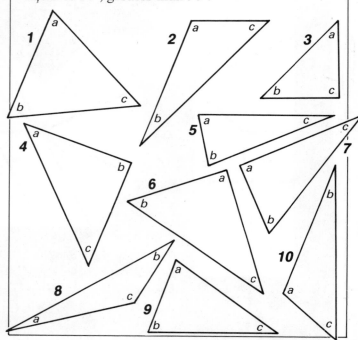

NOTATION

We can write

angle *a* is *less* than 90° as $a < 90°$

angle *a* is *equal* to 90° as $a = 90°$

angle *a* is *greater* than 90° as $a > 90°$

EXERCISE 2

1 In triangle 10 in Exercise 1, you should have found that

$$a > 90°, b < 90°, c < 90°$$

Describe the angles in triangles 1–9 in a similar way.

2 Try sketching triangles which have angles

$a = 90°,$	$b < 90°,$	$c < 90°$
$a = 90°,$	$b < 90°,$	$c > 90°$
$a = 90°,$	$b = 90°,$	$c = 90°$
$a < 90°,$	$b < 90°,$	$c < 90°$
$a > 90°,$	$b > 90°,$	$c < 90°$

ANGLE CLASSIFICATION

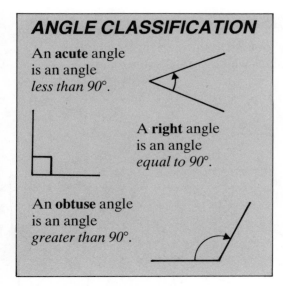

An **acute** angle
is an angle
less than 90°.

A **right** angle
is an angle
equal to 90°.

An **obtuse** angle
is an angle
greater than 90°.

EXERCISE 3

1 Use your 'paper-corner' to help you decide
which angles in these triangles are acute or
right or obtuse angles.

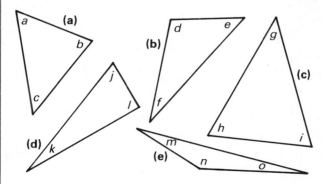

2 Draw *five* triangles of your own and describe
each of the angles in each triangle.

TRIANGLE CLASSIFICATION

We can describe triangles by looking at
the *size* of the angles:

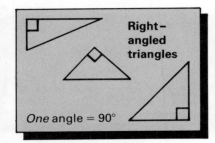

**Right-
angled
triangles**

One angle = 90°

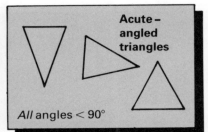

**Acute-
angled
triangles**

All angles < 90°

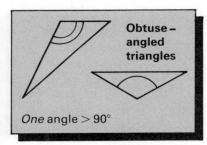

**Obtuse-
angled
triangles**

One angle > 90°

EXERCISE 4

1 Determine which of these triangles are
acute-angled, right-angled, obtuse-angled.

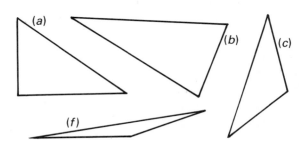

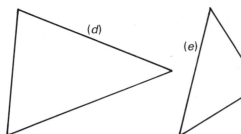

2 Draw two *acute*-angled triangles, *right*-angled triangles,
obtuse-angled triangles of your own.
Say which angles are *acute, right* or *obtuse* angles.

EQUAL SIDES

Look at these lines:

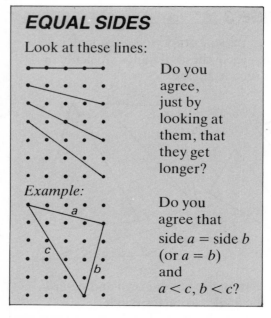

Do you agree, just by looking at them, that they get longer?

Example:

Do you agree that side a = side b (or $a = b$) and $a < c$, $b < c$?

EXERCISE 5

Decide by looking at these triangles whether any have sides which are the same length.

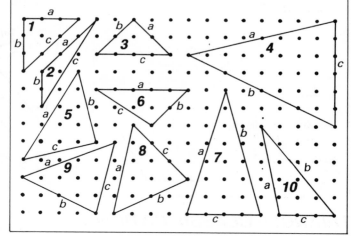

TRIANGLE CLASSIFICATION

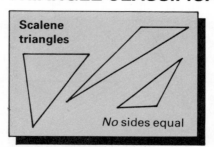

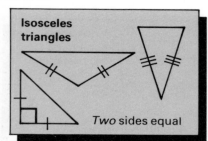

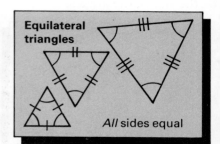

EXERCISE 6

1 Decide which of triangles 1–10 in Exercise 5 are scalene or isosceles.

2 Can you explain why it is not possible to draw an equilateral triangle on a square-dot lattice as above?

3 Describe the triangles on this isometric dot grid:

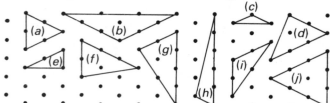

4 Triangle 1 in Exercise 5 is a *right-angled isosceles triangle*.
Describe all the other triangles in Exercise 5 and 6 in a similar way.

Investigation A

FINDING TRIANGLES

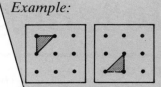

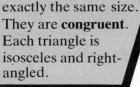

Example: These two triangles are exactly the same size. They are **congruent**. Each triangle is isosceles and right-angled.

(*a*) Using 9-dots as above, find the *eight* different triangles which are possible. (The two above count as one only.)

(*b*) Classify each of the triangles as in the example above.

(*c*) Are there any types of triangles which are impossible on the 9-dot square lattice?

(*d*) Which triangles are **similar** (same shape, different size)?

(*e*) Can you prove that you have found all possible triangles?

(*f*) Repeat the investigation for this arrangement of dots

(isometric dots):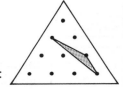

Investigation B

TRIANGLE TANGRAMS

(*a*) Cut out a rectangular piece of card 5 squares by 6 squares.

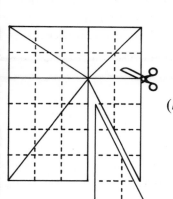

(*b*) Cut out the eight triangles as shown.

(*c*) Use the triangles to make other triangles:

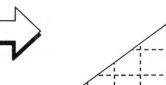

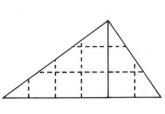

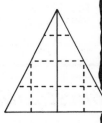

Make as many different triangles as possible.

(*d*) Use more than two triangles to make other triangles.

(*e*) Describe as accurately as you can each triangle you have found.

(*f*) Is an *equilateral* triangle possible?

Angles in triangles

Investigation *A*

PAPER TRIANGLES

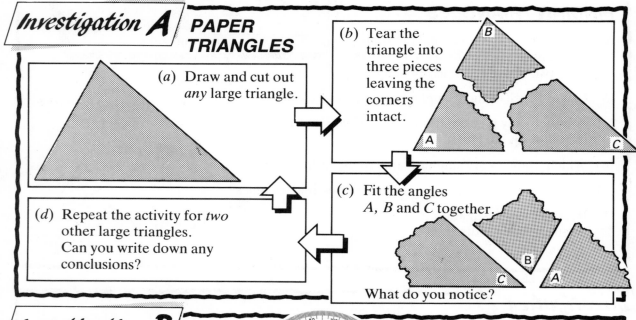

(*a*) Draw and cut out *any* large triangle.

(*b*) Tear the triangle into three pieces leaving the corners intact.

(*c*) Fit the angles A, B and C together.

What do you notice?

(*d*) Repeat the activity for *two* other large triangles. Can you write down any conclusions?

Investigation *B*

ANGLE SUMS

(*a*) Draw any three triangles in your book. Make each side at least 5 cm.

(*b*) Using a protractor, measure each angle in each triangle.

(*c*) Add up the three angles for each triangle. What do you notice?

Investigation *C*

SAME ANGLES

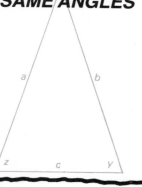

Drawn here are two isosceles triangles.

(*a*) What do you know about the lengths of sides *a* and *b* in each case?

(*b*) Measure the angles *x*, *y* and *z* in each. Put your answers in a table if necessary.

(*c*) What do you notice about the angles for each triangle? What do all three total? Are any angles the same size?

(*d*) Write down *two facts* about any isosceles triangle.

TRIANGLE FACTS

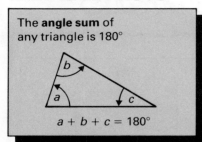

The **angle sum** of any triangle is 180°

$a + b + c = 180°$

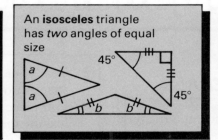

An **isosceles** triangle has *two* angles of equal size

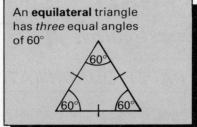

An **equilateral** triangle has *three* equal angles of 60°

EXERCISE

1 Find the missing angles in these triangles:

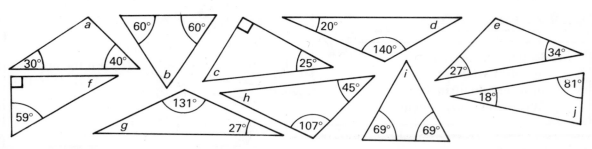

NOTATION

Sides which are the same length are marked like this:

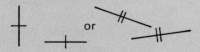

or

Angles which are the same size are marked with the same symbol:

2 Use the information given to find all of the missing angles:

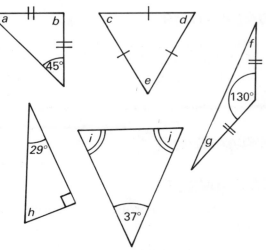

3 Which of these are possible triangles:

(*a*) three equal sides and one angle of 50°

(*b*) two equal sides and an angle of 35°

(*c*) two angles of 90°

(*d*) two angles of 55° and no equal sides

(*e*) one angle of 50°, one angle of 80° and two equal sides?

4 *Describe* and *draw* all of the triangles in questions 1. 2 and 3 where possible.

Angles in quadrilaterals

Investigation A

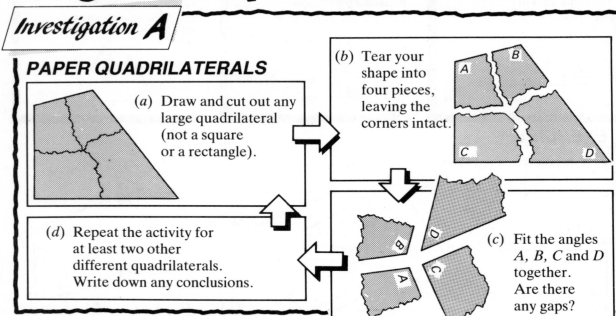

PAPER QUADRILATERALS

(a) Draw and cut out any large quadrilateral (not a square or a rectangle).

(b) Tear your shape into four pieces, leaving the corners intact.

(c) Fit the angles A, B, C and D together. Are there any gaps?

(d) Repeat the activity for at least two other different quadrilaterals. Write down any conclusions.

Investigation B

ANGLE SUMS

(a) Draw any four quadrilaterals. Make the length of each side at least 5 cm.

(b) Using a protractor, measure each of the four angles in each quadrilateral.

(c) For each quadrilateral, add up the four angles you have measured. What do you notice? Write down any conclusions.

Investigation C

SAME ANGLES

Drawn below are a square and a rectangle.

(a) Measure, using a protractor, the four angles in each.

(b) Find the *angle sum* for each shape.

(c) What can you say about each angle of a rectangle or a square?

(d) Write down any *facts* you know about squares and rectangles.

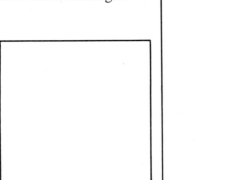

QUADRILATERAL FACTS

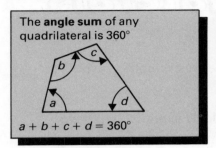

The **angle sum** of any quadrilateral is 360°

$a + b + c + d = 360°$

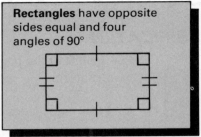

Rectangles have opposite sides equal and four angles of 90°

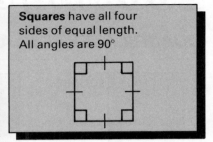

Squares have all four sides of equal length. All angles are 90°

EXERCISE

1 Calculate the size of the missing angle in each of these quadrilaterals.

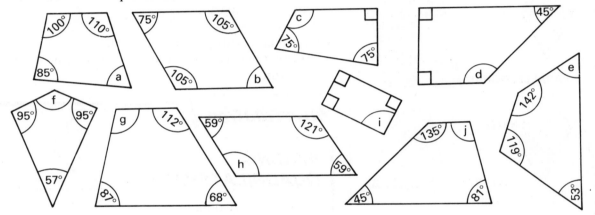

2 In these quadrilaterals, angles of the same size are marked with the same symbol.

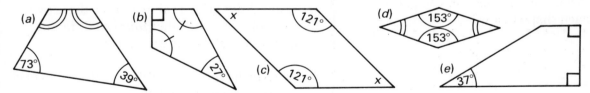

Write down the four angles for each quadrilateral.

3 Find the missing angle when

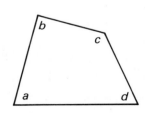

$a = 75°$, $b = 62°$, $c = 79°$. $d = 75°$, $c = 105°$, $a = 105°$.
$a = 86°$, $b = 107°$, $c = 120°$. $a = b = 60°$, $c = d$.
$a = b = 62°$, $d = 119°$. $a = b = 90°$, $c = 77°$.
$a = b = c = 90°$. $a = b = c = 110°$.
$a = b = c = 72°$. $a = b = c = 30°$.

Make a sketch of each quadrilateral.

Looking at quadrilaterals

QUADRILATERAL CLASSIFICATION

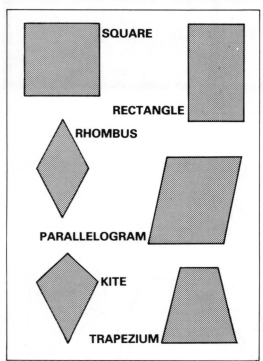

SQUARE

RECTANGLE

RHOMBUS

PARALLELOGRAM

KITE

TRAPEZIUM

On the left of the page are examples of types of quadrilaterals.

1   How many sides do *all* quadrilaterals have?

2   Write down anything you know about each type of quadrilateral. (Ask if you are not sure.)

3   Draw *three* different quadrilaterals for each type shown, if you can.

4   'A square is also a parallelogram'.
Write down as many other similar statements as you can.

Investigation

FINDING QUADRILATERALS

Here are two examples of quadrilaterals drawn on a 9-dot grid.

(a)   Using 9-dot grids as above, draw these two examples and the other *fourteen* different quadrilaterals which are possible.

(b)   Say which type of quadrilateral describes each of your sixteen drawings.

EXERCISE 1

Each shape below is a quadrilateral. What other names can you give to each shape below?

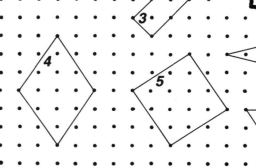

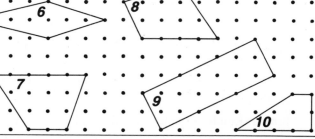

EXERCISE 2 EXTENSION

1 Copy out this table:

	Acute	Obtuse	Right
Scalene			
Isosceles			
Equilateral			

(*a*) Try to draw a triangle which will fit into each box.

(*b*) If a triangle is impossible to draw, try to explain why.

2 (*a*) Describe each of these quadrilaterals.

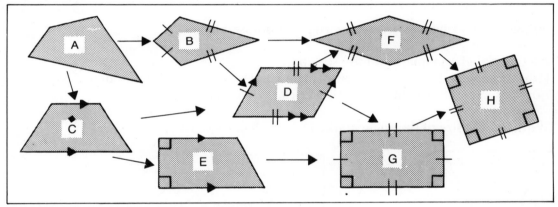

(*b*) What type of quadrilaterals are {D, G, F, H}?

(*c*) Can a square be a kite? Explain your answer.

(*d*) Follow the arrows between the quadrilaterals above and describe each change.

(*e*) Make a list of the quadrilaterals above which are in these sets:

{Quadrilaterals}   {Trapezia}   {Kites}   {Squares}
{Parallelograms}   {Rhombi}   {Rectangles}

3 Venn diagrams

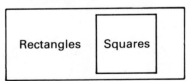

This Venn diagram tells us that
'All squares are rectangles'.

(*a*) What information does this Venn diagram give us?

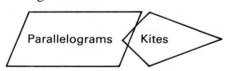

(*b*) Draw similar diagrams for other types of quadrilaterals.

Revision exercise

1   Look at the triangles below:

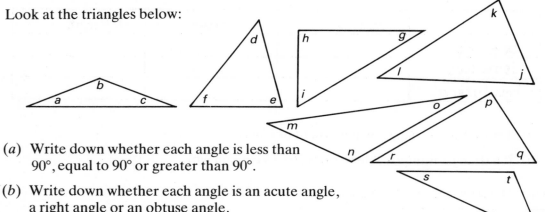

(*a*)   Write down whether each angle is less than 90°, equal to 90° or greater than 90°.

(*b*)   Write down whether each angle is an acute angle, a right angle or an obtuse angle.

(*c*)   Say which triangles are acute-, right- or obtuse-angled.

2   All the triangles in question 1 are scalene.
Draw triangles which are: (*a*) acute-angled *and* isosceles   (*b*) right-angled *and* isosceles   (*c*) obtuse-angled *and* isosceles   (*d*) equilateral.

3   Work out the size of the angle marked *x* in each of these triangles.

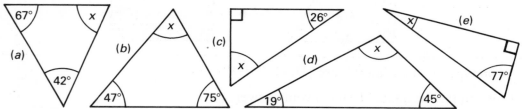

4   Work out the size of the two angles marked *x* and *y* in these isosceles triangles.

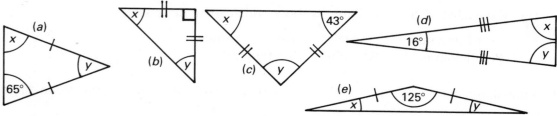

5   Work out the size of the missing angle in these quadrilaterals.

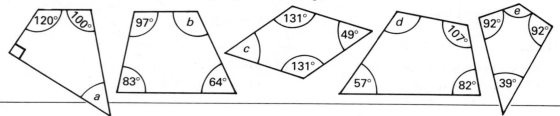

8. Algebra

n → 2n

Function machines

A function machine can be adjusted to run ten different programmes, like a washing machine. The diagram below shows what happened when function machine 0 was used.

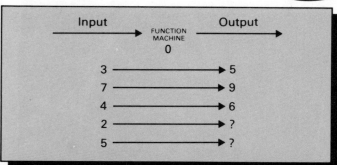

What does the machine do?
Function machine 0 adds 2 to each number put into it. We can predict further results:

$$2 \overset{+2}{\to} 4$$
$$5 \overset{+2}{\to} 7$$

Input	FUNCTION MACHINE 1	Output
1	→	5
7	→	11
4	→	8
9	→	?
3	→	?

EXERCISE 1

For each diagram, (*a*) describe what the function machine does, and (*b*) find the missing outputs.

Input	FUNCTION MACHINE 2	Output
2	→	1
8	→	7
5	→	4
1	→	?
7	→	?

Input	FUNCTION MACHINE 3	Output
3	→	6
9	→	18
6	→	12
1	→	?
8	→	?

Input	FUNCTION MACHINE 4	Output
2	→	8
3	→	12
6	→	24
4	→	?
9	→	?

Input	FUNCTION MACHINE 5	Output
6	→	2
3	→	1
12	→	4
21	→	?
15	→	?

Input	FUNCTION MACHINE 6	Output
8	→	$5\frac{1}{2}$
4	→	$1\frac{1}{2}$
7	→	$4\frac{1}{2}$
3	→	?
9	→	?

Input	FUNCTION MACHINE 7	Output
3	→	7
8	→	17
5	→	11
2	→	?
6	→	?

Input	FUNCTION MACHINE 8	Output
9	→	26
2	→	5
7	→	20
1	→	?
4	→	?

Input	FUNCTION MACHINE 9	Output
1	→	2
3	→	10
4	→	14
8	→	?
5	→	?

The function machines can also be made to work backwards:

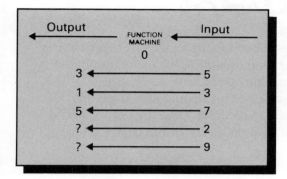

The effect of reversing the function machine is to change its function; function machine 0 now takes 2 away instead of adding it. We call this an **inverse** operation. The inverse of adding 2 is subtracting 2. We can still predict results:

$$0 \overset{-2}{\leftarrow} 2$$
$$7 \overset{-2}{\leftarrow} 9$$

EXERCISE 2

For each diagram, (*a*) describe the inverse operation, and
(*b*) find the missing outputs.

Output FUNCTION MACHINE	Input
1 ←	5
7 ←	11
4 ←	8
? ←	9
? ←	6

Output FUNCTION MACHINE 2	Input
2 ←	1
8 ←	7
5 ←	4
? ←	2
? ←	8

Output FUNCTION MACHINE 3	Input
3 ←	6
9 ←	18
6 ←	12
? ←	8
? ←	5

Output FUNCTION MACHINE 4	Input
2 ←	8
3 ←	12
6 ←	24
? ←	4
? ←	20

Output FUNCTION MACHINE 5	Input
6 ←	2
3 ←	1
12 ←	4
? ←	6
? ←	3

Output FUNCTION MACHINE 6	Input
8 ←	$5\frac{1}{2}$
4 ←	$1\frac{1}{2}$
7 ←	$4\frac{1}{2}$
? ←	7
? ←	$2\frac{1}{2}$

Output FUNCTION MACHINE 7	Input
3 ←	7
8 ←	17
5 ←	11
? ←	8
? ←	3

Output FUNCTION MACHINE 8	Input
9 ←	26
2 ←	5
7 ←	20
? ←	8
? ←	14

Output FUNCTION MACHINE 9	Input
1 ←	2
3 ←	10
4 ←	14
? ←	20
? ←	8

Investigation

Does every operation $(+, -, \div, \times)$ have an inverse? From the work you have already done, write down as many inverses as you can.

Letters for numbers

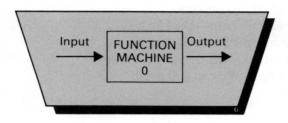

Input → FUNCTION MACHINE 0 → Output

We have described function machine 0 as carrying out the operation of 'add 2'. To every number we input, the machine adds 2.

There is a quick way of writing this: if x is any number ready to be input, then the output would be the same number and $+2$, that is, $x + 2$.

Function machine 0 would do $x \rightarrow x + 2$

We could then write **Input** $\rightarrow$ $\boxed{x \rightarrow x + 2}$ $\rightarrow$ **Output**

For a function machine which multiplies by 5, we would write:

$x \rightarrow 5x$ where $5x$ means $5 \times x$

For a function machine which multiplies by 7 and adds 2 we would write:

$x \rightarrow 7x + 2$

For a function machine which divides by 2, we would write:

$x \rightarrow \dfrac{x}{2}$

EXERCISE 1

Describe function machines 1 to 10 in Exercise 1 of the previous section in terms of letters.

EXERCISE 2

Describe inverse function machines 1 to 10 in Exercise 2 of the previous section in terms of letters.

EXERCISE 3

Find the output to the following function machines:

1 $7 \rightarrow \boxed{x \rightarrow x + 3} \rightarrow ?$ **2** $3 \rightarrow \boxed{x \rightarrow 5x} \rightarrow ?$ **3** $24 \rightarrow \boxed{x \rightarrow \frac{x}{6}} \rightarrow ?$

4 $9 \rightarrow \boxed{x \rightarrow x - 4} \rightarrow ?$ **5** $4 \rightarrow \boxed{x \rightarrow x + 3\frac{1}{2}} \rightarrow ?$ **6** $6 \rightarrow \boxed{x \rightarrow 7x} \rightarrow ?$

7 $5 \rightarrow \boxed{x \rightarrow 2x - 1} \rightarrow ?$ **8** $7 \rightarrow \boxed{x \rightarrow 4x - 3} \rightarrow ?$ **9** $3 \rightarrow \boxed{x \rightarrow 8 - 2x} \rightarrow ?$

10 $2 \rightarrow \boxed{x \rightarrow 3x + 1} \rightarrow ?$ **11** $8 \rightarrow \boxed{x \rightarrow \frac{2x + 1}{2}} \rightarrow$ **12** $5 \rightarrow \boxed{x \rightarrow x \times x} \rightarrow ?$

13 $3 \rightarrow \boxed{x \rightarrow 10 - 2x} \rightarrow ?$ **14** $4 \rightarrow \boxed{x \rightarrow 3x - 3} \rightarrow ?$ **15** $15 \rightarrow \boxed{x \rightarrow \frac{x}{5}} \rightarrow ?$

16 $7 \rightarrow \boxed{x \rightarrow 6x - 4} \rightarrow ?$ **17** $6 \rightarrow \boxed{x \rightarrow 8x} \rightarrow ?$ **18** $9 \rightarrow \boxed{x \rightarrow x + 8} \rightarrow ?$

19 $4 \rightarrow \boxed{x \rightarrow 3x - \frac{1}{2}} \rightarrow ?$ **20** $8 \rightarrow \boxed{x \rightarrow \frac{x}{2} + \frac{1}{2}} \rightarrow ?$

Flow charts

Flow charts help us order our thinking. A flow chart is a series of instructions which have been arranged in a special order, and can be used to explain how calculations are being done.

$$(2 \times 4) + (8 \div 2)$$

must be done in this order:

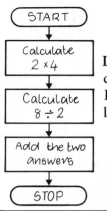

Do you remember the work we did on operations in Chapter 6? If not turn back and have a look now.

FLOW CHARTS AND ALGEBRA

EXERCISE 1

Draw flow charts for these problems:

1 $(2 + 3) \times 5$ **2** $36 \div (3 \times 2)$ **3** $5 + 3 - 2$

4 $18 - (10 + 3)$ **5** $(3 \times 6) + 7$ **6** $12 + (5 \times 3) - 14$

7 $8 \div (12 \div 6) + 3$ **8** $(20 \div 5) + (5 \times 3)$

For these problems you will have to think carefully about the write out your flow chart:

9 $3 \times 7 + 4$ **10** $13 - 12 \div 3 + 5$ **11** $14 + 3 \times 2 - 6$

12 $12 \div 3 + 7 \times 2$ **13** $5 \times 2 + 5 - 9$ **14** $12 \div 3 \times 2$

15 $6 \times 8 - 7 \times 2$

$x \rightarrow 2x + 1$ should be worked out in a special order: This flow chart clearly shows you what calculations need to be done, and also the order in which they are to be carried out.

Investigation

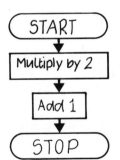

Use a calculator if you need to

Use your calculator to work through some of your flow charts in the exercise above. Do you get the right answer? Do the flow charts help you set out your work on the calculator in the correct order? If your calculator has parentheses (brackets) and a memory you might like to think about how these could help you do some of the problems.

EXERCISE 2

Draw flow charts for the following:

1 $x \rightarrow 3x - 1$ **2** $x \rightarrow 4x + 4$ **3** $x \rightarrow 10 - 2x$

4 $x \rightarrow 3x - \dfrac{1}{2}$ **5** $x \rightarrow 99 - 4x$ **6** $x \rightarrow \dfrac{x}{5} + 3$

7 $x \rightarrow \dfrac{3x}{4}$ **8** $x \rightarrow x \times x \times 3$ **9** $x \rightarrow \dfrac{x}{2} + \dfrac{1}{2}$

10 $x \rightarrow \dfrac{2x + 1}{2}$

Substitution

We have already seen that
function machines can be used
with any number in place of the
letter x. The same is true for
any expression using x.

If $x = 3$ then $2x - 4$ becomes $(2 \times 3) - 4 = 6 - 4 = 2$
If $x = 5$ then $2x - 4$ becomes $(2 \times 5) - 4 = 10 - 4 = 6$
If $x = 4$ then $\frac{1}{2}(x + 2)$ becomes $\frac{1}{2}(4 + 2) = \frac{1}{2}(6) = 3$
If $x = 7$ then $\frac{1}{2}(x + 2)$ becomes $\frac{1}{2}(7 + 2) = \frac{1}{2}(9) = 4\frac{1}{2}$

EXERCISE 1

1 If $x = 4$, find the value of (a) $3x$ (b) $x + 5$ (c) $2x - 3$ (d) $5x + 2$
(e) $2(x + 1)$ (a) $3(2x - 1)$ (g) $\frac{1}{2}(x + 4)$

2 If $x = 3$, find the value of (a) $5x$ (b) $x - 2$
(c) $x \times x$ (d) $2x - 3$ (e) $4x + \frac{1}{2}$
(f) $7(x - 3)$ (g) $\frac{1}{3}(x + 9)$

3 Find the value of $4x + 3$ when $x = 5$.

4 Find the value of $x \times x + 2x - 1$ when $x = 3$.

5 If $a = 2$ what would be the value of $3a$?

6 When $c = 8$ find the value of $4c + 5$.

7 What is $5d - 2$ when $d = 3$?

8 Calculate $2(6y + 4)$ when $y = 7$.

9 Work out the value of $3(4x - 3)$ when $x = 9$.

10 What is $2a(a + 2)$ when $a = 3$?

11 Work out the value of $2(3x + 5)$ when $x = 2$.

12 Calculate $4x + 7$ when $x = 5$.

13 If $y = 2\frac{1}{2}$, what would be the value of $2y + 3$?

14 What is $4(2a + 1)$ when $a = 9$?

15 Work out the value of $x \times x \times x$ when $x = 3$.

Investigation

$$\begin{array}{r} A\,B\,C\,D\,E \\ +\,A\,B\,C\,D\,E \\ \hline 1\,1\,8\,7\,2\,4 \end{array}$$

Can you find what numbers the letters represent?
Make up some problems of your own like this.

A function machine can have more than one input:

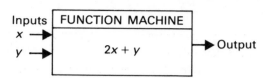
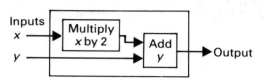

x and y have their own values.
If $x = 3$ and $y = 4$ then $2x + y$ becomes $(2 \times 3) + 4 = 6 + 4 = 10$

EXERCISE 2

Find the value of the following when $x = 3$, $y = 4$ and $z = 5$.

1 $2x + y$ **2** $2y + 3z$ **3** $4x + y$ **4** $y + 2z$ **5** $x + y + z$

6 $3y - z$ **7** $2x + 4y - 4z$ **8** $4x + y - 2z$ **9** $5x - 2y$ **10** $x + 3y - z$

11 $2x + 2y - 2z$ **12** $3x - y - z$ **13** $6x - 4y + 2z$ **14** $x + y - z$ **15** $8z - 6y - x$

16 $4y - 2x - 2z$

Find the value of the following when $a = 1$, $b = 2$, $c = 3$.

17 $2b - 3a$ **18** $2(b + 3a)$ **19** $3(2b - a)$ **20** $c - b$ **21** $\frac{1}{2}b + c$

22 $\frac{1}{2}(2c + b)$ **23** $\frac{b}{2} + a + c$ **24** $\frac{a + b + c}{2}$ **25** $5a + 2b - 3c$ **26** $4c \div b$

27 $4(a + b)$ **28** $5(a + b + c)$ **29** $c(a + b)$ **30** $b(2a + c)$ **31** $c(2c + b)$

32 $\frac{3c + a}{b}$ **33** $\frac{c}{3} + a$ **34** $2b - a$ **35** $a(b + c) + 2c$

What meaning does ab have?
$3a$ means $3 \times a$, so ab would mean $a \times b$.
If $a = 2$ and $b = 4$, $3a = 3 \times a = 3 \times 2 = 6$
$$ab = a \times b = 2 \times 4 = 8$$

EXERCISE 3

Find the value of the following when $a = 2$, $b = 5$ and $c = 8$.

1 ab **2** bc **3** $2ac$ **4** $2ab + 3$ **5** $3 + bc$

6 $ab - a$ **7** abc **8** $3bc$ **9** $50 - ac$ **10** $3c - b$

11 $ab \times ab$ **12** $4(ab + c)$ **13** $6(4 + ac)$ **14** $b - \dfrac{c}{a}$ **15** $\dfrac{2b - c}{a}$

16 $ac - ab$ **17** $2(b - 2)$ **18** $c - (b + a)$ **19** $\dfrac{bc}{a}$ **20** $ab - c$

Simplifying expressions

If $x = 4$, find the value of (a) $x + x + x + x$ (b) $4x$.
Can you explain why the answers are the same?
We simplify expressions to make them shorter:
$3x - x = 2x$ since $x + x + x - x = x + x = 2x$

EXERCISE 1

Simplify the following:

1 $x + x + x + x + x$ **2** $x + x + x - x + x$ **3** $3x + 2x$

4 $4x - 2x$ **5** $4x + 2x + x$ **6** $x + 2x + x$

7 $9x - x + 2x$ **8** $x + 8x - 5x$ **9** $x + 7x + 4x - 3x$

10 $5x + 2x - x - 4x$ **11** $6x - 4x + 3x$ **12** $4x + 5x - 9x$

13 $9x - 3x + 4x - 8x$ **14** $4x - 2x + 6x$ **15** $3x + 2x - x - x - 2x + 4x$

16 $7x + 2x - 3x$ **17** $10x - 7x + 6x$ **18** $13x - 2x + 9x - 11x + 7x$

All letters are different: they represent different values in an
expression. We must therefore keep them separate.
To simplify $x + x + y + y + x$: gather together the xs:
$x + x + x = 3x$, then the ys: $y + y = 2y$.
The answer is $3x + 2y$. We cannot simplify this any further.
Numbers should also be kept separate:

$$3x + x + y + 3 + y + 2$$
$$= 3x + x + y + y + 3 + 2$$
$$= 4x + 2y + 5$$

EXERCISE 2

Simplify the following:

1 $7x + 4y + 3x - 2y$ **2** $2x + y + x + y$ **3** $3x - x + 4y - 2y$

4 $2a + 4b + 4a + 2b$ **5** $p + q - p - q + 6p$ **6** $3x + y - x + 2y$

7 $m + 2n + m - 2n + m$ **8** $3s + 4t - 2s + 2t + s$ **9** $2a + b + 3a - b$

10 $5a + 3b - 2a - 3b - 3a$ **11** $7x + y + 8x - 4x + 9y$ **12** $8x + 4 + 3y + x - 2$

13 $p + 2q + 7 - p + q + 3$ **14** $7a + b + 8 - 4a + 9b + 7$ **15** $7t + s + 1 - 2t + s$

16 $9a + b - 6a + 2 - b + 3$ **17** $8e + f + 6 - 5 + 2f + 3e$ **18** $8m + 5n - 2m + 3n - 2m$

19 $7x + 3y + 1 - 2x - y - 1$ **20** $6p + q + 3 - 5p + 2q - 1$ **21** $2a + 7 + 4b + 5a + 2b$

22 $4b + 4c - 2b + a - 3c$ **23** $8x - 4x + y + 6y - x - 2y$ **24** $7m + 5n + 6 + 3n + m$

25 $5x + 2y - 3x + y + 7 + x + y - 2 + 4x - 2y$

Brackets are used in the same way as with numbers.
$2(x + 2y)$ means we have two of everything in the bracket.
So $2(x + 2y) = 2 \times x + 2 \times 2y = 2x + 4y$
The number outside the bracket mutliplies *everything* inside.

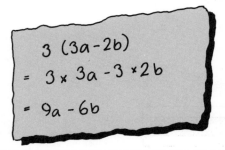

$$3(3a - 2b)$$
$$= 3 \times 3a - 3 \times 2b$$
$$= 9a - 6b$$

$$2(a - b) + 3(a + 3)$$
$$= 2 \times a - 2 \times b + 3 \times a + 3 \times 3$$
$$= 2a - 2b + 3a + 9$$
$$= 5a - 2b + 9$$

EXERCISE 3

Remove the brackets and simplify where possible:

1 $2(x + 1)$ **2** $5(a + b)$

3 $7(2 - x)$ **4** $6(3 - 2x)$

5 $4(3x - 4)$ **6** $3x + 3(x + 1)$

7 $7 + 2(3x + 4)$ **8** $4 + 2(3x - 1)$

9 $4(2x + 1) + 5$ **10** $2q + 8p + 2(p + q)$

11 $2a + b + 3(a + 2b)$ **12** $4s + t + 2(s + t)$

13 $4x + 5y + 3(3x - y)$ **14** $5(q + 3r) + 2q - 5r$

15 $3(x + 2) + 2(x + 1)$ **16** $5(2x + 1) + 2(x + 3)$

17 $3(6x + 4) + 4(x - 1)$ **18** $4(x + 1) - 3x - 2$

19 $3p + 8q + 3(p - 2q)$ **20** $2(3x + y + 4z) + 3(x + 3y - 2z)$

21 $4(a + 2b + 3) + 3(a + 4b - 3)$ **22** $5(x + y + 3) + 4(x - y) - 10$

23 $3(2x + 2y) + 2(x - y) + x$ **24** $7p + 2q + 4(p + 5 + 2q)$

25 $2(a + 2b) + 3(a - b)$ **26** $4x + 4(x - 2) + 2x$

27 $5(x + y) + 3(x - y) + 6y$ **28** $8(p + 2q) + 2(2p - 3q) + 4p$

29 $3(x + 2y) - 3(x + y) + 4(2x + 3y) + 7x$

30 $2(s + 3t) - 2(s + t) + 3(t + 2) - 7t - 6$

Simple expressions

Letters are used in expressions when we do not know a number.
By using letters it is still possible to write down a formula which
can then be used instead of numbers.
A piece of wood is 250 cm
long. A piece x cm long has been cut
off it. What is the length,
L cm, of the remaining piece?

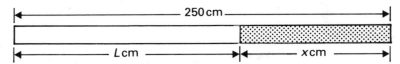

If x had been a number we would have taken it away from 250.
We can still do the same:

$$L = 250 - x$$

This is the expression we want: a simple expression or formula
using the letters L and x.

There are n ten-pence coins in a pile.
What is the total value, V, of the coins?

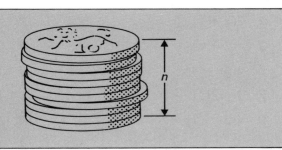

    1 coin would be 10p
    2 coins would be $2 \times 10p = 20p$
    3 coins would be $3 \times 10p = 30p$
    n coins would be $n \times 10p = 10n$ pence.
    The total value $V = 10n$ pence.

EXERCISE 1

Express the following in terms of a simple expression:

1

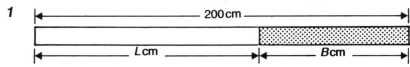

    A piece of wood is 200 cm long. It has a piece cut off it
    B cm long. What is the length, L cm, of the remaining piece?

2 A boy is now 12 years old. What will be his age, A, in
    Y years' time?

3 Find the total weight, W kg, of two parcels which weigh
    A kg and B kg.

4 A pen costs 20 pence. What would be the cost, C pence, of N similar pens?

5 I have to make a journey of M miles. How far have I to go, F miles, if I have already travelled 10 miles?

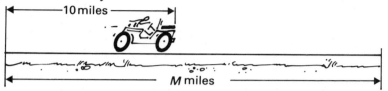

6 How far can the water level, L cm, rise in the jar before it overflows?

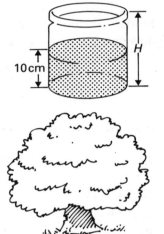

7 Julie is X years old, and her brother is 4 years younger than her. What age, A years, is her brother?

8 A car averages a speed of 60 m.p.h. on a motorway. How far will it go, M miles, in H hours?

9 A tree was 20 metres tall 5 years ago. It grows at a rate of T metres per year. What is its height, H metres, now?

10 A lorry weighs W tonnes. Its load weighs L tonnes. What is the total weight T tonnes?

EXERCISE 2

Give a simplified expression for each problem.

1

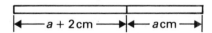

Two pieces of wood are of lengths $(a + 2)$ cm and a cm. What is the total length, T?

2 What is the total distance, D, around this square?

3 Ann is x years old. Her brother is twice her age. What is the total, T, of both their ages?

4 Three of the smaller cans can fit into the larger tin. What is the height, L, left at the top after the three cans have been put in?

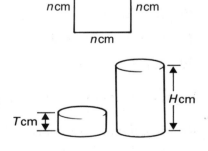

5 Ronald is 50 years old. His daughter is X years younger than him. How old, D years, was his daughter T years ago?

Revision exercise

Complete the function machines, and describe the machines in terms of letters:

1
$1 \rightarrow 5$
$2 \rightarrow 7$
$5 \rightarrow ?$
$7 \rightarrow ?$
$8 \rightarrow 19$

2
$1 \rightarrow 4\frac{1}{2}$
$3 \rightarrow 10\frac{1}{2}$
$6 \rightarrow 19\frac{1}{2}$
$9 \rightarrow ?$
$10 \rightarrow ?$

3
$2 \rightarrow 0$
$4 \rightarrow 4$
$5 \rightarrow ?$
$7 \rightarrow 10$
$9 \rightarrow ?$

4
$2 \rightarrow 1\frac{1}{2}$
$5 \rightarrow ?$
$1 \rightarrow 1$
$7 \rightarrow 4$
$12 \rightarrow ?$

5
$9 \rightarrow 40$
$2 \rightarrow ?$
$4 \rightarrow 15$
$5 \rightarrow ?$
$7 \rightarrow 30$

6
$4 \rightarrow 6$
$1 \rightarrow 9$
$7 \rightarrow ?$
$9 \rightarrow ?$
$2 \rightarrow 8$

7
$1 \leftarrow 3$
$3 \leftarrow 7$
$? \leftarrow 11$
$? \leftarrow 13$
$8 \leftarrow 17$

8
$3 \leftarrow 12$
$? \leftarrow 6$
$4 \leftarrow 11$
$6 \leftarrow 9$
$? \leftarrow 5$

Find the output to these function machines, and draw a flow chart to assist in their solution:

9 $3 \rightarrow \boxed{x \rightarrow 4x - 1} \rightarrow ?$ **10** $10 \rightarrow \boxed{x \rightarrow \frac{x}{4}} \rightarrow ?$

11 $6 \rightarrow \boxed{x \rightarrow \frac{x}{2} + 3} \rightarrow ?$ **12** $20 \rightarrow \boxed{x \rightarrow \frac{2x - 1}{3}} \rightarrow ?$

Find the value of the following expressions when $x = 2$, $y = 5$ and $z = 7$.

13 $3x$ **14** $2(y + z)$ **15** $3x - y$ **16** $y(z - x)$

17 $4 + xy$ **18** $xz - xy$ **19** $\frac{xy}{4}$ **20** xyz

21 $3(y - x) + z$ **22** $35 - \frac{3z}{x}$ **23** $z - (y - x)$ **24** $xy - (z - 4)$

Simplify:

25 $10x - 3x + 2x$ **26** $4x + 3x - x$ **27** $8x - 3x + 4x - 2x$

28 $3x + y - x$ **29** $3a + b + 2a - b$ **30** $3x + x + y + 4 + 2y$

31 $6p + 3q - 4p + q + 5$ **32** $4b + c - 4b + 2c$

33 $3m + 2n + 1 - m + n + 5$ **34** $9x - 3x + 3y - 3x + 1$

35 $2p + 2q + 2 - 2p + 2q$ **36** $6x + 2x - x + 5x - 2x - 9x - x$

37 $4x + 3y + 2(x + 2y)$ **38** $2(x + 2y) + 3(3x + y)$

39 $3(x + y + 1) + 2(x - y) - 3$ **40** $3(2x + y) - 3(x + y) + 4(2x + y)$

Express the following in terms of letters:

41 Josephine has x coins each of value 50p. What is the value, in pence, of all the coins?

42 A car is y years old. It was bought 4 years ago. Write down an expression for the age of the car when it was first bought.

9. Area and Perimeter

FREE FITTING ADVICE

REMNANT 10' × 10'

If you make one continuous cut in the large remnant, the three pieces will fit your 12'×9' room exactly!

CARPET CENTRE

REMNANT 8' × 1'

10' × 10'

2 PIECES

8' × 1'

1 PIECE

12' × 9'

3 PIECES

+

=

Area

HOW BIG?

1 How big is your hand?

2 Who has the largest hand in your class?

3 How might you measure your hand size?

4 How large is the hand below?

WHAT CAN WE MEASURE?

1 Handspan (thumb to little finger).

2 Hand length (wrist to end of longest finger).

3 How much space it covers (how many squares).

DEFINITION

The amount of space a shape covers is called its **area**.

UNITS

Each square shown has a side of 1 cm.
Each square is **1 square centimetre** or **1 cm²**.

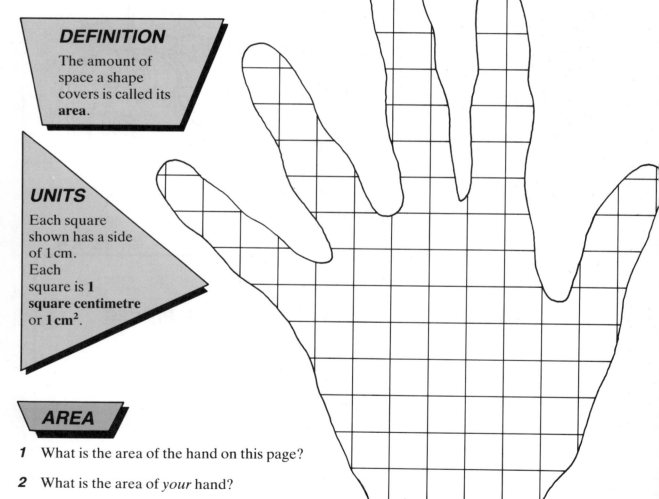

AREA

1 What is the area of the hand on this page?

2 What is the area of *your* hand?

3 In what way might you place your hand on a sheet of paper to draw around it, so that its area is easier to work out?

4 Use graph paper to find the area of your hand more accurately.

SQUARES AND RECTANGLES

What is the area of this rectangle?
There are 4 rows of 9 squares.
How does this help you to find the *area*?
How many more rectangles (or squares)
can you draw with the same area? Write
down the length and width of each.

EXERCISE 1

1   Copy and complete this table
for rectangles $(a) - (f)$.

	Length	Width	Area
(a)			
(b)			
(c)			
(d)			
(e)			
(f)			

2   Draw *five* more rectangles or
squares of your own. Add the
length, width and area of each
to your table.

3   What do you notice if you
multiply the length by the
width for each rectangle?

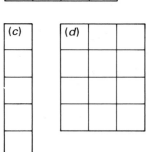

(a)   (b)

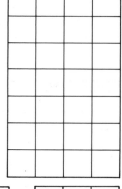

(c)   (d)

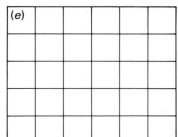

(e)   (f)

FORMULA

The **area** of a *rectangle* or *square* is
found by mutliplying its **length** by
its **width**.

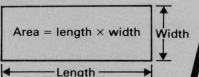

Area = length × width   Width

Length

EXERCISE 2

1   Write down the lengths and widths of six
rectangles with an area of $60\,cm^2$.

2   Work out the areas of squares with
sides:

(a) 1 cm   (b) 3 cm   (c) 6 cm   (d) 8 cm

(e) 10 cm   (f) 11 cm   (g) 15 cm   (h) 20 cm

(i) 30 cm   (j) 40 cm

Perimeters

PACING

Sarah walks around her classroom.
It takes her 72 paces.
Her teacher, who is
much taller, takes
36 paces.

DEFINITION

The distance around the edge of your classroom is called the **perimeter** of your classroom. The distance around the edge of any shape is called its **perimeter**.

Questions
Does the information tell us the size of the classroom? Explain your answer. What is the size of your classroom? Pace it out. Measure it.

EXERCISE 1 MEASURING

1 Measure, using a ruler, the perimeter of
(*a*) your desk (*b*) your exercise book
(*c*) your text book. Give your answers in centimetres (cm).

2 Who has the largest head in your class?
Measure the perimeter of your head as shown.

3 Find some other objects and measure their perimeters.

EXERCISE 2 ESTIMATING

1 On a running track the distance from start to finish is normally 400 metres.

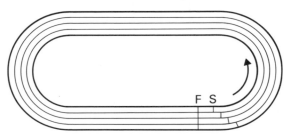

This is the perimeter of the *inside* of the track.
Can you estimate the length of the perimeter of the *outside* of the track?

2 Without measuring, see if you can write down reasonable estimates of the perimeters of:

(*a*) a hockey pitch   (*b*) a football pitch

(*c*) the staff car park   (*d*) the playground

(*e*) the school playing fields

(*f*) your school site.

Make a plan of each, showing any you have estimated.

3 What is the special name given to the perimeter of a circle?

AREAS AND PERIMETERS

EXERCISE 3

1 Find the area and perimeter of each of these rectangles:

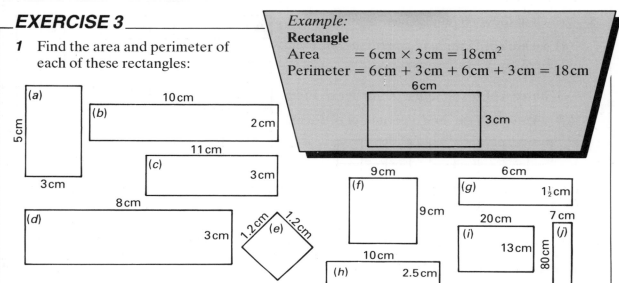

Example:
Rectangle
Area $= 6\,\text{cm} \times 3\,\text{cm} = 18\,\text{cm}^2$
Perimeter $= 6\,\text{cm} + 3\,\text{cm} + 6\,\text{cm} + 3\,\text{cm} = 18\,\text{cm}$

6 cm
3 cm

(a) 5 cm, 3 cm
(b) 10 cm, 2 cm
(c) 11 cm, 3 cm
(d) 8 cm, 3 cm
(e) 1.2 cm, 1.2 cm
(f) 9 cm, 9 cm
(g) 6 cm, $1\tfrac{1}{2}$ cm
(h) 10 cm, 2.5 cm
(i) 20 cm, 13 cm
(j) 7 cm, 80 cm

2 Find, by measuring, the areas of the front faces of these objects:

(a) CORNO FLAKES
(b) GREATEST HITS VOL.2
(c) WASHO AUTO POWDER
(d) (cassette)
(e) WISH YOU WERE HERE
(f) 3ᴾ (stamp)

Measure this stamp. Explain why the area of the stamp may not be correct using these measurements.

3 Find the area and perimeter of the rectangle which is:

(a) 12 cm by 2 cm   (b) 4 cm by 20 cm   (c) 8 cm by 9 cm

(d) 12 cm by 7 cm   (e) 13 cm by 5 cm   (f) 11 cm by 9 cm

(g) 30 cm by 3 cm   (h) 10 cm by 18 cm   (i) 45 cm by 20 cm

(j) 30 cm by 18 cm   (k) 17 cm by 7 cm   (l) 22 cm by 8 cm

(m) 90 cm by 90 cm   (n) 30 cm by 45 cm   (o) 14 cm by 15 cm

(p) 12 cm by 40 cm   (q) 8.1 cm by 2 cm   (r) 10 cm by 3.5 cm

(s) $4\tfrac{1}{2}$ cm by 12 cm   (t) 3.7 cm by 8.5 cm

EXERCISE 4

1 Which of these rectangles has:

  (a) an area of 12 cm² *and* a perimeter of 16 cm.

  (b) an area of 12 cm² *and* a perimeter of 14 cm.

  (c) an area of 16 cm² *and* a perimeter of 16 cm.

  (d) an area of 7 cm² *and* a perimeter of 16 cm.

Example:

This square has an area of 25 cm²:

$$25\,cm^2 = 5\,cm \times 5\,cm$$

so its sides all have length 5 cm.
Its perimeter is
5 cm + 5 cm + 5 cm + 5 cm = 20 cm.

2 Work out the perimeter of the square with area
  (a) 4 cm² (b) 36 cm² (c) 49 cm² (d) 144 cm².

3 Work out the area of the square with perimeter
  (a) 4 cm (b) 36 cm (c) 12 cm (d) 44 cm.

4 Work out the perimeter of the square with area
  (a) 0.04 m² (b) 1.44 m² (c) 0.64 m²
  (d) 2.25 m².

5 Work out the area of the square with perimeter
  (a) 1.2 m (b) 0.4 m (c) 3.6 m (d) 10 m.

6 Copy and complete these tables for rectangles.

(a)

Length	Width	Perimeter	Area
	1 cm		24 cm²
	2 cm		24 cm²
	3 cm		24 cm²
	4 cm		24 cm²
	5 cm		24 cm²
	6 cm		24 cm²
	8 cm		24 cm²
	10 cm		24 cm²
15 cm			24 cm²
18 cm			24 cm²

(b)

Length	Width	Perimeter	Area
		40 cm	100 cm²
		40 cm	96 cm²
		40 cm	99 cm²
		40 cm	36 cm²
		40 cm	91 cm²
		40 cm	19 cm²
		40 cm	64 cm²
		40 cm	75 cm²
		40 cm	84 cm²
		40 cm	9.75 cm²

Investigation A

RECTANGLES

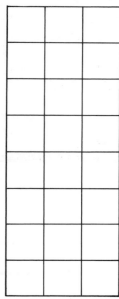

(*a*) What is the area of the rectangle?

(*b*) Using whole numbers only, find as many rectangles as you can with the same area.

(*c*) Work out the perimeter of each rectangle.

(*d*) Record your results in a table like this:

Length	Width	Area	Perimeter
8 cm	3 cm	$\cdots$ cm^2	$\cdots$ cm
.	.		
.	.		
.	.		

(*e*) Which rectangle has the shortest perimeter?

(*f*) Using decimal values, can you find a shorter perimeter of a rectangle with area 24 cm^2.

(*g*) Find the shortest perimeter for the rectangle with area
(i) 25 cm^2 (ii) 36 cm^2 (iii) 100 cm^2 (iv) 48 cm^2
(v) 40 cm^2.

(*h*) Find the largest area for the rectangle with perimeter
(i) 20 cm (ii) 16 cm (iii) 30 cm (iv) 39 cm
(v) 90 cm.

Investigation B

RABBIT ENCLOSURE

Tim and Sarah are given 20 ft of netting to make a rectangular rabbit enclosure against the garden fence. They want to make the enclosure as large as possible.

(*a*) Investigate the area for other widths. Record your results in a table.

(*b*) Find the largest enclosure which can be made if the netting is
(i) 12 ft (ii) 16 ft (iii) 100 ft (iv) 10 ft (v) 30 ft
(vi) 11 m (vii) 15 m long.

(*c*) Can you find a quick way of working out the maximum area for any length of fencing?

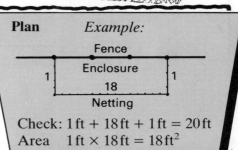

Plan   *Example:*

Fence

Enclosure

1   18   1

Netting

Check: 1 ft + 18 ft + 1 ft = 20 ft
Area   1 ft × 18 ft = 18 ft^2

Investigation C

CUTTING OUT RECTANGLES

Take a rectangle 5 cm by 7 cm.

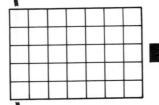

Cut out a
rectangle
3 cm by 2 cm.
What area
is left?

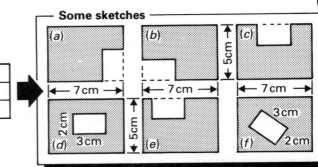

Draw any more 'cut-outs' you can.
Is the remaining area the same in all cases?
Explain how the *total* perimeter of the remaining shape
changes when you cut the 3 cm by 2 cm rectangle from
a different place.

Investigation D

NUMBERS

Each of these numbers has been cut from a rectangular sheet 16 cm by 20 cm.

If each ☐ is 4 cm by 4 cm, work out

(*a*) the area of each number   (*b*) the area which has been cut out
(*c*) the total perimeter for each number.

EXERCISE 5

Work out the area and perimeter of each of these shapes.
(You will have to work out some of the lengths of the
sides first.)

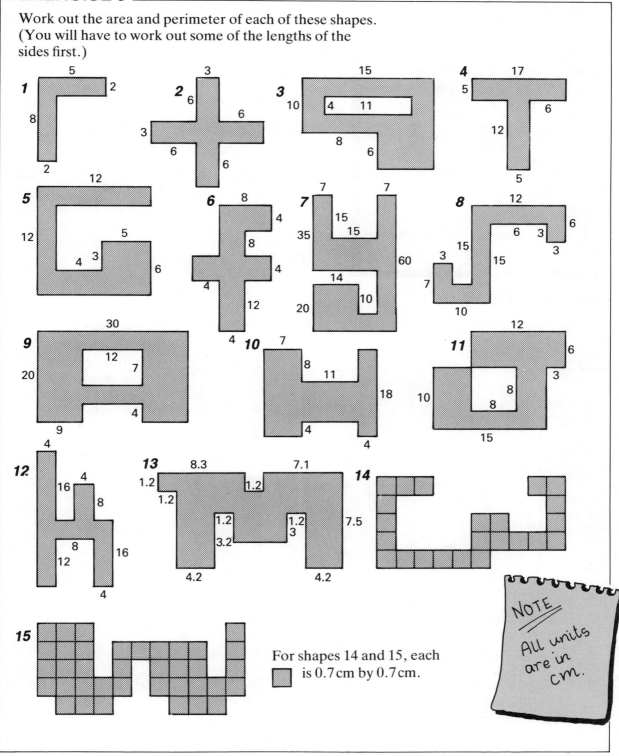

For shapes 14 and 15, each
☐ is 0.7 cm by 0.7 cm.

NOTE
All units
are in
cm.

Tiling

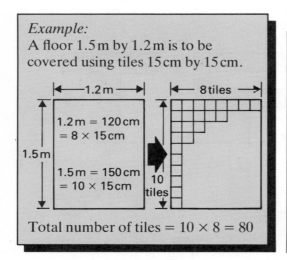

Example:
A floor 1.5 m by 1.2 m is to be covered using tiles 15 cm by 15 cm.

1.2 m = 120 cm
= 8 × 15 cm

1.5 m = 150 cm
= 10 × 15 cm

10 tiles

8 tiles

Total number of tiles = 10 × 8 = 80

EXERCISE 1

1 What is the area of the floor in m²?

2 What is the area of the floor in cm²?

3 What is the area of one tile in cm²?

4 What is the area of one tile in m²?

5 How many tiles are required to cover a similar area if a tile is (*a*) 10 cm by 10 cm
(*b*) 20 cm by 20 cm   (*c*) 25 cm by 20 cm
(*d*) 30 cm by 30 cm   (*e*) 25 cm by 20 cm
(*f*) 30 cm by 40 cm   (*g*) 0.1 m by 0.2 m
(*h*) 0.15 m by 0.1 m?

EXERCISE 2

1 Work out how many tiles are needed to cover the areas below when one tile is

(*a*) 20 cm by 20 cm
(*b*) 10 cm by 15 cm
(*c*) 30 cm by 12 cm
(*d*) 0.25 m by 0.4 m
(*e*) 0.5 m by 0.6 m.

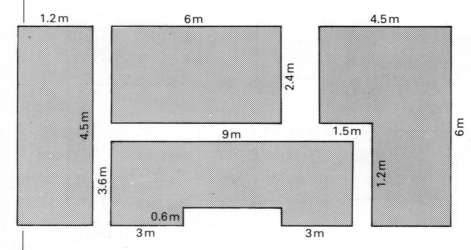

2 Calculate the area of each tile in (*a*) cm²   (*b*) m².

3 Calculate the area of each room in (*a*) cm²   (*b*) m².

4 Paving slabs cost £3.75 for the 0.9 m by 0.6 m size and £2.65 for the 0.6 m square size. How much would it cost to pave a rectangular area which measures 10.8 m by 7.8 m in (*a*) the 0.9 m × 0.6 m size   (*b*) the 0.6 m × 0.6 m size?

Using formulas

RECTANGLES

Area = length × width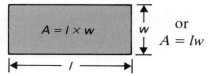

This can be shortened to:

$A = l \times w$ or $A = lw$

Perimeter = length + width + length + width $\qquad P = l + w + l + w$

    or   = 2 × length + 2 × width $\qquad$ or $P = 2l + 2w$

    or   = 2 × (length + width) $\qquad$ or $P = 2(l + w)$

EXERCISE 1

1 Find A, if (*a*) $l = 5\,\text{cm}$, $w = 4\,\text{cm}$ (*b*) $l = 12\,\text{cm}$, $w = 3.5\,\text{cm}$
    (*c*) $l = 1.2\,\text{m}$, $w = 0.7\,\text{m}$ (*d*) $l = 37\,\text{m}$, $w = 11.6\,\text{m}$.

2 Find P, if (*a*) $l = 5\,\text{cm}$, $w = 4\,\text{cm}$ (*b*) $l = 10\,\text{cm}$, $w = 8\,\text{cm}$
    (*c*) $l = 4.1\,\text{m}$, $w = 3.2\,\text{m}$.

SQUARES

EXERCISE 2

Find A and P, if (*a*) $l = 3\,\text{cm}$
(*b*) $l = 9\,\text{cm}$ (*c*) $l = 1.3\,\text{m}$
(*d*) $l = 1.5\,\text{m}$ (*e*) $l = 0.6\,\text{m}$
(*f*) $l = 4.2\,\text{m}$.

Area $A = l \times l$ or $A = l^2$
Perimeter $P = l + l + l + l$ or $P = 4l$

PROGRAMS

1 RUN the program using the data
    (*a*) 5, 4   (*b*) 10, 8   (*c*) 15, 7.5.
    What does the program do?

2 Change the program so that it finds (*a*) the
    perimeter of a rectangle   (*b*) the *area* of a
    square   (*c*) the *perimeter* of a square.

3 If you know the area of a rectangle and its length,
    how would you calculate its width?
    Write a program to (*a*) find the width of a rectangle
    when you know the area and length   (*b*) find the
    length of a side of a square when you know the area.

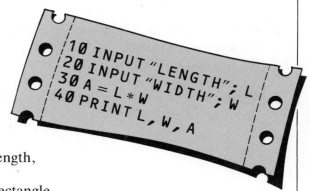

```
10 INPUT "LENGTH"; L
20 INPUT "WIDTH"; W
30 A = L * W
40 PRINT L, W, A
```

Revision exercise

1 Find the perimeter and area of these shapes.

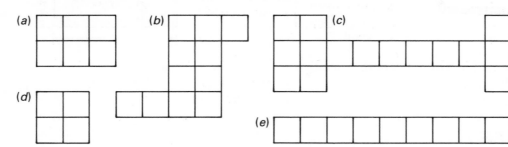

2 Work out the perimeter and area of these shapes.

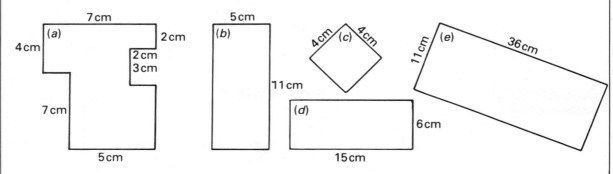

3 Find the area of the rectangle with dimensions:

(a) length = 10 cm, width = 2 cm   (b) length = 25 cm, width = 11 cm

(c) length = 15 cm, width = 4 cm   (d) length = 4.5 cm, width = 3 cm.

(e) length = 9 cm, width = 7 cm

4 If $A = lw$, find (a) A when $l = 14.5$ cm, $w = 12$ cm
(b) l when $A = 65$ cm^2, $w = 6.5$ cm
(c) w when $A = 567$ cm^2, $l = 31.5$ cm.

5 Work out how many tiles are required to cover
this floor space if one tile is

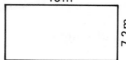

(a) 0.3 m by 0.1 m
(b) 0.3 m by 0.2 m
(c) 0.6 m by 0.1 m
(d) 0.3 m by 0.3 m.

6 For question 5, find (a) the area of each tile
(b) the area of the floor space
(c) the perimeter of the floor space.

10. Directed numbers

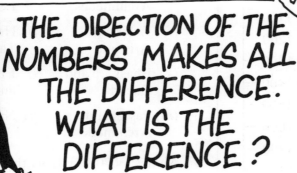

Starting points

When we count, we do so relative to a **starting point**.
One such example is the way in which we record historical events.

BC . . . AD

We use the Christian calendar to indicate events in time.

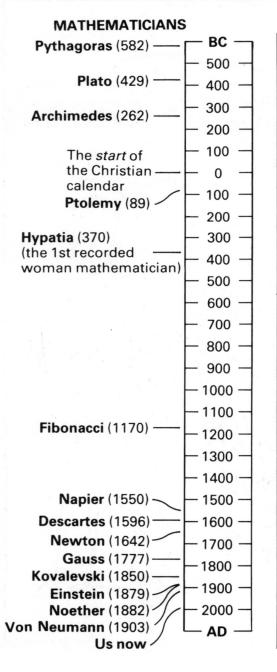

MATHEMATICIANS

Pythagoras (582)

Plato (429)

Archimedes (262)

The *start* of the Christian calendar

Ptolemy (89)

Hypatia (370)
(the 1st recorded woman mathematician)

Fibonacci (1170)

Napier (1550)
Descartes (1596)
Newton (1642)
Gauss (1777)
Kovalevski (1850)
Einstein (1879)
Noether (1882)
Von Neumann (1903)
Us now

BC
500
400
300
200
100
0
100
200
300
400
500
600
700
800
900
1000
1100
1200
1300
1400
1500
1600
1700
1800
1900
2000
AD

EXERCISE 1

1 Write each mathematician's date of birth as a year BC or AD.

2 Make a copy of the chart and add these:

Pascal AD1623	Aristotle 384BC
Euclid 300BC	Tartaglia AD1500
Hero AD75	Eratosthenes 276BC
Euler AD1707	Leibnitz AD1646
Bhaskara AD1114	Diophantus 250BC

3 How many years apart are the chart dates for

(a) Fibonacci and Gauss

(b) Einstein and Hypatia

(c) Archimedes and Plato

(d) Pythagoras and Euclid

(e) Plato and Ptolemy

(f) Von Neumann and Plato

(g) Descartes and Archimedes

(h) Diophantus and Leibnitz

(i) Euler and Aristotle

(j) Hero and Tartaglia

(k) Bhaskara and Euclid

(l) Eratosthenes and Pascal

(m) Pascal and Archimedes

(n) Napier and Plato

4 Ahmes (3070BC) wrote the first known work on mathematics.
If we put Ahmes on a mathematical calendar, roughly how much longer would the chart have to be?

OTHER STARTING POINTS

EXERCISE 2

1

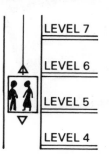

LEVEL 7

LEVEL 6

LEVEL 5

LEVEL 4

A lift in an office block moves *up* or *down*.
Copy and complete this table:

Enters at floor	5	4	. . .	5	10
Change in floors	up 3	down 3	down 2		
Leaves at floor			7	10	0

What name is normally given to floor level 0?

2 A bank account statement consists of *debits* (pay out) and *credits* (pay in). If too much money is taken out, the account becomes *overdrawn* (DR).

Copy and complete the bank statement.

Baroyds Midwest Bank plc			
Date	Credit	Debit	Balance
B/F	—	—	£15.20
5 JAN	£45.00	—	. . .
5 JAN	—	£3.75	. . .
6 JAN	£9.86	—	. . .
6 JAN	. . .	. . .	£6.31DR
6 JAN	£101.37	—	. . .
7 JAN	. . .	. . .	£11.62

NOTATION

Directed numbers are numbers with a + or − sign in front of them.
For example: +7, −3, +1.8, ...
For the lift above, 'up 3' can now be written as +3. How can we write 'down 3
'Enter floor 5' then 'up 3' then 'Leaves at floor 8' can be written as 5 + (+3) =
Write the other lift journeys in the same way.

EXERCISE 3

Timetable arrival time	Minutes difference	Actual arrival time
0805	+8	
0834	-3	
0910	+17	
0947		0946
1007	-5	
	+20	1054
1133		1128
1207	-9	
1245	+27	
	-13	1301

1 *Arrival times*
Buses and trains run according to set timetables. Sometimes the buses and trains are late, sometimes they are early.

(*a*) Copy the table on the left.

(*b*) If +8 means '8 minutes late', what does −3 mean?

(*c*) Complete the table.

2 How can we now write (*a*) credit £45
(*b*) debit £3.75 (*c*) £6.31DR?

Temperatures

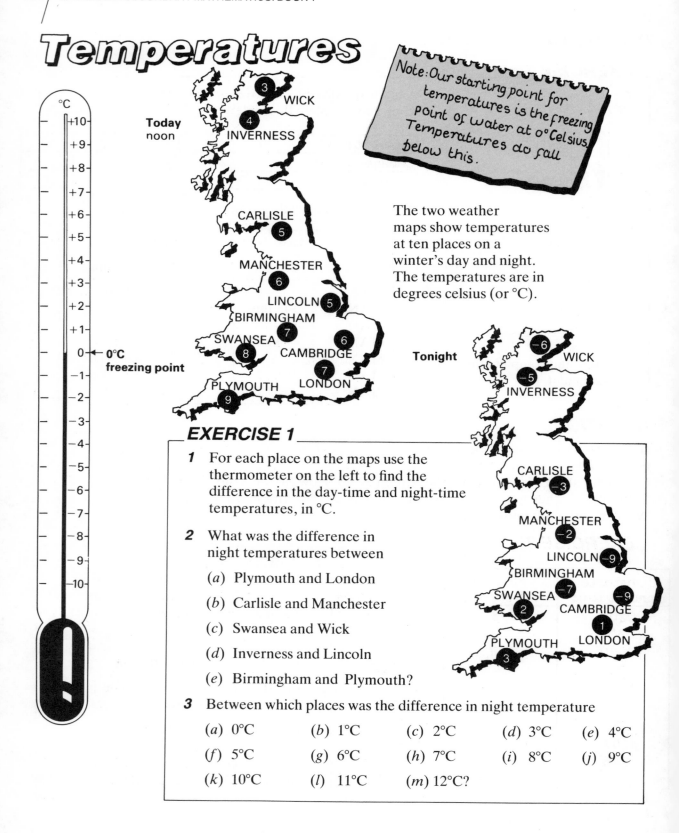

Note: Our starting point for temperatures is the freezing point of water at 0°Celsius. Temperatures do fall below this.

The two weather maps show temperatures at ten places on a winter's day and night. The temperatures are in degrees celsius (or °C).

Today noon

WICK 3
INVERNESS 4
CARLISLE 5
MANCHESTER 6
LINCOLN 5
BIRMINGHAM
SWANSEA 8
CAMBRIDGE 6
PLYMOUTH 9
LONDON 7

Tonight

WICK −6
INVERNESS −5
CARLISLE −3
MANCHESTER −2
LINCOLN −9
BIRMINGHAM −7
SWANSEA 2
CAMBRIDGE −9
PLYMOUTH 3
LONDON 1

°C thermometer: +10, +9, +8, +7, +6, +5, +4, +3, +2, +1, 0 ← 0°C freezing point, −1, −2, −3, −4, −5, −6, −7, −8, −9, −10

EXERCISE 1

1 For each place on the maps use the thermometer on the left to find the difference in the day-time and night-time temperatures, in °C.

2 What was the difference in night temperatures between

(a) Plymouth and London

(b) Carlisle and Manchester

(c) Swansea and Wick

(d) Inverness and Lincoln

(e) Birmingham and Plymouth?

3 Between which places was the difference in night temperature

(a) 0°C   (b) 1°C   (c) 2°C   (d) 3°C   (e) 4°C

(f) 5°C   (g) 6°C   (h) 7°C   (i) 8°C   (j) 9°C

(k) 10°C   (l) 11°C   (m) 12°C?

EXERCISE 2

1 (*a*) Write down the
temperature on
each thermometer.

(*b*) What would be
the new readings
if the temperature
(i) rose by 4°
(ii) fell by 6°?

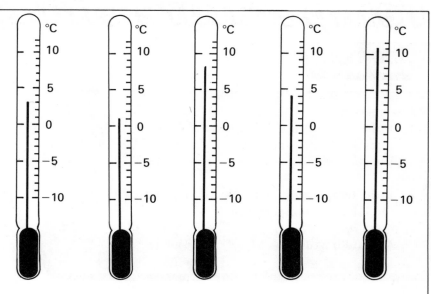

2 (*a*) Write down the
temperature on
each thermometer.

(*b*) What would be
the new reading
if the temperature
(i) rose by 7°
(ii) fell by 3°?

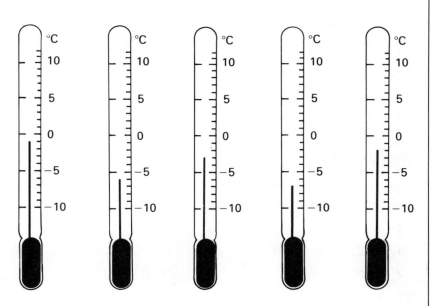

3 Copy and complete this table.

Start temperature	17°C	−12°C	. . .	. . .	. . .
Change in temperature	down 25°	up 44°	down 7°	down 33°	up 21°
New temperature	. . .	. . .	17°	−12°	8°

Temperature changes

ADDITION

Examples:

1 If the temperature is 4°C and then *rises* by 7°C,
then the new temperature is: 4°C + 7°C = 11°C
We could write (+4) + (+7) = +11

2 If the temperature is 4°C and then *falls* by 7°C,
then the new temperature is:
4°C + (−7)°C = −3°C
We could write (+4) + (−7) = −3

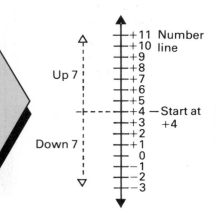

EXERCISE 1

Rewrite these temperature changes as number additions and find
each final temperature when the initial temperature is

1 −2°C and then rises by 3°C.

2 −2°C and then falls by 3°C.

3 5°C and then falls by 6°C.

4 0°C and then falls by 3°C.

5 7°C and then rises by 6°C.

EXERCISE 2

Draw a number line labelled from −16 to +16. Use your line
to help you with these additions.

1 (+3) + (+2)	**2** (+1) + (−5)	**3** (−7) + (+2)
4 (−2) + (+6)	**5** (−3) + (−1)	**6** (0) + (−7)
7 (+6) + (−6)	**8** (−10) + (+3)	**9** (−7) + (−3)
10 (−11) + (+6)	**11** (+9) + (−17)	**12** (−8) + (−2)
13 (−3) + (+3)	**14** (−3) + (0)	**15** (−6) + (−6)
16 (+1.5) + (−1)	**17** (−3) + (+1.5)	**18** (−1.5) + (−3)
19 (−1.7) + (+11.3)	**20** (+7) + (−2.4)	**21** (+4.6) + (+5.7)
22 (−9.2) + (−8.7)	**23** (+0.7) + (0.5)	**24** (+0.7) + (−0.3)
25 (+0.7) + (−0.1)	**26** (+13.6) + (−9.8)	**27** (−13.6) + (+9.8)
28 (−6.2) + (−6.2)	**29** (+10.7) + (−11.8)	**30** (−0.3) + (−0.8)

Temperature differences

SUBTRACTION

EXAMPLES:

1 If the temperature is 5°C and it was 2°C, then the temperature *change* is a rise of 3°C.
So the **difference** is: 5°C − 2°C   = 3°C
We could write $(+5) - (+2) = +3$

2 If the temperature is −3°C and it was −2°C, then the temperature *change* is a fall of 1°C.
So the **difference** is: $(-3)°C - (-2)°C = -1°C$
We could write $(-3) - (-2)$ = −1

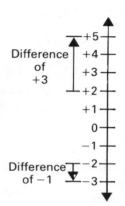

Difference
of
+3

Difference
of −1

EXERCISE 1

Rewrite these temperature differences as number subtractions
and find each difference.

1 The temperature is −3°C and it was 4°C.   **2** The temperature is +5°C and it was −2°C.

3 The temperature is −3°C and it was −4°C.   **4** The temperature is 0°C and it was −2°C.

5 The temperature is −7°C and it was −9°C.

EXERCISE 2

Use a number line to work out these differences.

1 $(+4) - (+2)$	**2** $(+5) - (0)$	**3** $(+6) - (-1)$
4 $(-3) - (+6)$	**5** $(-3) - (-6)$	**6** $(-10) - (+5)$
7 $(+11) - (+5)$	**8** $(+11) - (-5)$	**9** $(+15) - (+20)$
10 $(+15) - (-20)$	**11** $(-15) - (+20)$	**12** $(-15) - (-20)$
13 $(-2) - (-7)$	**14** $(-2) - (+7)$	**15** $(+11) - (-7)$
16 $(-19) - (-18)$	**17** $(-19) - (-17)$	**18** $(+17) - (+18)$
19 $(-10) - (-10)$	**20** $(0) - (+7)$	**21** $(0) - (-7)$
22 $(+2.5) - (+3.5)$	**23** $(-1.6) - (-3.7)$	**24** $(-0.7) - (+0.7)$
25 $(-16.4) - (+20)$	**26** $(-9.7) - (-9.7)$	**27** $(+1.7) - (-3.9)$
28 $(+99) - (-99)$	**29** $(0) - (-9.9)$	**30** $(-3.7) - (+8.9)$

Equalities

TURTLE WALKS

Imagine a turtle on a number line.

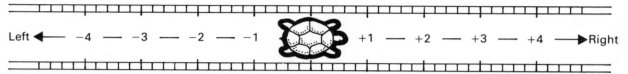

Left ◄— −4 — −3 — −2 — −1   +1 — +2 — +3 — +4 —►Right

A turtle walk of +3 means forward 3 units
              −3 means backwards 3 units.

| A turtle walk of: + (+3) will mean 'face right', walk forwards 3 units | 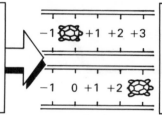 | − (+3) will mean 'face left', walk forwards 3 units | 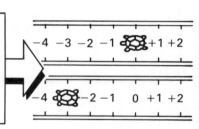 |

Check that these walks will end at +3 and −3 respectively.

EXERCISE 1

If the turtle starts at 0 each time, find where the turtle walks to after these walks. Write each turtle walk in words.

1 + (+2)   **2** − (+2)   **3** + (−2)   **4** − (−2)   **5** + (−4)

6 − (+5)   **7** + (−7)   **8** − (−1)   **9** + (+4)   **10** − (+6)

EXERCISE 2

1 Work out where the turtle finishes after these walks.

(*a*) 3 + (−1)   (*b*) (−3) + (−1)   (*c*) 4 + (+5)

(*d*) 7 − (−2)   (*e*) 7 + (−2)   (*f*) (−4) + (+5)

(*g*) 3 − (+2)   (*h*) 8 + (−6)   (*i*) (−8) + (+2)

(*j*) (+5) − (−3)   (*k*) (−5) − (−3)   (*l*) (+2) − (−3)

(*m*) (+4) + (+4)   (*n*) (−3) + (−3)   (*o*) (−3) − (−3)

(*p*) 0 − (−2)   (*q*) 0 + (−2)

(*r*) 0 − (+2)   (*s*) (−6) − (−7)

(*t*) (−11) − (−10)

NOTATION

We can write *positive* numbers without a sign. For example, +1 = 1, +2 = 2, +3 = 3, and so on.

Example:
3 − (−1) means start at +3, face left, walk backwards 1 unit. The turtle should finish at +4 *or* 4.

Note: 3 − (−1) also gives the same answer as 3 + 1.

Inequalities

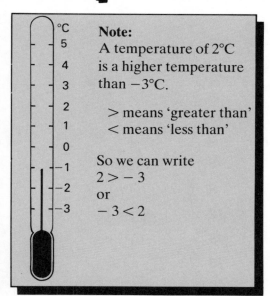

Note:
A temperature of 2°C
is a higher temperature
than −3°C.

> means 'greater than'
< means 'less than'

So we can write
2 > −3
or
−3 < 2

EXERCISE 1

Place these sets of temperatures in order with
the coldest first:

1 0°,   −3°,   4°,   −2°,   6°

2 10°,   −70°,   −35°,   12°

3 11°,   15°,   −7°,   −1°,   6°

4 −7°,   −5°,   −6°,   −8°

5 14°,   −13°,   12°,   −11°

6 6°,   −6°,   7°,   −1°

7 2.5°,   −3.5°,   1.5°,

8 9.7°,   −11.2°,   4.4°,   −2.7°

9 0.8°,   0.87°,   0.78°,   −0.5°

10 7.6°,   −1.5°,   −8.2°,   0.6°

EXERCISE 2

Insert either '=', '<', or '>' in the box to make each statement correct.

1 0☐5   **2** 0☐−3   **3** −2☐0   **4** 6☐0

5 −3☐5   **6** 3☐−3   **7** −2☐2   **8** 8☐−6

9 −3 + 6☐2   **10** 4 + 7☐12   **11** −4 + (−7)☐−12

12 −7 − 7☐0   **13** −9 + 11☐2   **14** −3 − 9☐−12

15 −8 + 8☐0   **16** −2 − 7☐−5   **17** 10 − 11☐1

18 −10 + 11☐1   **19** −3 − 5☐−8   **20** −9 + 7☐−3

Say whether each of these statements is true or false:

21 −3 > −2   **22** −5 > −3 + −1

23 (−2) + (−7) = (−2) − (+7)   **24** 5 − (−2) = 0 − (−7)

25 4 + (−3) = (−4) + (+3)   **26** −1 > −2 > −3

27 −(−5) = +5   **28** 4 + (−7) − (−2) = +1

29 4 − (−2) < 5 + (−2) − (−1) < −7   **30** (−9) − (−7) > (−7) − (−9)

Rewrite the false statements, using the appropriate sign, to make them correct.

Missing numbers

Note:
Think of the '+' sign to mean 'and then'.
Think of the '−' sign to mean 'the difference between'.

EXERCISE 1

Find the number missing from the boxes.

1 $\square + 5 = 2$	**2** $10 + \square = 7$	**3** $\square + (-3) = -6$
4 $\square - 5 = 3$	**5** $\square - 5 = -3$	**6** $10 - \square = 3$
7 $10 - \square = -13$	**8** $(-2) - \square = -4$	**9** $(-2) - \square = 0$
10 $8 - \square = 10$	**11** $(-8) - \square = -15$	**12** $(-7) - \square = 1$
13 $4 + \square = 0$	**14** $\square + (-6) = 0$	**15** $\square - (-6) = 0$
16 $(-5) - \square = -3$	**17** $\square - (-2) = 6$	**18** $12 - \square = 18$
19 $0 - \square = 10$	**20** $0 + \square = -5$	

Example:
At 6 p.m. the temperature is −1°C.
The temperature had fallen by 7°C from midday.
What was the midday temperature?

Midday temp.

We could write this as

$$(\text{midday temp.}) + (-7)°C = -1°C$$
or $\qquad \square + (-7)°C = -1°C$
now $\qquad 6°C + (-7)°C = -1°C$
so $\qquad\qquad \square = 6°C$

6 P.M.

So the midday temperature must have been 6°C.

─6°C

falls 7°

─ −1°C

EXERCISE 2

Look at the 6 p.m. temperatures and the temperature changes below. Use them to find the original midday temperature.

6 p.m. temperature	Change from midday
12°C	down 4°C
−5°C	up 1°C
−7°C	down 3°C
6°C	up 2°C
6°C	down 7°C
−3°C	up 2°C
−3°C	down 5°C
−10°C	down 4°C
−1°C	up 3°C
−6.5°C	up 1.8°C

EXERCISE 3

In these questions the temperature is represented by t. Find t.

1 $t + 7 = 10$ **2** $t + 7 = 0$ **3** $t + 7 = -3$

4 $10 - t = 4$ **5** $10 - t = 0$ **6** $10 - t = -20$

7 $t - 5 = 3$ **8** $t - 5 = 0$ **9** $t - 5 = -4$

10 $t - (-2) = 5$ **11** $t - (-2) = 0$ **12** $(-7) - t = -4$

13 $(-7) - t = 3$ **14** $-1 + t = -7$ **15** $-3 + t = 0$

16 $t - (-2) = 1$ **17** $(-30) - t = -1$ **18** $t + (-15) = -30$

19 $t - (-15) = -30$

Limits

Investigation

CALCULATORS

Switch on your calculator.
Add a number less than 10.
Add another number so that the total
is still less than 10.
Keep on going.
Stop if you go over 10.
Note down your additions and totals.
Try to get as close to 10 as possible.

EXTENSION

EXERCISE 1

1 What is the *largest* number
less than 10 you can get to
on your calculator?

2 Starting at 20, subtract numbers so that
the answer is still greater than 10.

3 What is the *smallest* number greater than
10 you can get on your calculator?

EXERCISE 2

1 Write down *any* five numbers between:

  (*a*) 10 and 10.5   (*b*) 33 and 35   (*c*) 62.1 and 62.2

  (*d*) 6.3 and 6.35   (*e*) 0.83 and 0.84

2 Using your calculator, write down the *largest* number less than
   (*a*) 10.5   (*b*) 35   (*c*) 62.2   (*d*) 6.35   (*e*) 0.84

3 Using your calculator, write down the *smallest* number greater than
   (*a*) 10   (*b*) 33   (*c*) 62.1   (*d*) 6.3   (*e*) 0.83

4 Write down whether -1.5 is greater than or less than
   (*a*) 1   (*b*) 0   (*c*) -1 (*d*) -2 (*e*) -1.4999

Revision exercise

1 Calculate how many years difference there are between:
   (*a*) 55 BC and 55 AD   (*b*) BC 250 and AD 1989   (*c*) BC 275 and BC 82

2 A lift in a store starts at floor 5. It then travels
   (*a*) *up* 3 floors   (*b*) *down* 4 floors   (*c*) *down* 3 floors   (*d*) *up* 6 floors.
   Work out at which floor the lift arrives each time it moves *up* or *down*.

3 The first lift journey in question 2 can be written as 5 + (+3) = 8.
   Write the other three journeys in the same way.

4 Copy and complete this bank statement

Credit	Debit	Balance
—	—	£100.00
£36.75	—	...
—	£73.80	...
£9.48	—	...

5 Work out temperature change from day to day:

Sunday		Monday		Tuesday		Wednesday		Thursday		Friday		Saturday	
noon	mid-night	noon	mid-night	noon	mid-night	noon	mid-night	noon	mid-night	noon	mid-night	noon	mid-night
11°C	4°C	8°C	1°C	5°C	0°C	6°C	-2°C	7°C	-3°C	4°C	-1°C	6°C	-5°C
−7°C	+4°C	...	...	...	...	...	...	...	...	...	...	...	Change

6 Work out

   (*a*) $(-7) + (+3)$ (*b*) $(0) + (-3)$ (*c*) $(-2) + (-1)$ (*d*) $(-9) + (+8)$

7 Work out

   (*a*) $(+2) - (+5)$ (*b*) $(-3) - (-2)$ (*c*) $(5) - (-2)$ (*d*) $(-7) - (-7)$

8 Insert one of the symbols $<$, $=$ or $>$ in each box to make the statements correct.

   (*a*) $-3 \square 0$ (*b*) $-8 \square -9$ (*c*) $(-7) + (-7) \square 0$ (*d*) $(-5) + (-3) \square -7$
   (*e*) $(-2) - (4) \square -6$ (*f*) $6 - (-2) \square -8$ (*g*) $(-3) - (-4) \square -1$

9 Solve these equations for *x*.

   (*a*) $(-2) + x = 7$ (*b*) $6 - x = 8$ (*c*) $x - (-1) = 6$ (*d*) $x - (-1) = -5$

11. Coordinates

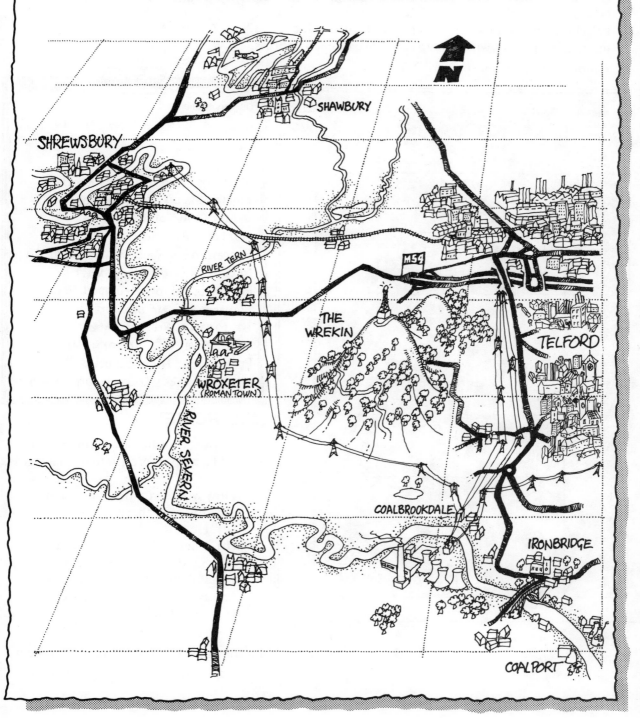

Maps

Derek is a delivery man who works for the gas board. Every day he picks up his list of deliveries. To help him find the places he has to visit he uses a local map, and writes down the map reference of each address.

Example: Peveril Close D7

Delivery Name

Delivery Day   Dockets included

Addresses Summary:

Hastings Road off Heys Road
Maple GR. off Nursery Road.
Walker Av. off A665
Harlech Av., Half Acre
Parren Thorn Road off Heywood Rd.
Milton Rd. off Heys Rd.
Parkville Rd. off Heywood Rd.
Heaton St. Nr station
St. Mary's Rd. off A56
The Drive off Rectory Ln.
Prestwich High School
St. Margaret's Church off A665

EXERCISE

1 Copy the addresses summary and add a map reference to each address.

2 How would you describe the map references of these roads:
(*a*) Heys Road
(*b*) Cuckoo Lane, Half Acre
(*c*) Sandgate Road (over M62)
(*d*) Polefield Road, Half Acre
(*e*) Rectory Lane, Prestwich
(*f*) Bury Old Road (A665).

3 Write down the main road in each of these map references:

(*a*) B7   (*b*) B1   (*c*) D6   (*d*) D4   (*e*) E7   (*f*) B3.

Road maps

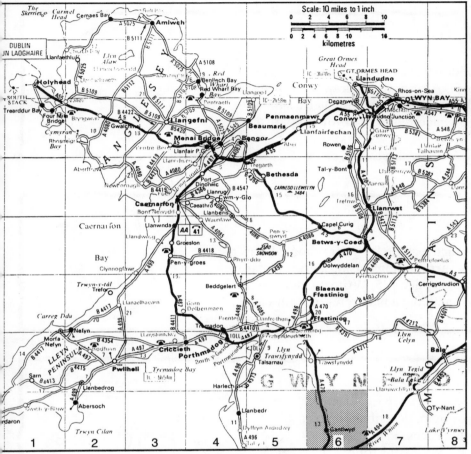

Road maps also use map references to refer to places. Ganllwyd has a map reference of 6–1 since it is in the shaded square which is labelled 6 across the bottom of the map, and 1 up the side of the map.

EXERCISE

Which towns have the following map references:

1 2–8	**2** 7–4	**3** 5–4	**4** 3–7	**5** 3–3
6 7–1	**7** 1–1	**8** 2–5	**9** 3–2	**10** 1–2

Find the map reference for each of these towns:

11 Holyhead, Anglesey   **12** Bangor   **13** Porthmadog, Gwynedd

14 Colwyn Bay, North Wales **15** Caernarfon   **16** Amlwch, Anglesey

17 Betws-y-Coed, Snowdonia **18** Pwllheli   **19** Ffestiniog   **20** Llangefni

21 List the map reference squares in which there is (a) no land (b) land, but no towns.

Drawing maps

Investigation A

Use a local map to write down the references of the roads or places around your school. Alternatively draw your own sketch map of the area around your school, and use a grid similar to that shown on the map on page 124 to help you prepare a list of map references.

Investigation B

Is it possible to produce such a guide for your school? Draw a map of the school and its surroundings, using a grid similar to the one shown in the map on page 125. Write an index of all the places on your map, including a map reference for each.

Investigation C

Using an ordnance survey map, describe a route taken in terms of map references. Pass your description to a friend and see if your route can be followed.

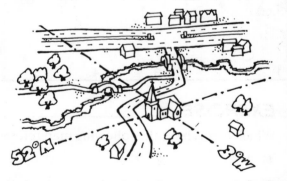

Ordnance Survey maps

Ordnance Survey maps use an accurate map referencing system using 6 figures.

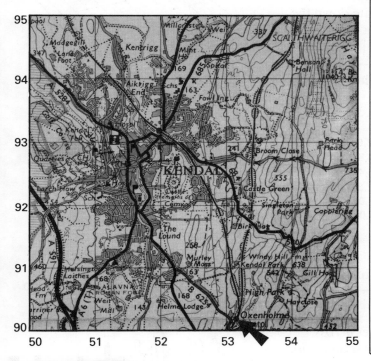

Oxenholme station, indicated by the arrow, is in square 53–90. We can give the station an accurate reference by estimating how far across the square it is.

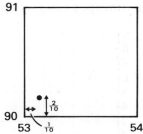

We estimate it as being $\frac{1}{10}$ across the square, and give it a horizontal reference of 53**1**. It is also approximately $\frac{2}{10}$ up the square, and we give it a vertical reference of 90**2**. The complete map reference of Oxenholme station is therefore 531902.

EXERCISE

Describe what is to be found at the following map references:

1 520905	**2** 541920	**3** 514904	**4** 506927
5 540943	**6** 511922	**7** 546909	**8** 526948

What would be the map references of each of the following:

9 Kendal station **10** Kendal castle

11 The hospital on the A5284 road

12 The second hospital in Kendal

13 Mint House on the A6

14 The place where the two railway lines meet

15 The railway bridge near Birk House

Positive coordinates

Remi has a lighting board in which he can put pegs that light up. The board is numbered so he can write down the position of each peg.

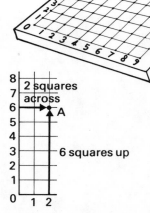

He puts in some pegs and writes down their position:

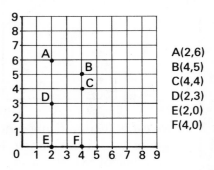

A(2,6)
B(4,5)
C(4,4)
D(2,3)
E(2,0)
F(4,0)

Can you describe how he was using the numbers?

Point A is 2 squares *across* and 6 squares *up*.
Remi then wrote down (2, 6)
          ↑ ↑
squares across   squares up

Point E is 2 squares *across* but it has moved 0 squares up. E could be written as (2, 0).

Points described as (2, 6), (2, 0) are called **coordinates**. The brackets are the normal notation when writing down coordinates.

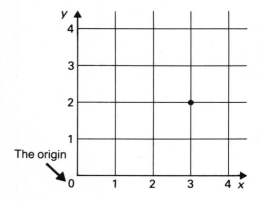

The horizontal axis (across the page) is called the *x* axis. The vertical axis (up the page) is called the *y* axis. Coordinates (3, 2) have two parts:
        ↑ ↑
the *x* coordinate the *y* coordinate

Why do you think the number 3 is called the *x* coordinate?

EXERCISE 1

1 Write down the coordinates of each of these points.

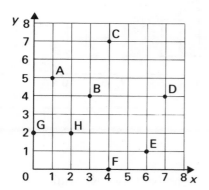

2 Copy the grid below and mark on it the following points:
A(1,1), B(4,2), C(7,5), D(2,5), E(3,3), F(0,6), G(5,5), H(4,0), I(7,6), J(6,7).

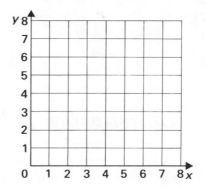

3 Remi would like to see his name in lights. Using grids like the one in question 2 show how Remi could light up each letter of his name. Write out a list of coordinates for each letter.

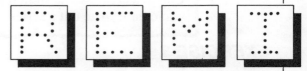

EXERCISE 2

Plot the following series of points, joining them up in the order they are written:

1 (5,2), (6,2), (5,1), (2,1), (1,2), (2,2), (2,3), (3,3), (3,4), (4,4), (4,3), (5,3), (5,2), (2,2).

2 (2,1), (4,2), (6,1), (4,2), (4,5), (6,4), (4,5), (2,4), (4,5), (4,6), (3,6), (3,8), (5,8), (5,6), (4,6).

3 (4,1), (2,1), (1,0), (1,2), (2,3), (2,7), (3,9), (4,7), (4,3), (5,2), (5,0), (4,1).

4 (3,0), (3,3), (2,3), (1,4), (1,6), (2,7), (5,7), (6,6), (6,4), (5,3), (4,3), (4,0).

5 (2,0), (2,2), (1,3), (1,4), (2,5), (6,5), (7,6), (8,6), (10,4), (10,1), (9,1), (9,3), (8,3), (7,2), (7,0), (6,0), (6,2), (3,2), (3,0).

Write down the coordinates of each point:

6

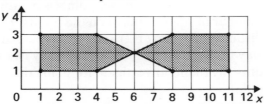

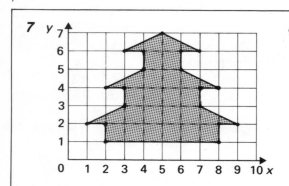

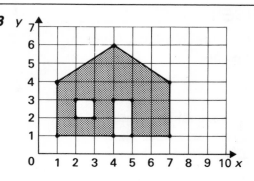

Investigation A

All the pictures in questions 1–5 of Exercise 2 can be drawn without taking your pen off the paper, without having to stop and start again. Can you create some similar pictures of your own? For each picture you create write out a series of coordinates to help others draw your pictures.

EXERCISE 3

For each pair of coordinates plot the points, joint them with a line, and write down the coordinates of the midpoint of the line:

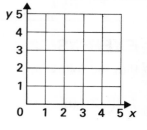

1 (1,1), (3,3) **2** (3,1), (3,5) **3** (1,2), (5,4) **4** (5,2), (1,4)

5 (2,1), (2,4) **6** (4,2), (1,3) **7** (0,4), (4,1) **8** (5,4), (1,1)

Find the coordinates of the midpoints of these shapes:

9 (1,1), (3,1), (3,3), (1,3)   **10** (2,1), (6,1), (6,5), (2,5)

11 (2,0), (4,0), (4,4), (2,4)   **12** (0,0), (4,0), (4,4), (0,4)

13 (1,4), (4,4), (4,2), (1,2)   **14** (1,2), (3,4), (5,2), (3,0)

15 (3,4), (4,2), (2,1), (1,3)

Investigation B

The distance between two points is measured in terms of the number of squares between the points. For example, the distance between (1,2) and (1,5) is 3. Can you find an easy way to find the distance between any two points, without drawing them? Investigate for many different pairs of points.

Move and draw

The commands 'MOVE' and 'DRAW' are used to give instructions in creating diagrams on a coordinate grid. The 'MOVE' command is an instruction to move to a new position without drawing. The 'DRAW' command is used to draw a line from the previous position to a new position.

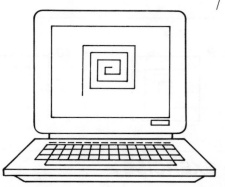

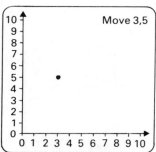
Move 3,5

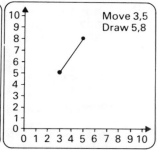
Move 3,5
Draw 5,8

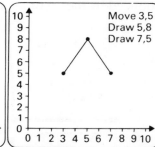
Move 3,5
Draw 5,8
Draw 7,5

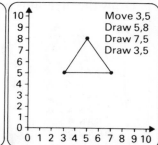
Move 3,5
Draw 5,8
Draw 7,5
Draw 3,5

The instructions can also be used on a computer, but in this case the scale on the axes is 100 times as large, e.g. MOVE 300,500, and the actual axes are not shown on the screen. When you have drawn each shape type CLS to clear the screen.

```
10 CLS
20 MOVE 300, 500
30 DRAW 500, 800
40 DRAW 700, 500
50 DRAW 300, 500
```

EXERCISE 1

Write a series of instructions to produce these diagrams, starting from the point indicated.

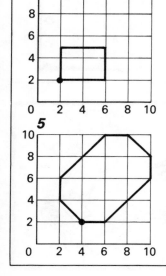

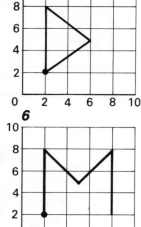

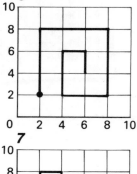

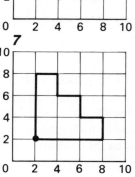

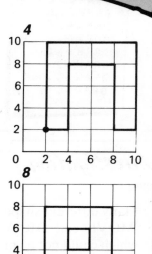

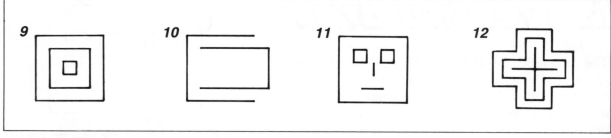

EXERCISE 2

Draw the diagrams produced by these commands:

1

```
MOVE 2, 2
DRAW 2, 6
DRAW 6, 6
DRAW 6, 4
DRAW 4, 4
DRAW 4, 2
DRAW 2, 2
```

2

```
MOVE 0, 2
DRAW 2, 6
DRAW 6, 4
DRAW 0, 2
```

3

```
MOVE 0, 2
DRAW 0, 4
DRAW 4, 6
DRAW 8, 4
DRAW 8, 2
DRAW 4, 0
DRAW 0, 2
```

4

```
MOVE 0, 3
DRAW 2, 4
DRAW 3, 6
DRAW 4, 4
DRAW 6, 3
DRAW 4, 2
DRAW 3, 0
DRAW 2, 2
DRAW 0, 3
```

5

```
MOVE 4, 8
DRAW 6, 8
DRAW 8, 6
DRAW 8, 2
DRAW 6, 0
DRAW 4, 0
DRAW 2, 2
DRAW 2, 6
DRAW 4, 8
MOVE 4, 6
DRAW 6, 6
DRAW 6, 2
DRAW 4, 2
DRAW 4, 6
```

6

```
MOVE 4, 4
DRAW 4, 6
DRAW 6, 6
DRAW 6, 4
DRAW 4, 4
MOVE 4, 2
DRAW 2, 2
DRAW 2, 4
MOVE 2, 6
DRAW 2, 8
DRAW 4, 8
MOVE 6, 8
DRAW 8, 8
DRAW 8, 6
MOVE 6, 2
DRAW 8, 2
DRAW 8, 4
```

7

```
MOVE 0, 6
DRAW 0, 0
DRAW 4, 0
DRAW 4, 4
DRAW 6, 4
DRAW 6, 0
DRAW 10, 0
DRAW 10, 6
DRAW 5, 10
DRAW 0, 6
DRAW 10, 6
MOVE 1, 4
DRAW 3, 4
DRAW 3, 2
DRAW 1, 2
DRAW 1, 4
MOVE 7, 4
DRAW 9, 4
DRAW 9, 2
DRAW 7, 2
DRAW 7, 4
```

8

```
MOVE 1, 6
DRAW 1, 10
DRAW 2, 8
DRAW 3, 10
DRAW 3, 6
MOVE 3, 4
DRAW 5, 8
DRAW 7, 4
MOVE 4, 6
DRAW 6, 6
MOVE 10, 4
DRAW 8, 4
DRAW 7, 2
DRAW 8, 0
DRAW 10, 0
```

Investigation

Many different shapes can be produced using 'MOVE' and 'DRAW'. Can you find any shapes which could not be produced? Discuss other ways to see if you can find methods which may work to produce approximations to these shapes.

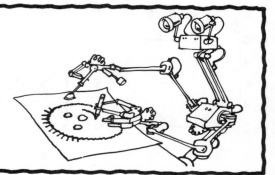

Positive and negative coordinates

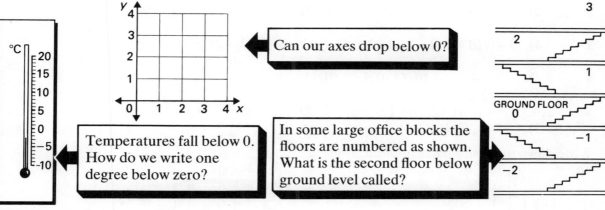

Can our axes drop below 0?

Temperatures fall below 0. How do we write one degree below zero?

In some large office blocks the floors are numbered as shown. What is the second floor below ground level called?

We can extend the axes of our graphs in the same way:

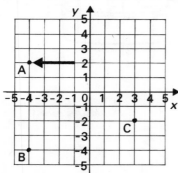

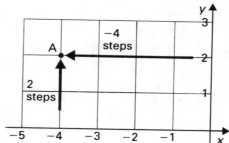

Point A has the coordinates $(-4,2)$.
Point B has the coordinates $(-4,-4)$.
Point C has the coordinates $(3,-2)$.

EXERCISE 1

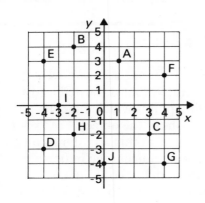

1 Write down the coordinates of each of the points on the left.

2 Draw a new pair of axes and mark the following points:

A(4,1), B(−1,1), C(−3,1), D(−5,−2), E(2,−5), F(0,−3), G(−2,2), H(−5,0), I(1,1), J(−4,4).

3 Draw a new pair of axes and mark the following points:

A(4,2), B(2,1), C(0,0), D(−2,−1), E(−4,−2), F(−2,4), G(−1,2), H(1, −2), I(2,−4).

EXERCISE 2

Plot the following points, joining them up in the order they are written:

1 $(-3,-4), (-3,4), (1,4), (2,3), (2,1), (1,0), (-3,0), (0,0), (2,-4)$

2 $(2,-4), (-2,-4), (-3,-3), (-3,3), (-2,4), (2,4), (3,3), (3,-3), (2,-4)$

3 $(-3,4), (3,4), (0,4), (0,-2), (-1,-3), (-2,-3), (-3,-2)$

4 $(-3,4), (-3,-4), (-3,0), (1,4), (-3,0), (1,-4)$

5 $(-3,-3), (-2,-4), (2,-4), (3,-3), (3,-2), (2,-1), (-2,1), (-3,2),$
$(-3,3), (-2,4), (2,4), (3,3)$

Write down the coordinates of these points:

6

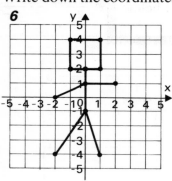

7

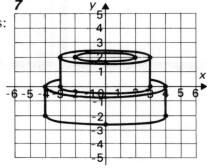

8

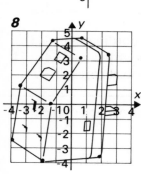

9

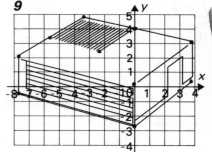

Investigation A

Write down the coordinates you would use to mark out each of the letters of your name. Is it possible to create every letter in this way?

Investigation B

Questions 8 and 9 in Exercise 2 show how a picture can be 'digitised', that is, turned into a number of important points which indicate some of the dimensions of the object. Find your own pictures to 'digitise' in this way. Draw a pair of axes over them, indicate the important points, and write them out as coordinates. Which objects will be difficult to digitise in this way?

Lines

$(3,4), (3,-3), (3,0), (3,2), (3,-1)$

What do these coordinates have in common? Plot the points.

What can you say about the points you have just plotted?

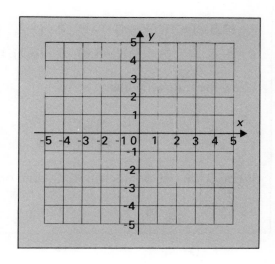

$(3,4)$
$(3,2)$
$(3,0)$ All the points had 3
$(3,-1)$ as the x-coordinate.
$(3,-3)$

The points are all in a line: join them up with a line, and that line passes through the point on the x axis where x is 3. We call this line: $x = 3$ as all points on the line have an x coordinate of 3.

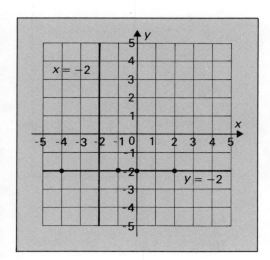

$(2,-2), (-4,-2), (-1,-2), (0,-2)$

What do these coordinates have in common?
The y coordinates are all -2.
When we plot the points and join them up we have drawn a line called $y = -2$
Notice that we label each line clearly.
We can extend the line to the left, and to the right, as there is no real 'end' to such a line: it is as long as you want to make it.

To draw the line $x = -2$:
The line $x = -2$ must have all points with an x coordinate of -2:

$(-2, \ ), (-2, \ ), (-2, \ ), (-2, \ )$

Copy these coordinates and fill in some y coordinates of your own. Plot the points, join them up, and you will have the line $x = -2$ as shown above.

EXERCISE 1

Write down the equation of the line we would obtain if we were to plot each series of points:

1 $(1,5), (1,3), (1,-4)$ **2** $(-2,-4), (0,-4), (3,-4)$ **3** $(0,5), (2,5), (-3,5)$

4 $(-5,-5), (-5,5), (-5,0)$ **5** $(0,2), (-2,2), (4,2)$ **6** $(0,0), (0,4), (0,8)$

Draw the following lines:

7 $x = 4$ **8** $y = -3$ **9** $x = -1$ **10** $x = 2$

11 $y = 3$ **12** $x = -4$ **13** $y = 0$ **14** $y = -5$

Write down two points you would find on each of these lines:

15 $x = 5$ **16** $y = -1$ **17** $x = -3$ **18** $y = 7$ **19** $x = -8$ **20** $x = 10$

EXERCISE 2

What would we call the line which joins each of the following pair of points?

1   A and D   **2**   E and H   **3**   A and C

4   C and F   **5**   G and H   **6**   B and D

7   B and E   **8**   I and J   **9**   G and F

10   H and J

Find the point where each pair of lines cross:

11 $x = 2$ and $y = 4$ **12** $x = -2$ and $y = 2$ **13** $x = -1$ and $y = 3$

14 $x = 0$ and $y = -4$ **15** $x = 3$ and $y = -3$ **16** $x = -5$ and $y = -5$

17 $x = 5$ and $y = 0$ **18** $x = -7$ and $y = 4$ **19** $x = 8$ and $y = -5$

20 $x = -9$ and $y = -2$

Investigation

Can you describe a quick way of writing down the point where two such lines cross?

Using letters

1

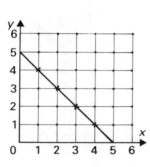

(a) Complete this table of coordinates:

x coordinate	0	1	2	3	4	5
y coordinate	5	4				

(b) Add the x and y coordinates together. What do you notice?

(c) Write down an equation for the graph:
$x + y = ?$

2

x coordinate	0	1	2	3	4	5
y coordinate	2	3	4			

(a) What rule do you think connects the x and y coordinates?

(b) Complete the table.

(c) Complete the graph using the table.

$y =$

3

(a) Complete the table.

x	0	1	2	3
y	0	2		

(b) What is the rule?

(c) The equation is $y = ?$

4

x	1	2	3	4	6	12
y	12	6				

(a) Complete the table from the graph.

(b) Multiply the coordinates together. What do you notice?

(c) Write down an equation: $xy = ?$

(d) Draw a graph for $xy = 24$.

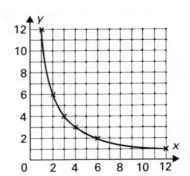

SPACE BATTLES

The game is played on three levels between two players.

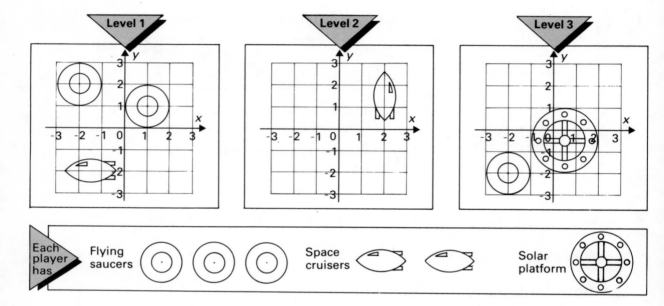

Rules

1 Each player begins with three boards as shown.

2 Each player has three flying saucers, two space cruisers, and one solar platform, which he draws, to the exact sizes shown above, on the boards. Each player may choose the level on which to draw each space-craft. A player's opponent does not know the location of any of his space-craft.

3 Each player, in turn, chooses a point at which to fire, (for example, (2,1) on level 2). If an opponent has a space-craft drawn on this point, he must declare it, and remove the space-craft. A hit on any part of an opponent's vehicle destroys it.

4 When a player has lost all his space vehicles the game finishes and the opponent has won.

Revision exercise

1 On a pair of axes plot the following points and join them up:

(1,3), (4,3), (8,1), (11,1), (11,3), (8,3), (4,1), (1,1), (1,3).

2 On a pair of axes plot the following points and join them up:

$(-2,-2)$, $(-1,-1)$, $(-1,2)$, $(0,3)$, $(1,2)$, $(1,-1)$, $(2,-2)$, $(-2,-2)$.

3 Write down the coordinates of the midpoint of the line joining each pair of points:

(*a*) (2,3), (4,1)   (*b*) (0,0), (4,5)   (*c*) (1,4), (5,0)

(*d*) $(-4,-3)$, (2,1)   (*e*) $(5,-1)$, $(2,-3)$ (*f*) $(4,2)$, $(3,-3)$

4 Find the coordinates of the midpoint of these shapes:

(*a*) (2,5), (4,3), (2,1), (0,3)   (*b*) (1,5), (4,5), (4,2), (1,2)

5 Draw the diagram produced by these MOVE and DRAW commands:

(*a*)   (*b*)   (*c*)

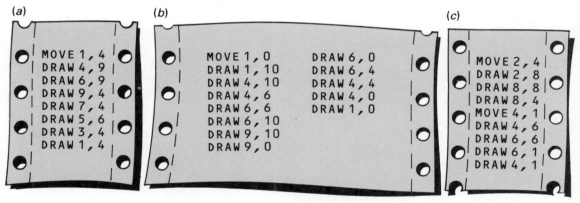

```
MOVE 1, 4
DRAW 4, 9
DRAW 6, 9
DRAW 9, 4
DRAW 7, 4
DRAW 5, 6
DRAW 3, 4
DRAW 1, 4
```

```
MOVE 1, 0      DRAW 6, 0
DRAW 1, 10     DRAW 6, 4
DRAW 4, 10     DRAW 4, 4
DRAW 4, 6      DRAW 4, 0
DRAW 6, 6      DRAW 1, 0
DRAW 6, 10
DRAW 9, 10
DRAW 9, 0
```

```
MOVE 2, 4
DRAW 2, 8
DRAW 8, 8
DRAW 8, 4
MOVE 4, 1
DRAW 4, 6
DRAW 6, 6
DRAW 6, 1
DRAW 4, 1
```

6 On a pair of axes draw these lines:

(*a*) $x = -2$ (*b*) $y = 3$ (*c*) $y = -2$
(*d*) $x = 4$ (*e*) $x = 0$ (*f*) $y = 5$
(*g*) $y = 0$

7 Find the point where each pair of lines cross:

(*a*) $x = 1, y = 3$ (*b*) $x = 0, y = -2$
(*c*) $x = -2, y = 3$

8

x	0	1	2	3	4	5
y	1	3	5			

Find the rule for working out the y coordinates. Draw a pair of axes, plot the points, and find the equation of the line: $y = ?$

9 Repeat question 8 with this table.

x	0	1	2	3	4
y			0	-1	-2

12. Measure: capacity and mass

Capacity

Capacity is a measure of how much liquid a container holds. The flagon shown can hold 4 litres. The measuring scale on the side also shows millilitres. How many millilitres are there in a litre?

LITRES ML
4 — — 4000
— 3500
3 — — 3000
— 2500
2 — — 2000
— 1500
1 — — 1000
— 500

Investigation

The numbers on the scale on the side of the flagon are not spaced out evenly. Why do you think this is? You can test your ideas for yourself:

Use a glass bowl, and add equal measures of water, marking on the side of the bowl the level of water after each measure has been added. What do you notice about the distances between the marks you have made?

The units used to measure capacity are:

10 ml = 1 cl	millilitre (ml)
100 cl = 1 *l*	centilitre (cl)
1000 ml = 1 *l*	litre (*l*)

A medicine spoon is normally 5ml

EXERCISE 1

Estimate the capacity of the following:

1 A teacup   **2** An egg cup   **3** A bath   **4** A washing-up bowl

5 A mug   **6** A milk pan   **7** A car radiator   **8** A hot-water bottle

9 Match up the object with the amount:

A household bucket

A can of fizzy drink

A milk bottle

A tin of paint

A washing machine

| 70 *l* | 300 ml | 2.5 *l* | 600 ml | 9 *l* |

> 2 *l* 450 ml = 2000 ml + 450 ml = 2450 ml
>
> We could also write 2450 ml as 2.450 *l*
> so 2*l* 450 ml = 2450 ml or 2.450 *l*

EXERCISE 2

Copy and complete the tables:

	Mixed units	Litres	Milli-litres
1	2*l* 200 ml		
2	3*l* 150 ml		
3	2*l* 830 ml		
4	1*l* 20 ml		
5	0*l* 800 ml		
6	1*l* 200 ml		
7	4*l* 950 ml		
8	5*l* 950 ml		
9	3*l* 20 ml		
10	2*l* 100 ml		
11	2*l* 5 ml		
12	3*l* 225 ml		

	Mixed units	Litres	Centilitres	Milli-Litres
13			2.4 cl	
14			1.2 cl	
15		3.042 *l*		
16		1.155 *l*		
17				3420 ml
18				1532 ml
19	1*l* 20 cl			
20	2*l* 90 cl			
21			32.4 cl	
22		5.1 *l*		
23				980 ml
24			96.5 cl	
25		4.2 *l*		

26 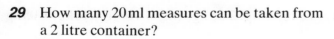 The medicine bottle holds 25 cl. How many 5 ml spoonfuls are there in the bottle?

27 Martin, an asthmatic, has two 5 ml doses of ventolin syrup each day. How many litres of ventolin syrup will he have in a year of 365 days?

28 How many 15 cl cups of orange squash can you pour out of a large 1½ litre container?

29 How many 20 ml measures can be taken from a 2 litre container?

30 What total capacity, in litres, is needed to fill 80 cans each of capacity 50 cl?

For each question write the capacities in order, smallest first.

31 3*l* 335 ml, 2.4 cl, 4.2*l*, 100 ml, 1.031*l*, 1300 ml, 25 cl, 180 ml

32 1.512*l*, 3.5 cl, 3800 ml, 39 cl, 3.72*l*, 250 ml, 2*l* 20 ml, 2305 ml

33 81 cl, 2.31*l*, 830 ml, 2*l* 900 ml, 4 cl, 8 ml, 0.517*l*, 115 ml

34 2.157*l*, 1850 ml, 40 cl, 970 ml, 5.1*l*, 7.9 cl, 1*l* 250 ml, 120 ml

Mass

Mass is measured in grams. The units used to measure mass are:

100 mg = 1 g	milligram (mg), gram (g)
1000 g = 1 kg	kilogram (kg)
1000 kg = 1 t	tonne (t)

A 10p coin weighs about 10g

A bag of sugar weighs 1 kg

The milligram is only used for weighing very small objects.

EXERCISE

Estimate the mass of each of the following:

1 A £1 coin   **2** A 5p coin   **3** A 50p coin   **4** Yourself

5 A small car   **6** An elephant

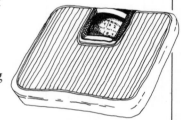

Write in terms of grams:

7 2 kg   **8** 1 kg 350 g   **9** 2 kg 10 g   **10** 1 kg 155 g

Write in terms of kg only:

11 2 t   **12** 500 g   **13** 2 t 400 kg   **14** 700 g   **15** 3.4 t

16 1 t 10 kg   **17** 50 g   **18** 2 t 900 kg

Write in terms of tonnes only:

19 20 000 kg

20 3 t 300 kg

21 500 kg

22 5600 kg

23 3 t 20 kg

24 250 000 kg

25 250 kg

For each question write the masses in order, smallest first.

26 2 kg, 1200 g, 8.5 kg, 3 t, 700 kg, 400 g, 1400 kg, 50 kg

27 1540 g, 3400 g, 1.5 kg, 0.35 kg, 670 g, 2.5 t, 350 kg, 20.5 kg

28 2750 g, 1.75 t, 3 kg, 68 kg, 4500 kg, 4500 g, 850 g, 575 g

29 2350 kg, 72 kg, 550 g, 2.25 kg, 1.25 t, 4100 g, 910 kg, 1.05 kg

30 2.15 t, 1.75 kg, 1200 kg, 3100 g, 95 kg, 780 kg, 375 g, 9500 g

The heaviest man in the world was Jon Minnock of Washington, who weighed 635 kg. The lightest human was Lucia Zarate of Mexico, who weighed 2.125 kg at the age of 17. The heaviest load ever lifted was the roof of the Montreal Velodrome weighing 37 194 tonnes.

Scales and dials

We will need to read scales and dials frequently in our daily lives.
Reading instruments requires estimation, and a knowledge of
decimal places.

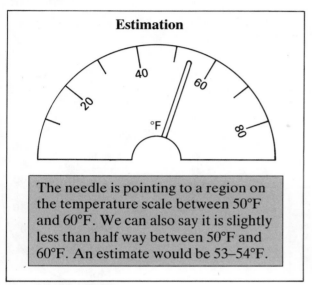

Estimation

The needle is pointing to a region on
the temperature scale between 50°F
and 60°F. We can also say it is slightly
less than half way between 50°F and
60°F. An estimate would be 53–54°F.

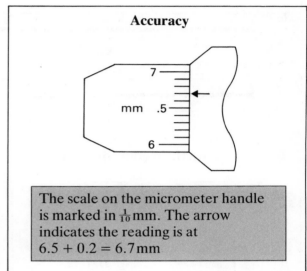

Accuracy

The scale on the micrometer handle
is marked in $\frac{1}{10}$ mm. The arrow
indicates the reading is at
$6.5 + 0.2 = 6.7$ mm

EXERCISE

1 Estimate or give an accurate reading for each dial:

2 Give the temperature in
(i) °C and (ii) °F

3 What is the
reading on
each of
these dials?

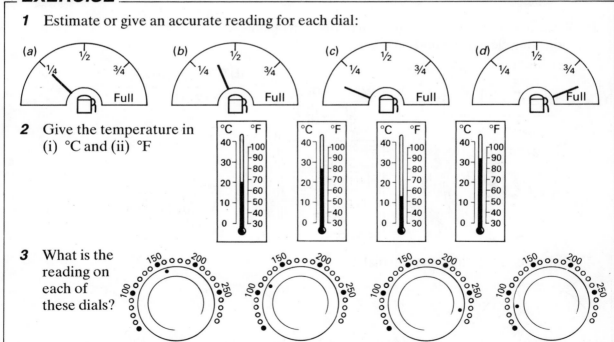

4 Give the speed in (i) km per hour (ii) miles per hour.

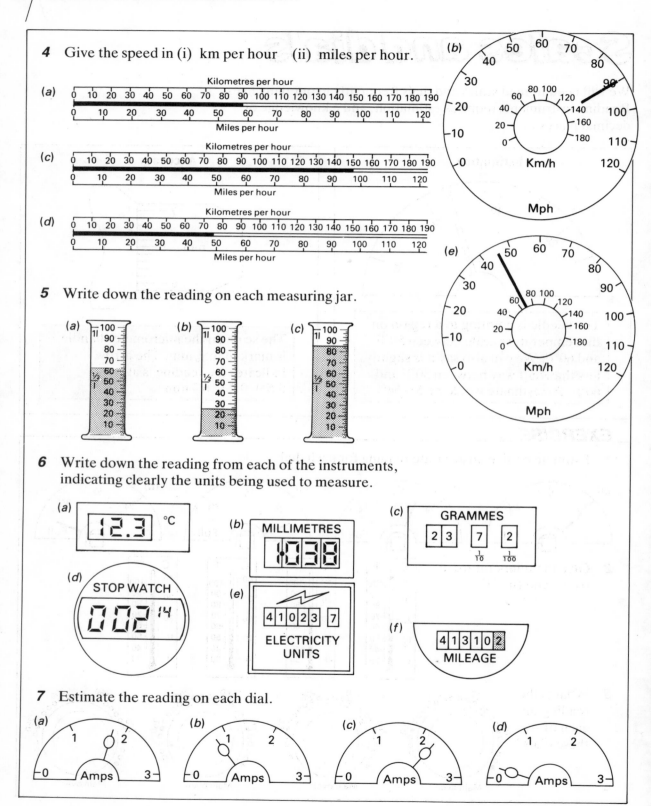

(a)

Kilometres per hour
0 10 20 30 40 50 60 70 80 90 100 110 120 130 140 150 160 170 180 190

0 10 20 30 40 50 60 70 80 90 100 110 120
Miles per hour

(c)

Kilometres per hour
0 10 20 30 40 50 60 70 80 90 100 110 120 130 140 150 160 170 180 190

0 10 20 30 40 50 60 70 80 90 100 110 120
Miles per hour

(d)

Kilometres per hour
0 10 20 30 40 50 60 70 80 90 100 110 120 130 140 150 160 170 180 190

0 10 20 30 40 50 60 70 80 90 100 110 120
Miles per hour

5 Write down the reading on each measuring jar.

6 Write down the reading from each of the instruments, indicating clearly the units being used to measure.

(a) `12.3` °C

(b) MILLIMETRES `1038`

(c) GRAMMES `2 3 7 2` $\frac{1}{10}$ $\frac{1}{100}$

(d) STOP WATCH `002`¹⁴

(e) `4 1 0 2 3 7` ELECTRICITY UNITS

(f) `4 1 3 1 0 2` MILEAGE

7 Estimate the reading on each dial.

(a) 0 1 2 3 Amps

(b) 0 1 2 3 Amps

(c) 0 1 2 3 Amps

(d) 0 1 2 3 Amps

Revision exercise

Copy and complete the tables.

	Litres/ml	Litres	Centilitres	Millilitres
1	3l 100 ml			
2	2l 90 ml			
3		3l		
4			4 cl	
5				500 ml
6			5.3 cl	
7		5.115l		
8				1500 ml
9	3l 350 ml			
10				6500 ml
11			12.9 cl	
12		5.01l		
13	2l 900 ml			
14			39.5 cl	
15				3450 ml

	Mixed units	Kilograms	Grams
16	2 kg 300g		
17			3400 g
18		2.1 kg	
19			800 g
20		4.01 kg	

	Mixed units	Tonnes	Kilograms
21		3.3 t	
22	3t 150 kg		
23			5400 kg
24		9.41t	
25			20 kg

For each question write the measurements in order, smallest first:

26 1.312*l*, 1850 ml, 2*l* 900 ml, 7.8 cl, 0.517*l*, 130 ml, 1.3*l*

27 1*l* 205 ml, 2870 ml, 81 cl, 45 ml, 1*l* 100 ml, 2.5 cl, 3.72*l*

28 400 ml, 840 cl, 2.4 cl, 1*l* 400 ml, 130 ml, 1.04*l*, 25 cl

29 1.8 t, 4600 g, 900 kg, 2.5 kg, 3 t, 3100 g, 1.05 kg, 400 g

30 780 kg, 1.8 t, 700 kg, 1400 g, 2750 g, 1.7 kg, 40000 g, 700 g

31 How many 5 ml spoonfuls are there in a 30 cl medicine bottle?

32 How many 20 cl cups of squash could be poured from a container of capacity 5 litres?

33 A lorry has a maximum weight restriction of 5 t. What is the maximum weight of its load if the empty lorry weighs 2.8 t?

34 How many 200 g ball bearings can be placed in a container with a maximum load of 1 tonne?

35 Estimate the voltage shown on each of these dials.

(a)
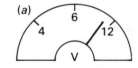

(b)
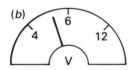

(c)
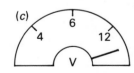

(d)
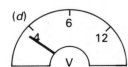

13. Symmetry

Line symmetry

Investigation A

PAPER CUTTING

Follow these instructions:

 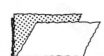

What do you notice?

Take a sheet of paper.

Fold the sheet down the middle.

Draw and cut out a shape of your own design on the folded edge.

Open out your sheet of paper.

Note: Each fold is called a **line of symmetry**.

Investigation B

INK DEVILS

Fold . . .

    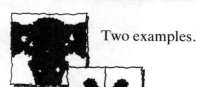

Two examples.

. . . flat.

Take a sheet of paper.

Put some ink or paint on the paper.

Fold your sheet of paper in half.

Open up your sheet.

Investigation C

POLYGONS

Fold a sheet of paper. Draw and cut the right-angled triangle shown (angle about 70°). Open up your sheet. You should have an isosceles triangle.

70° Decide exactly what triangle needs to be cut from a folded sheet to give each of these unfolded shapes:

(a) an equilateral triangle
(b) a kite
(c) a square
(d) a rhombus (which is not a square)
(e) an obtuse-angled isosceles triangle
(f) a re-entrant quadrilateral.

Show your cut-out triangle and your final shape.

Investigation **D**

PENTOMINOES

5 squares
touching on
at least
one side.

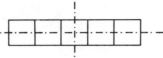

2 lines of symmetry.

1 line of symmetry.

Find other
pentominoes
which have
at least one
line of symmetry.

Investigation **E**

9-DOTS

Line of
symmetry

This heptagon has *one* line of symmetry.
Investigate other symmetrical polygons on 9-dots.

Investigation **F**

HEXAGONS

This hexagon has 0
lines of symmetry.

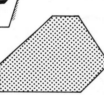

Draw hexagons with

(*a*) 1 line of symmetry
(*b*) 2 lines of symmetry
(*c*) 3 lines of symmetry
(*d*) 6 lines of symmetry

Are there any hexagons with 4 or 5 lines of symmetry?
Explain your answers.

Investigation **G**

TRIANGLES → QUADRILATERALS

Use *four* triangles
like this:
What symmetrical quadrilaterals
can you make?
Draw and describe each one.

Investigation **H**

ALPHABET

'A' has *vertical*
line symmetry.

Draw the rest of the alphabet carefully.

'B' has *horizontal*
line symmetry.

Draw in all lines of symmetry for each
letter.

EXERCISE

1 Copy each diagram. Complete each shape.

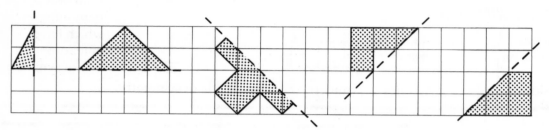

2 Trace each pattern below. Complete the patterns.

3 Each of these regular polygons has *one* line of symmetry drawn.

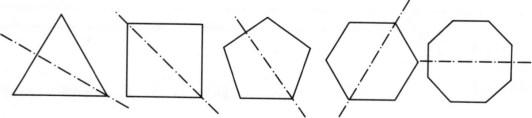

Trace these polygons and draw in all the other lines of symmetry.

4 What name is given to a line which is a line of symmetry of a circle?
How many lines of symmetry does a circle have?

Coordinates

A line of symmetry
acts like a mirror,
and produces an
image or a **reflection**.

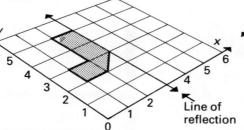

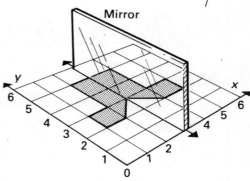

Mirror

Line of
reflection

EXERCISE

1

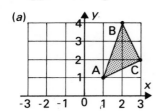

Line of
symmetry

Point	Reflections
A (3,5)	A (3,5)
B (1,4)	H (5,4)
C (,)	G (,)
D (,)	F (,)
E (,)	E (,)

(a) Copy and complete the
diagram and table.

(b) Why are the
reflections of
points A and E
the same?

2 Copy and complete these diagrams:

(a)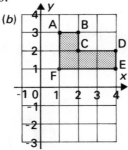

(b)

(c)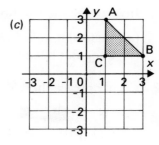

Lines of symmetry are, in (a), the y axis, in (b), the x axis, in (c) the y axis, then the x axis.

Draw up a coordinates table for each reflection.

3 Plot each of these sets of points on separate diagrams:

(a) (4,0), (5,3), (2,4), (1,1), (4,0).

(b) (1,1), (2,1), (3,2), (4,1), (5,2), (2,5), (1,4), (2,3), (1,2), (2,1).

(c) (2,1), (3,1), (4,2), (4,3), (3,4), (2,4), (1,3), (1,2), (2,1).

Join the points up in the order plotted for each set.
Draw in the lines of symmetry for each diagram.

Rotational symmetry

DEFINITIONS

Rotate this *equilateral triangle* through 120° . . .

. . . it looks the same.

Another rotation . . .

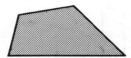

. . . it looks the same.

Another rotation . . .

. . . it is back to its original position.

There are 3 positions in which the triangle looks the same when rotated 120° clockwise three times. We say that the equilateral triangle has **rotational symmetry of order 3**.

The point about which the triangle turns is called the **centre of rotation**.

This irregular quadrilateral only looks the same when rotated back to its original position.

We say it has **rotational symmetry of order 1**.

EXERCISE 1

1 Investigate the rotational symmetry of

   (*a*) quadrilaterals   (*b*) a regular pentagon
   (*c*) a regular hexagon   (*d*) a semicircle   (*e*) a circle.

2 Copy or trace these diagrams.

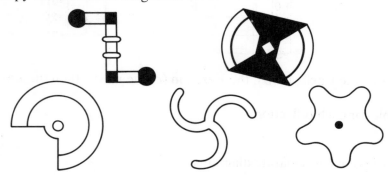

   (*a*) Write down the order of rotational symmetry for each.

   (*b*) State how many axes of symmetry each shape has.

3 The letter 'H' has rotational symmetry of order 2. Work out the order of rotational symmetry for the rest of the alphabet.

COORDINATES

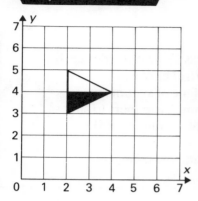

Example:
The shape on the grid at the left has been rotated about *centre* (4,4).

The final shape has *rotational symmetry of order 2.*

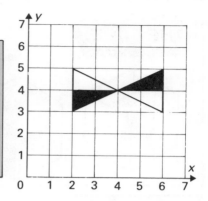

EXERCISE 2

1 For the example above

   (*a*) rotate the shape, centre (4,4), so that the final shape has rotational symmetry of order 4.

   (*b*) rotate the shape, centre (2,3), so that the final shape has rotational symmetry of order 2.

   (*c*) rotate the shape, centre (2,3), so that the final shape has rotational symmetry of order 4.

2 For the shape on the right, rotate it so that the final diagram has rotational symmetry.

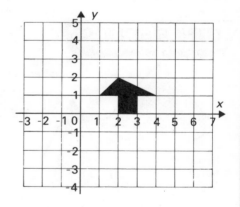

   (*a*) order 4, centre (4,1)
   (*b*) order 2, centre (3,−2)
   (*c*) order 4, centre (0,0)
   (*d*) order 4, centre (2,1).
   Draw a separate diagram for each.

3 Look at each of these shapes. Write down the order of rotational symmetry and centre of rotation for each one.

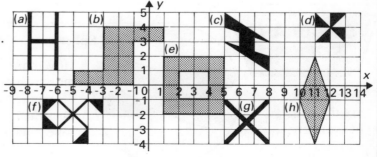

Plane symmetry

THE CUBE

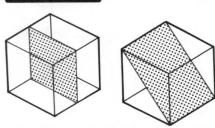

Each 'slice' of a cube, as shown, divides each cube into two *symmetrical* halves.
Each slice is called a **plane of symmetry**.
Draw diagrams, on isometric paper, to show other possible planes of symmetry of the cube.
What shape is each plane of symmetry?

THE CUBOID

This cuboid slice divides the solid into two equal halves, but *not* into two symmetrical halves.
There are three possible planes of symmetry for the cuboid.
Draw diagrams to show them.
Describe the shape of each plane of symmetry.

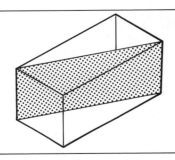

OTHER SOLIDS

Regular octahedron

Regular tetrahedron

Square-based pyramid

Make sketches of all the possible planes of symmetry of these solids.
Describe the shape of each plane of symmetry.
Look at the tetrahedron below.
Is the 'slice' shown a plane of symmetry?
Explain your answer.

CIRCULAR SOLIDS

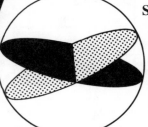

What shape are the planes of symmetry shown?

Sphere
How many more planes of symmetry does the sphere have?

The cylinder
Draw some other possible planes of symmetry for the cylinder.

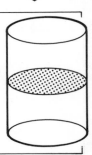

Rotating solids

EXTENSION

THE CUBE

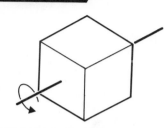

The line through the cube shows an **axis of symmetry**.
When the cube is rotated, there are four positions where it looks the same.
The cube has **rotational symmetry of order 4**.
Draw sketches to show other possible axes of symmetry.
Write down the 'order of rotation' for each axis.

OTHER SOLIDS

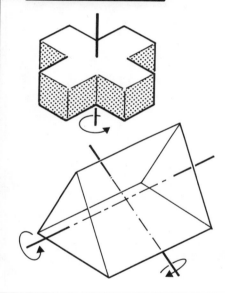

One axis of symmetry has been shown for this solid.
How many other axes of symmetry does it have?
What is the order of rotational symmetry of the solid for each axis?
How many axes of rotational symmetry do these solids have?
Sketch them.
Draw your own solid with rotational symmetry.

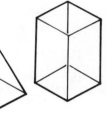

There are two axes of rotational symmetry shown for the triangular prism.
How many more axes are possible?
How many planes of symmetry does it have?
Try sketching the solid and its planes of symmetry.

CIRCULAR SOLIDS

How many axes of symmetry does each of these solids have?
How many planes of symmetry does each have?

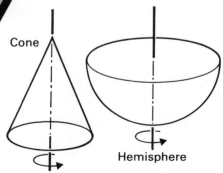

Cone

Hemisphere

For each axis, what is the order of rotational symmetry?
Investigate the sphere.

Revision exercise

1 (*a*) Say whether or not these shapes have line symmetry.

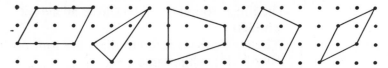

(*b*) Copy each shape and draw in all the lines of symmetry.

2 (*a*) State whether or not these shapes have rotational symmetry.

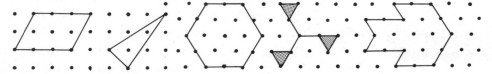

(*b*) What order of rotational symmetry does each possess?

3 Make a copy of this diagram. Show the position of the shape after a reflection in

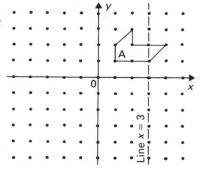

(*a*) the *y* axis

(*b*) the *x* axis

(*c*) the line $x = 3$.

4 Make another copy of the diagram in question 3. Show the final shape which results from rotating shape A to give it

(*a*) rotational symmetry of order 2, centre $(1,1)$

(*b*) rotational symmetry of order 4, centre $(3,1)$

(*c*) rotational symmetry of order 4, centre $(2,-1)$.

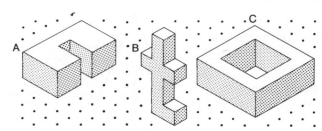

5 (*a*) Say whether or not each of these solids has rotational symmetry. State the order of rotational symmetry.

(*b*) Draw diagrams to show any planes of symmetry.

14. Statistics

Collecting data

Ali and Samantha run the school shop. Crisps are sold regularly, but they are never sure how many boxes of each flavour they need to order. The answer to their problem can be found by conducting a **survey**.

Plain	𝍸 𝍸 ||	12
Cheese and onion	𝍸 ||||	9
Salt and vinegar	𝍸 𝍸 |||	13
Beef	||||	4
Roast chicken	𝍸 |||	8
Smokey bacon	𝍸 ||||	9

To conduct a survey we need a **data collection sheet**. This lists the things we need to know. Ali and Samantha usually sell six flavours of crisp. They make a mark on the sheet each time they sell a bag of crisps, using a sheet for each day:

The marks are called **tallies**. The tallies are recorded in groups of five: 𝍸 to make them easier to count. The results can be written on a **data summary sheet** like this

	Mon	Tue	Wed	Thu	Fri	Total
Plain	12	13	16	12	8	
Cheese and onion	9	10	12	12	9	
Salt and Vinegar	13	13	11	10	8	
Beef	4	5	8	7	6	
Roast chicken	8	10	9	6	7	
Smokey bacon	9	12	11	11	9	

EXERCISE 1

1 Complete the totals on the data summary sheet.

2 Which was the most popular flavour of crisp?

3 On which day did Ali and Samantha sell the most crisps?

4 On which day did they sell the least crisps?

5 Which was the least popular flavour?

6 On which day did they sell the most beef flavoured crisps?

7 Which was the most popular flavour on Friday?

8 On which day were most beef and roast chicken flavoured crisps sold?

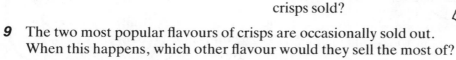

9 The two most popular flavours of crisps are occasionally sold out. When this happens, which other flavour would they sell the most of?

10 Crisps are bought every four weeks in boxes of 48 packets. How many boxes of each flavour would you want to buy on the basis of this survey?

EXERCISE 2

Listed below are some suggestions of surveys which could be conducted by students. For each survey draw a data collection sheet and a data summary sheet.

1 Two senior pupils are conducting a survey, over a week, on punctuality. They record the number of pupils entering the main school gate during five-minute intervals starting fifteen minutes before the first bell, and fifteen minutes after.

2 Sadiah and Rozina are interested in birthdays. They carry out a survey to record the day of the week on which each person's birthday falls this year.

3 Mark would like to find the number of hours of sunshine each day of a week. Describe how he could conduct his survey.

4 Lisa is conducting a survey to find which of the subjects taught at school are most popular. She writes out all the subjects studied as a basis for her investigation.

Grouped data

Mary wishes to investigate the amount of pocket money received by students each week. She carefully writes out every amount between £0 and £1.50. The list is so long it is very difficult to use.

Can you suggest another way for Mary to organise the information?

When we have many items to consider, we group them together to make it possible to conduct a survey. Can you suggest a way of grouping together amounts of money for Mary's survey? Mary decided to group her data in 10ps as shown in her data collection sheet:

Pocket money survey					
0-10p			81-90p		
11p-20p			91p-£1.00		
21p-30p			£1.01-£1.10		
31p-40p			£1.11-£1.20		
41p-50p			£1.21-£1.30		
51p-60p			£1.31-£1.40		
61p-70p			£1.41-£1.50		
71p-80p			£1.51-£1.60		

Copy this data collection sheet and insert tallies for her information (given below). Finally total the tallies.

£1, £1.20, 85p, 50p, 75p, £1.25, 90p, 85p, £1.10, £1.00, 90p, £1.30, 70p, £1.00, 90p, £1.20, £1.00, 85p, £1.30, £1.50, £1.05, £1.40, 90p, 85p, 70p, 85p, £1.00, £1.20, 90p, 75p, £1.00, £1.05, £1.20, £1.10, 85p, 95p, £1.00, 75p, £1.00, 90p, £1.00, £1.20, 90p, 95p, £1.00, £1.15, 50p, 80p, £1.30, 90p, £1.00, £1.05

Notice the groups are all of the same size: exactly 10 pence. Which group of pocket monies was the most popular?

EXERCISE

Listed below are some survey results which require grouping of the data. For each survey, draw a data collection sheet and insert the data given.

1 The heights of children in centimetres has been recorded in a survey:

163	155	161	149	158	148	159	163
168	146	148	143	150	152	141	158
154	168	155	166	149	147	152	163
156	157	153	140	162	144	154	158
163	163	153	155	164	156	167	165
143	160	142	169	166	169	159	148
157	146	165	140	151	161	143	150

2 The amounts of money expected to be collected from a sponsored run:

£5.50	£2.45	£20.90	£15.20	£5.60	£3.30	£8.75	£2.48
£6.00	£1.02	£13.20	£10.84	£7.10	£6.40	£5.60	£8.76
£7.20	£12.35	£6.58	£4.35	£16.95	£2.25	£0.75	£11.11
£4.85	£8.42	£0.80	£3.90	£11.76	£10.67	£8.25	£9.54
£2.30	£3.45	£15.85	£7.80	£9.15	£12.00	£7.79	£14.30
£5.40	£5.57	£12.10	£6.93	£13.00	£7.68	£0.90	£4.35

3 The marks achieved in an examination:

52 78 34 26 39 40 22 57 92 45 83 36 21 67 59 10 82 39 43
21 56 42 63 23 36 94 59 45 58 71 60 12 34 47 78 48 62 53
62 51 32 35 45 66 54 57 75 80 66 54

Investigation

Is there something you consider worth investigating?
Decide on a topic, prepare a data collection sheet, and conduct your own survey.

Bar charts

Ali and Samantha want to illustrate the sales figures for each day of the week. They decide to use a **bar chart**.

On which day were the most plain crisps sold?
On which day were the least plain crisps sold?
The bar chart helps us to find the answers to these questions easily.

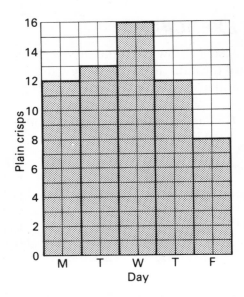

EXERCISE 1

Draw bar charts for the other flavours of crisps in Ali and Samantha's survey.

EXERCISE 2

Draw bar charts for the information contained in these tables:

1

Number of books needed for school				
8	5	12	7	10
Mon	Tues	Wed	Thu	Fri

2

Number of children in each lunchtime activity			
13	10	5	2
School dinner	Sand-wiches	Go home	Other

3

Number of hours of sunshine per day				
8	7	6½	5	7½
Mon	Tues	Wed	Thu	Fri

4

Average daily maximum temperature in London (°F)						
57	62	67	70	70	65	59
Apr.	May	Jun.	Jul.	Aug.	Sep.	Oct.

5

Number of children belonging to each family					
Families	3	10	8	5	4
Children in family	1	2	3	4	5+

6

Method of transport to school				
16	3	6	2	3
Walk	Bus	Car	Train	Others

Bar charts can also be used to display grouped data. Mary is using these axes to show the results of her survey on pocket money. Refer back to her data collection sheet. Copy and complete the bar chart.

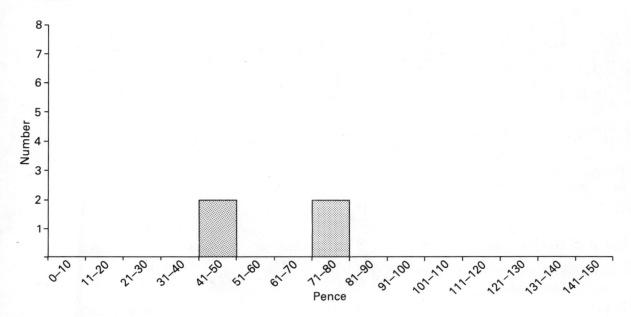

EXERCISE 3

Draw a bar chart for each of the questions in the exercise on grouped data on page 163.

EXERCISE 4

Draw a bar chart for the results you obtained as part of the investigation above. Can you suggest any other way to present the information?

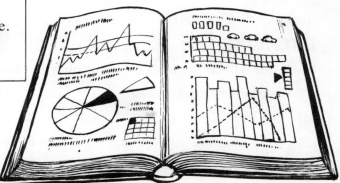

A database

Simon is collecting information about his friends' likes and dislikes with regard to particular types of food. He conducts a survey, and collects his information using a data collection sheet:

	A	B	C	D	E	F	G	H
Name:	Chips	Potatoes	Rice	Peas	Beans	Sprouts	Cabbage	Tomatoes
Jenny	✓	✗	✓	✓	✓	✓	✗	✗
Mandy	✓	✓	✗	✓	✗	✗	✓	✓
Paul	✓	✓	✓	✓	✓	✓	✓	✗
Josie	✓	✓	✗	✗	✓	✗	✗	✗
Chris	✓	✗	✓	✓	✓	✗	✗	✓

To help him investigate this information he puts the data into a short program on the computer. He is setting up his own **database**.

He has data on 25 of his friends ——

Spare line for any questions ——

All the information from the data collection sheet has been put in these data statements.
A tick is represented by a 1.
A cross is represented by a 0.

```
10 FOR X = 1 TO 25
20 READ N$, A, B, C, D, E, F, G, H
30
40 GOTO 60
50 PRINT N$
60 NEXT X
100 DATA "JENNY", 1, 0, 1, 1, 1, 1, 0, 0
110 DATA "MANDY", 1, 1, 0, 1, 0, 0, 1, 1
120 DATA "PAUL", 1, 1, 1, 1, 1, 1, 1, 0
130 DATA "JOSIE", 1, 1, 0, 0, 1, 0, 0, 0
140 DATA "CHRIS", 1, 0, 1, 1, 1, 0, 0, 1
```

Simon can then use the computer to ask questions about the data.
For example, if he wants to find which of his friends like chips and beans he would type in:
30 IF A = 1 AND E = 1 THEN 50, and then RUN the program.
If he wants to find those who do not like sprouts and cabbage he would type in:
30 IF F=0 OR G=0 THEN 50, and then RUN the program.

EXERCISE 1

Write down the statements Simon would type in to find those who:

1 like cabbage and sprouts
2 do not like tomatoes
3 like chips
4 like chips, but not potatoes
5 do not like rice or tomatoes
6 like rice, peas and beans
7 do not like sprouts, cabbage or tomatoes
8 would like a meal including rice, beans and tomatoes
9 would not like a dinner which included potatoes and cabbage
10 like all the foods mentioned.

The computer program could be changed easily so that data from any investigation could be processed. By changing the program we can use the computer to ask more questions. Ali and Samantha might have wanted to ask which flavours of crisp are liked. As there are 6 flavours of crisp they need the name, and details for each flavour:

```
10  FOR X = 1 TO 30
20  READ N$, P, CO, SV, B, RC, SB

100 DATA "ROBERT", 1, 1, 0, 1, 0, 0
```

For 30 people. Change as necessary.
Can you guess what the initials mean?

As Robert likes plain, cheese & onion and beef crisps.

EXERCISE 2

Write out programs for the following surveys, and if possible some sample data.

1 A survey to discover the types of television programme people like, such as sport, news, etc.

2 A survey to find out which of the subjects taught at school are liked.

3 A detailed investigation to discover the sports people enjoy watching.

4 Market research to determine which chocolate bars are popular.

5 A survey to find out which of the current top ten records are liked by a small sample of people.

EXTENSION: PROGRAMS AND QUESTIONS

A further change could be to insert an extra few lines as follows:

```
5   LET N = 0
55  LET N = N + 1
65  PRINT "TOTAL NUMBER ="; N
```

1 What effect does this have on the program?

2 How would you explain the question:

IF A=1 AND (B=0 OR C=0) THEN 50

3 A menu offers chips, with either peas or sprouts. What statement would you use to find those who would like the meal?

Investigation

Carry out one of the surveys detailed above, and enter the data on a computer. Write a series of questions to investigate the data, and describe what you find.

Pictograms

A pictogram is a graph where the symbol represents a group of units or numbers. Ali and Samantha could have shown the sales figures in terms of a pictogram:

1 bag of crisps is represented by $\frac{1}{4}$ of the symbol:

= 4 bags of crisps

Monday

Plain	Cheese and onion	Salt and vinegar	Beef	Roast chicken	Smokey bacon

How would 2 bags of crisps be shown?

EXERCISE 1

Draw pictograms for the following information, using the given symbols:

1

Number of books needed for school.				
8	5	12	7	10
Mon	Tue	Wed	Thu	Fri

= 2 Books

2

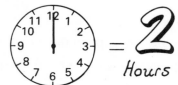
= 2 Hours

Hours spent on activities each day.				
8	7	2	1½	5½
Sleeping	Working	Eating	Travelling	Other

3

Goals scored in a season					
23	10	5	8	30	19
Alan	Gary	Mat	Louise	Sanchez	Noel.

= 4 Goals

4

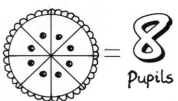
= 8 Pupils

Pupils with birthdays on these days						
24	32	20	16	28	19	21
Sun	Mon	Tue	Wed	Thu	Fri	Sat

5

Number of Christmas trees bought from local shops.						
	40	48	37	22	30	18	29
Shops	A	B	C	D	E	F	G.

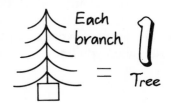
Each branch = 1 Tree

EXERCISE 2

Some pictograms use more complex symbols:

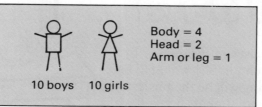

Write down the number of (*a*) boys (*b*) girls
in each group:

Draw pictograms for each of these groups:

7 14 boys, 16 girls

8 23 boys, 15 girls

9 28 boys, 28 girls

10 19 boys, 30 girls

11 25 boys, 21 girls

12 3 boys, 23 girls

Investigation

While working through this chapter you
will have prepared your own surveys.
Present your data in terms of pictograms,
selecting your own symbol to use.
Which symbols did you find
easiest to use?

MY SURVEY

Bar charts and grouped data

Sandra is a prefect who organises refreshments during a parents evening at school. She would like to know which part of the evening will be the busiest. A sample of the times of the appointments booked with teachers are as follows:

7.30	8.15	8.00	8.15	7.45	8.45	7.35	8.20	7.50
8.45	8.00	8.30	8.45	8.15	7.55	8.40	7.50	8.40
8.25	7.45	8.50	8.35	8.30	8.30	8.20	8.05	7.50
8.10	8.55	7.40	8.10	8.10	8.25	8.15	8.15	8.35
8.30	7.40	8.45	8.20	8.00	8.20	8.35	7.50	
7.55	8.40	8.05	8.30	7.50	8.50	8.20	8.25	

Sandra uses a data collection sheet which groups these times in $\frac{1}{4}$-hour intervals:

Times (pm)	Tallies	Frequency
7.30 – 7.44	IIII	4
7.45 – 7.59		
8.00 – 8.14		
8.15 – 8.29		
8.30 – 8.44		
8.45 – 9.00		

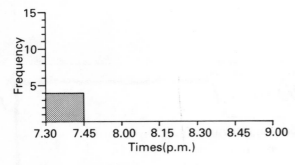

In drawing the bar chart the first bar finishes just before 7.45, as the first interval only includes those times up to 7.44 p.m. The horizontal scale used here is called a **continuous** scale.

EXERCISE

1 Copy and complete the data collection sheet and bar chart.

2 During which time interval will Sandra be busiest?

3 Which will be her quietest interval?

Interpretation of graphs and charts

EXERCISE

1 (*a*) What was the average daily maximum temperature in Turkey in
(i) May (ii) July (iii) October?

(*b*) What was the average daily maximum temperature in London in (i) May
(ii) July (iii) September?

(*c*) What was the difference in average daily maximum temperature between Turkey and London in (i) April
(ii) June?

(*d*) In which month was the difference in temperatures (i) the greatest
(ii) the least?

(*e*) In which month was the minimum hours of sunshine per day recorded in
(i) Turkey (ii) London?

2 The charts give temperature information for two Italian resort areas: the Adriatic and Neapolitan Rivieras.

(*a*) Which is the warmer resort?

(*b*) What is the maximum temperature difference between London and (i) the Adriatic Riviera (ii) the Neapolitan Riviera?

(*c*) In which month is the maximum temperature difference between the two resorts?

(*d*) Which resort had more sunshine?

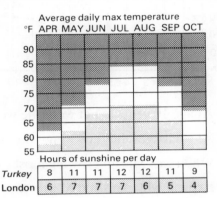

Average daily max temperature

Hours of sunshine per day

	APR	MAY	JUN	JUL	AUG	SEP	OCT
Turkey	8	11	11	12	12	11	9
London	6	7	7	7	6	5	4

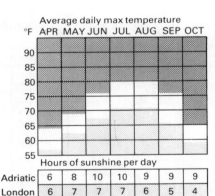

Average daily max temperature

Hours of sunshine per day

	APR	MAY	JUN	JUL	AUG	SEP	OCT
Adriatic	6	8	10	10	9	9	9
London	6	7	7	7	6	5	4

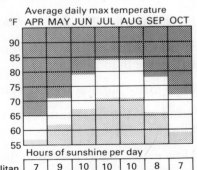

Average daily max temperature

Hours of sunshine per day

	APR	MAY	JUN	JUL	AUG	SEP	OCT
Neapolitan	7	9	10	10	10	8	7
London	6	7	7	7	6	5	4

3 Ann and Martin were weighed each birthday.

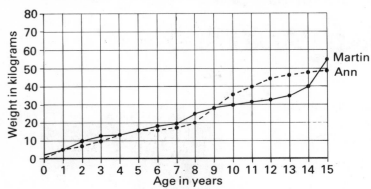

(*a*) At age 10 years, what were the weights of (i) Ann (ii) Martin?

(*b*) At what ages did they weigh the same?

(*c*) When was Martin growing most rapidly?

(*d*) Explain why Ann and Martin may have differed in weight between their 4th and 5th birthdays.

(*e*) About how old were they both when their weights differed the most?

4 The bar chart shows a survey of families living in a small village in Wales.

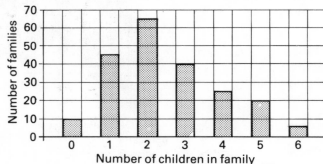

(*a*) How many families had (i) one child (ii) 4 children?

(*b*) How many families had (i) more than 3 children (ii) more than 2 children?

(*c*) How many families took part in the survey?

(*d*) What was the total number of children who lived in families with just 2 children?

(*e*) How many children lived in the village?

(*f*) What was the maximum number of children in any one family?

5

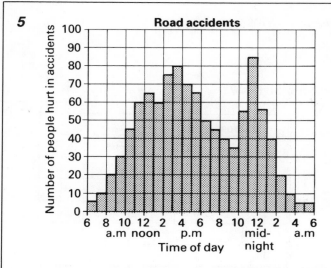

Road accidents

(a) How many people were hurt
    in road accidents at these times:
    (i) 9–10 a.m.   (ii) 6–7 p.m.
    (iii) 9–10 p.m.   (iv) 4–6 a.m.?

(b) During which times were the lowest
    figures recorded? Why do you think
    this is?

(c) During which times was it most
    dangerous on the roads? Why do you
    think this is?

(d) What is the most dangerous time on
    the roads *during the day*? Can you
    explain this?

6 (a) How many people were employed in
    (i) 1986   (ii) 1989   (iii) 1987
    (iv) 1990?

(b) Between which years was there the
    largest fall in the number of people
    employed?

(c) From 1986 to 1989, how many people
    left the factory?

(d) How many extra people were
    employed in 1990?

(e) Draw the symbols which would
    represent (i) 1400 people   (ii) 1700
    people.

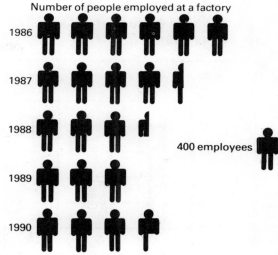

Number of people employed at a factory

400 employees

7

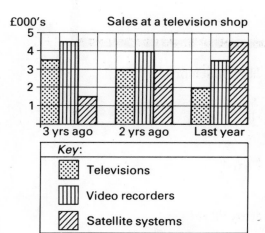

£000's   Sales at a television shop

Key:
Televisions
Video recorders
Satellite systems

(a) What value were the sales of video
    recorders
    (i) 3 years ago   (ii) 2 years ago
    (iii) last year?

(b) Which item has gradually increased
    its sales figures? Can you explain why?

(c) Which item has had a gradual fall in
    its sales figures? Why do you think
    this is?

(d) By how much did the sales of satellite
    systems increase (i) 2 years ago
    (ii) last year?

8 (*a*) What was the interest rate in (i) February (ii) June (iii) November?

(*b*) What was the lowest interest rate?

(*c*) In which month were interest rates at their highest?

(*d*) What was the highest interest rate?

(*e*) Between which months was the smallest increase in rates?

(*f*) Between which months was the sharpest decrease in rates?

(*g*) What is the difference between the highest and lowest rates?

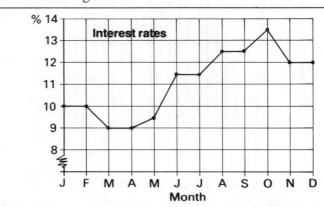

9

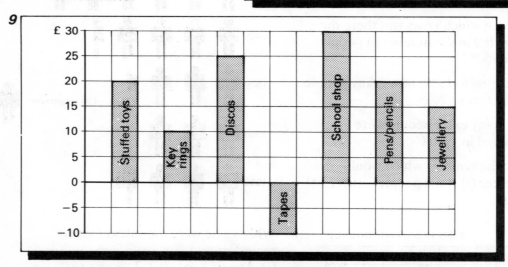

(*a*) Which was the most successful business? How much profit did it make?

(*b*) Which two enterprises made the same profit?

(*c*) How much profit was made in jewellery?

(*d*) Why is 'tapes' shown below the horizontal axis?

(*e*) What was the least successful business?

(*f*) What was the total amount of money made by all the enterprises?

Revision exercise

Prepare tally tables and graphs to represent each of the
following sets of data. Decide which of the sets of data
will need grouping.

1 Colours of new cars being ordered by clients at a garage:

> blue, white, red, blue, brown, black, red, brown, blue,
> white, red, blue, yellow, grey, black, blue, white, red,
> red, orange, black, white, red, orange, yellow, red,
> blue, yellow, grey, blue, brown, black, red, orange,
> white, blue, blue, grey, white, blue, black, white, blue,
> blue, orange, red, red, brown, black, red, blue, grey.

2 Amounts of bonus earned at a factory:

> £25.00, £32.50, £22.50, £38.00, £29.00, £30.00, £14.00,
> £19.50, £28.00, £9.00, £26.00, £37.00, £18.90, £22.00,
> £27.00, £20.00, £34.00, £31.75, £25.00, £29.00, £22.00,
> £37.50, £21.25, £11.50, £23.00, £29.50, £35.00, £38.00,
> £33.50, £18.70, £29.50, £25.00, £19.00, £14.00, £27.50,
> £14.00, £25.50, £29.00, £8.00, £10.50, £27.50, £18.50,
> £16.25, £31.00, £21.50, £14.25, £17.00, £9.00

3 Errors (in mm) detected in parts made in a company:

> $0, 1, 4, 3, -1, -3, 0, 1, -2, 0, 4, 3, -3, 1, 2, 0, 0, 1, 1,$
> $0, -2, -3, 0, 3, 4, 0, -3, 0, 0, 4, 2, 1, -1, 0, -1, 5, 4,$
> $-4, -2, 3, 4, 5, 0, -1, -1, 1, 3, 2, 1, 0, 0, 0, 3, 2, -1,$
> $-2, 0, 3, 4, 0, -1, 1, -2, -3, 1, 3, -1, -2, 0, 4, 1, 2,$
> $3, -3, 0, 1, -1, 0, -2, 3, 2, 5, -4, 5, 0, 6, 4, 2, 1, 0,$
> $-1, 0, 2, 4, -2, -3, 0, 3, 0, 4, -5, -4, 3, 0, 1, 1, 1, 2,$
> $-1, -1, 1, 0, 0$

4 Numbers attending several sports meetings:

9432	5427	12415	8417	6513	1046	7863	10411
4312	11307	10502	9412	13507	15103	18112	8403
1403	18503	7747	12401	14559	6001	5019	13147
7607	13412	4454	5043	10040	9090	3023	14389
9442	12019	3043	8470	2412	7092	13052	7437
14537	16053	5545	2653	7832	8012	11012	12953
12012	3742	8432	13532	15099	7453	9099	10329

15. Maps and bearings

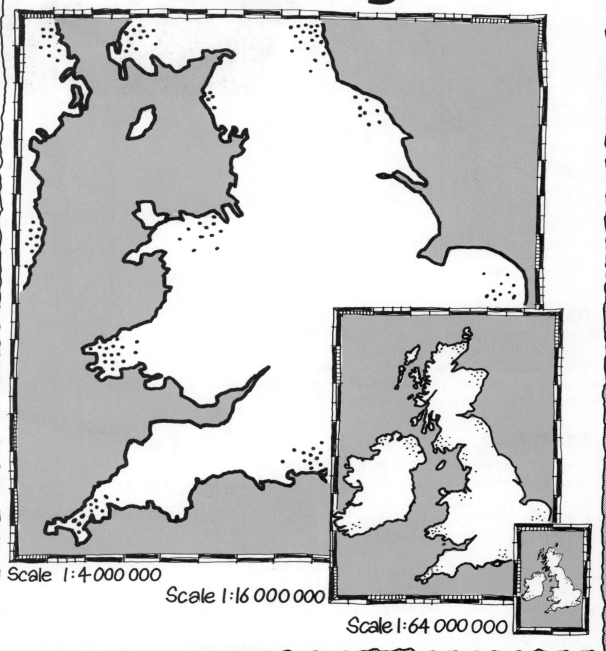

Scale 1:4 000 000

Scale 1:16 000 000

Scale 1:64 000 000

Mapwork

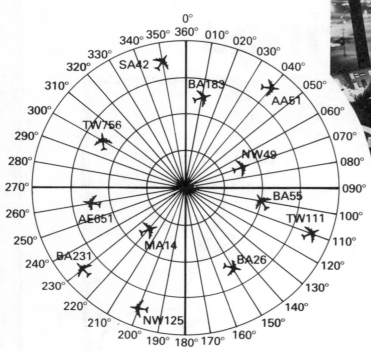

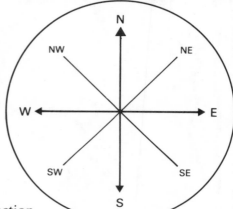

In Chapter 2 we used compass points to indicate angle direction. Bearings are more accurate than compass points. Flight AA51 above is at a bearing of 040° on the radar. Notice each bearing is represented by a three-figure number. A bearing of 1° would be written as 001°. Why do you think this is? A bearing is always measured clockwise from the North line, at 0°.

EXERCISE 1

Copy and complete the table to show the bearing of each aircraft on the radar.

Aircraft	Bearing
AA51	040°
AE651	
BA26	
BA55	
BA183	
BA231	

Aircraft	Bearing
MA14	
NW49	
NW125	
SA42	
TW111	
TW756	

EXERCISE 2

What bearing is used in place of these compass points?

1. North
2. South
3. West
4. East
5. North-West
6. North-East
7. South-East
8. South-West

Bearings

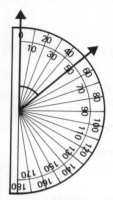

Bearings are measured in the same way as we measured angles. Remember to place the base line of the protractor at 0° on the North line. The bearing is 050°.

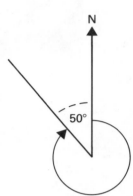

Bearings are always measured in a *clockwise* direction. The angle shown is the bearing required: a reflex angle. We could measure the acute angle, 50°, and calculate the bearing:

$$360° - 50° = 310°$$

EXERCISE 1

Measure and write down each bearing.

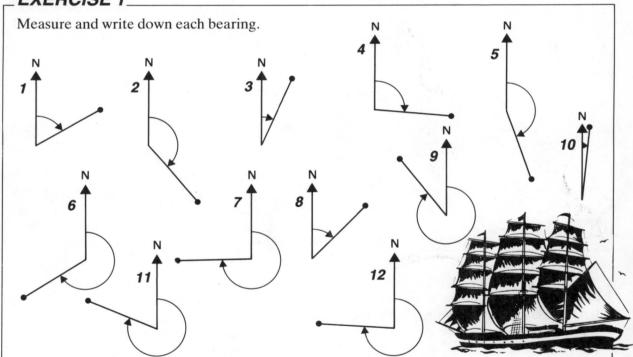

EXERCISE 2

Draw the following bearings:

1	070°	**2**	150°	**3**	100°	**4**	040°	**5**	175°
6	020°	**7**	200°	**8**	225°	**9**	105°	**10**	340°
11	205°	**12**	305°	**13**	145°	**14**	030°	**15**	235°

Maps

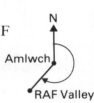

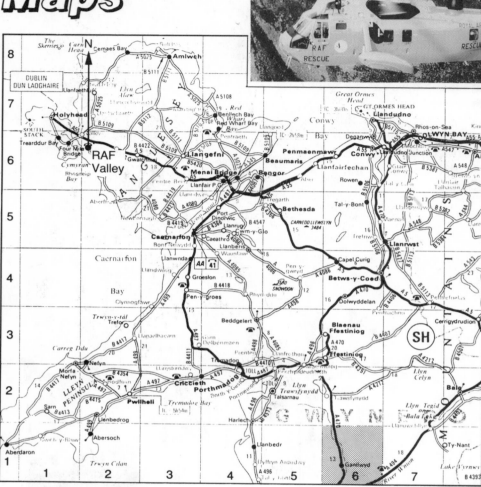

RAF Valley in Anglesey has an emergency rescue service. Whenever anyone suffers a serious injury, either in the Irish Sea, or in North Wales, the RAF rescue helicopter is called out to assist in the rescue.

The airfield at RAF Valley in (2–6) is indicated by the North line.

EXERCISE 1

Find the bearing the helicopter would fly from RAF Valley to the following places, for which map references are also given:

1 Amlwch (3–8)   **2** Bangor (4–6)

3 Colwyn Bay (7–6) **4** Snowdon (5–4)

5 Nefyn (2–3)   **6** South Stack (1–7)

7 Beddgelert (4–3) **8** Capel Curig (6–4)

9 Llandudno (6–7)   **10** The Skerries (1–8)

Having rescued the injured, the helicopter sometimes returns directly to RAF Valley. In order to find the bearing back to RAF Valley you will need a North line:

EXERCISE 2

Find the bearing the helicopter would fly from the places in Exercise 1 back to RAF Valley.

Investigation

Compare your answers from Exercise 1 with Exercise 2. What can you say about the bearings both to and from a pair of points?
Can you describe a way to calculate one bearing after being given the other?

EXERCISE 3

Find the bearing needed to fly between these places:

1 Snowdon (5–4) to Conway (6–6)

2 Betwys-y-Coed (6–4) to Porthmadog (4–2)

3 Llangefni (3–6) to Llanrwst (7–5)

4 Caernarfon (3–5) to Llanbedr (4–1)

5 Pwllheli (2–2) to Beaumaris (5–6)

Scales

Diagrams and maps are frequently drawn **to scale**. The measurements given on the plan or map are not the actual measurements, but scaled-down measurements.

```
0   1   2   3   4   5   6 Km
```

This scale is a very easy scale to use:

$1\,\text{cm} = 1\,\text{km}$

Every 1 cm in length represents 1 km.

```
0   5   10   15   20   25   30 Km
```

This scale is $1\,\text{cm} = 5\,\text{km}$
What does 10 mm represent? $10\,\text{mm} = 1\,\text{cm} = 5\,\text{km}$
What does 1 mm represent?

$1\,\text{mm} = \frac{1}{10}\,\text{cm}$ or $\frac{1}{10}$ of $5\,\text{km} = 0.5\,\text{km}$

EXERCISE 1

Find the distances represented by these lines on a scale of
(*a*) 1 cm = 1 km   (*b*) 1 cm = 5 km.

1 ├─────────┤   **2** ├─────────┤   **3** ├─────────┤   **4** ├──┤

5 ├───────────────┤   **6** ├──────────┤

7 ├─────────────────┤   **8** ├────────────────────────┤

Find the distances represented by these lines on a scale of 1 cm = 20 km.

9 ├──────────┤   **10** ├──────────┤   **11** ├──────────┤

12 ├────────┤   **13** ├──────────────┤

14 ├──────────┤   **15** ├────────────┤

This sketch-map of the British Isles is drawn to a scale of 1 cm to 100 km.

Scale   1:10 000 000

```
0     100    200    300
          Km
```

EXERCISE 2

Find the approximate distances between:

1 London and Norwich

2 Newcastle and Edinburgh

3 Liverpool and Cardiff

4 Aberdeen and Edinburgh

5 London and Liverpool

6 Glasgow and Edinburgh

7 Liverpool and Manchester

8 Newcastle and Manchester

9 London and Cardiff

10 Newcastle and Norwich.

Investigation

Using a piece of string, can you estimate the distance around the coast of the British Isles?

EXERCISE 3

1 Estimate the distance from Lands End to John O'Groats.

2 What is the return distance between Liverpool and Douglas, Isle of Man?

3 What is the approximate distance of a flight from London to Liverpool, then to Edinburgh, and back to London?

4 Find the approximate distances of the journeys:

(*a*) London – Liverpool – Manchester – London

(*b*) Newcastle – Aberdeen – Glasgow

(*c*) Cardiff – Edinburgh – Norwich – Cardiff

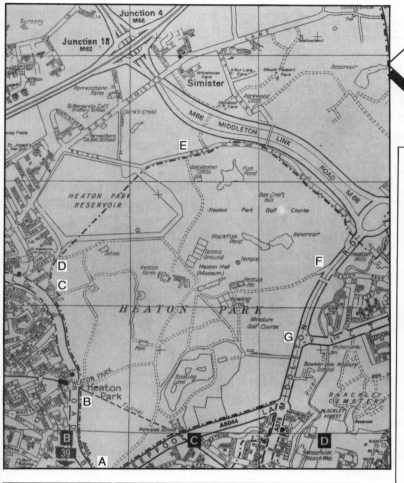

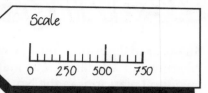

Scale

0   250   500   750

EXERCISE 4

Give your answers in metres.

1 What is the maximum width of Heaton Park reservoir?

2 What is the maximum length of the boating lake in the park?

3 What is the direct distance between these places in the park:

 (*a*) Heaton Farm to the Dog Kennel Cottages

 (*b*) Heaton Park Station to Heaton Hall Museum

 (*c*) Temple to Parkside School?

4 What is the perimeter of the park, indicated by the dotted line?

5 Find the direct distances from the Temple to each of the Park Entrances A–G.

6 Using the paths indicated in the park, estimate the distances between:

 (*a*) Entrance G and the Museum

 (*b*) Entrance F and Heaton House

 (*c*) Entrance B and the pool.

7 What is the length of Sheepfoot Lane?

8 What is the length of the railway tunnel between Heaton Park station and Bowker Vale station?

FOOTPATH

Bearings and scales

In order to describe a journey we need both a bearing and a distance. The map below shows the major oil platforms in the North Sea, and the location of the three main heliports serving the platforms from Aberdeen, Kirkwall and Lerwick.

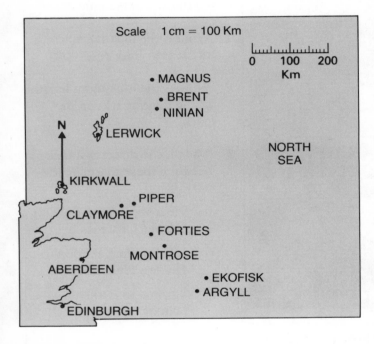

To make a flight from Kirkwall to Claymore we need a bearing and a distance:

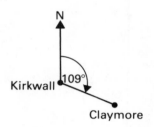

The bearing, as measured on the map, is 109°.
The distance, as measured on the map, is 3.3 cm.
The scale of the map is 1 cm = 50 km
So 3.3 cm = 3.3 × 50 km = 165 km.
The flight details are: bearing 109° for 165 km

EXERCISE 1

Find the flight details for the following journeys:

1 Lerwick to Magnus   2 Aberdeen to Argyll   3 Lerwick to Ninian

4 Kirkwall to Piper   5 Brent to Lerwick   6 Ekofisk to Forties

7 Aberdeen to Montrose   8 Lerwick to Magnus to Claymore to Kirkwall

9 Aberdeen to Ekofisk to Argyll to Edinburgh

10 Kirkwall to Piper to Forties to Aberdeen.

11 Which oil platform is nearest to (a) Lerwick   (b) Kirkwall   (c) Aberdeen?

12 Find the flight details for a journey from Lerwick to Magnus, Brent and Ninian, returning to Lerwick.

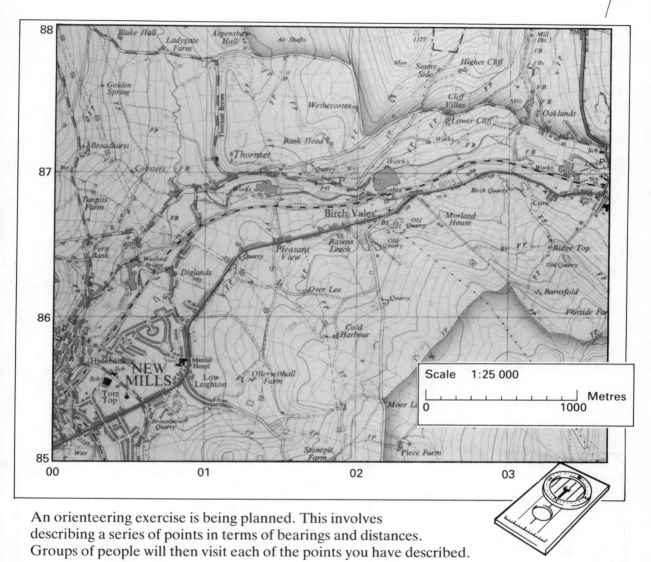

An orienteering exercise is being planned. This involves
describing a series of points in terms of bearings and distances.
Groups of people will then visit each of the points you have described.

EXERCISE 2

In terms of bearings and distances, describe the following orienteering stages:

1 New Mills school (004856) to Thornset school (012872) to Birch Vale
Station (023868).

2 Moor Lodge (023854) to Morland House (026867) to Oaklands (033874).

3 Aspenshaw Hall (013878) to Wethercotes (020875) to Cliff Villas (026875).

4 Cold Harbour (018858) to Ravens Leach (019866) to Diglands (009863).

5 Stonepit Farm (018850) to Watford Bridge (006864) to Birch Vale Station
(023868) to Sunny Side (026877).

Planning journeys

The diagram shows part of the motorway system. This type of diagram is called a **network** since it shows the network of motorways connecting the towns and cities.

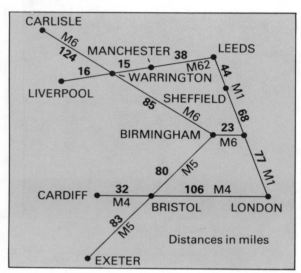

Distances in miles

EXERCISE 1

What is the minimum distance between these places by motorway?

1 Carlisle and London

2 Leeds and Birmingham

3 Liverpool and Cardiff

4 Exeter and Leeds

5 London and Manchester

6 Carlisle and Sheffield

7 Liverpool and London

8 Warrington and Bristol

Investigation A

A delivery firm based in London needs to make a delivery to each of the towns in the diagram. Describe the single journey which will give the least mileage, visit all the places, and return to London.

Investigation B

Is London the best location for the firm? Plan a route based on another place in the diagram, other than London, to give the minimum mileage. Is this a better location than London?

A company based in Taunton needs to make a delivery to three towns in the network diagram, returning to Taunton after the deliveries have been made. The deliveries can be made in several different ways:

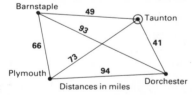

Distances in miles

Taunton → Barnstaple → Plymouth → Dorchester → Taunton = 250 miles.
Taunton → Plymouth → Barnstaple → Dorchester → Taunton = 273 miles.
Taunton → Barnstaple → Dorchester → Plymouth → Taunton = 309 miles.

The first route is therefore the shortest.

EXERCISE 2

Find the shortest route to make a call at all the places
indicated in each network diagram below and return
to the company base after all deliveries have been made.

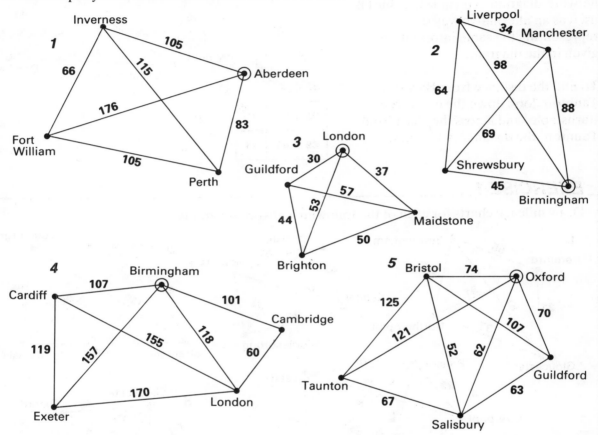

Investigation C

Using a local map, plan a route for
either a postman or a refuse
collection service. You
should minimise the
actual distance
travelled.

Mileage charts

Compare the mileage chart with the network diagram. The mileage chart is used as an alternative way of representing the same information given in the diagram.

To find the distance from Barnstaple to Taunton: look down the chart from Barnstaple, and across the chart from Taunton: the distance is 49 miles.

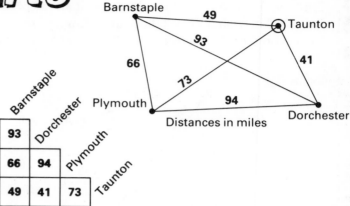

Barnstaple			
93	Dorchester		
66	94	Plymouth	
49	41	73	Taunton

EXERCISE 1

Draw mileage charts for each of the following network diagrams.

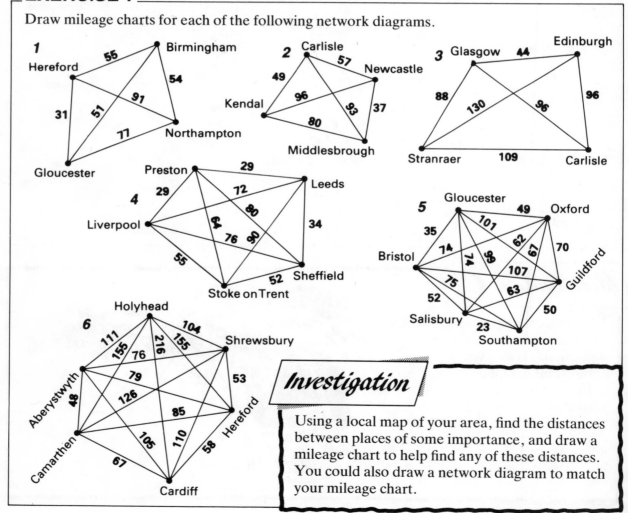

Investigation

Using a local map of your area, find the distances between places of some importance, and draw a mileage chart to help find any of these distances. You could also draw a network diagram to match your mileage chart.

EXERCISE 2

```
Aberdeen
445  Aberystwyth
420  114  Birmingham
493  125   81  Bristol
458  214  100  144  Cambridge
490  105  103   45  179  Cardiff
221  224  196  277  264  289  Carlisle
576  282  176  186  125  238  372  Dover
125  320  292  373  335  385   96  449  Edinburgh
569  201  157   76  220  121  353  248  450  Exeter
165  430  392  473  460  485  196  568  144  549  Fort William
145  320  292  373  360  385   96  468   44  449  100  Glasgow
439  111  148  206  248  216  212  339  308  282  408  308  Holyhead
105  486  458  539  493  549  262  607  158  618   66  166  474  Inverness
383  199   90  171   85  193  181  202  258  247  377  277  200  427  Lincoln
341  104   93  161  168  169  120  273  216  237  316  216   92  382  118  Liverpool
503  211  105  115   54  167  301   71  378  172  497  397  268  536  131  202  London
340  136   80  161  151  172  119  256  215  236  315  215  124  373   84   35  185  Manchester
235  273  207  288  230  304   57  345  110  364  253  148  247  268  159  155  274  132  Newcastle
475  276  166  221   62  241  289  174  366  282  485  385  293  498  105  220  114  185  264  Norwich
670  306  268  185  329  228  458  354  542  111  651  545  394  703  350  340  281  342  465  390  Penzance
 81  354  329  406  370  411  136  483   45  483  105   61  351  112  290  251  415  251  150  400  590  Perth
547  201  128   76  131  121  324  143  421  105  520  420  273  579  188  221   77  208  324  193  217  454  Southampton
319  205  130  211  150  244  121  264  194  287  317  217  188  352   75   99  193   64   84  181  391  227  245  York
```

MILEAGE CHART - BRITAIN

Motorways, primary routes, and 'A' roads have been used to calculate distances.

Find the distances between:

1 Holyhead and Cardiff

2 Bristol and Manchester

3 Aberdeen and Lincoln

4 Exeter and Inverness

5 Norwich and Dover

6 Southampton and London

7 Penzance and Glasgow

8 Fort William and Edinburgh

9 Perth and Inverness

10 Aberystwyth and Newcastle.

11 How far would a journey take from Newcastle to Manchester, then to Liverpool, and back to Newcastle?

12 The mileage recorder on a coach shows 64592 when it leaves Southampton. What will it show after calling in order at
(*a*) Birmingham   (*b*) Manchester   (*c*) Carlisle?

13 A car's mileage recorder shows 36002 upon leaving Fort William. What will it show at (*a*) Edinburgh   (*b*) Newcastle
(*c*) Lincoln   (*d*) London?

14 A coach makes a return trip from London to Holyhead, stopping at Birmingham en route. What mileage will it have done?

15 According to the mileage chart, (*a*) which two places are the nearest   (*b*) which two places are the furthest away?

Revision exercise

Draw the following bearings:

1 080°   **2** 115°   **3** 245°   **4** 350°   **5** 130°

6 025°   **7** 190°   **8** 295°   **9** 165°   **10** 310°

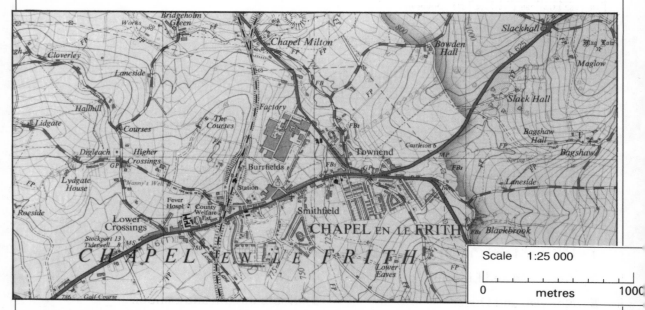

Scale   1:25 000

0   metres   1000

Find (*a*) the bearing and (*b*) the distance in metres of the following places from the station.

11 Bowden Hall   **12** Slack Hall   **13** Lydgate House

14 Hallhill   **15** Bagshaw Hall   **16** Roeside

17 What is the true distance across the map, in metres?

18 How far is the railway station from the junction in the railway line?

Find the shortest route to make a call at the places indicated in each network diagram, from the headquarters indicated.

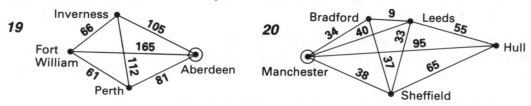

Draw a mileage chart for each of these network diagrams.

16. Time and timetables

Time

> 30 days hath September,
> April June and November.
> All the rest have 31, save
> February alone,
> which has but 28 days clear,
> and 29 in every leap year.

CALENDAR

	January	February	March
Su	**1** 8 15 22 29 —	— 5 12 19 26 —	— 5 12 19 26
M	**2** 9 16 23 30 —	— 6 13 20 27 —	— 6 13 20 **27**
Tu	3 10 17 24 31 —	— 7 14 21 28 —	— 7 14 21 28 —
W	4 11 18 25 —	1 8 15 22 —	1 8 15 22 29 —
Th	5 12 19 26 —	2 9 16 23 —	2 9 16 23 30 —
F	6 13 20 27 —	3 10 17 24 —	3 10 17 **24** 31 —
Sa	7 14 21 28 —	4 11 18 25 —	4 11 18 25 —

	April	May	June
Su	— 2 9 16 23 30	— 7 14 21 28 —	— 4 11 18 25
M	— 3 10 17 24 —	1 8 15 22 **29** —	— 5 12 19 26
Tu	— 4 11 18 25 —	2 9 16 23 30 —	— 6 13 20 27 —
W	— 5 12 19 26 —	3 10 17 24 31 —	— 7 14 21 28 —
Th	— 6 13 20 27 —	4 11 18 25 —	1 8 15 22 29 —
F	— 7 14 21 28 —	5 12 19 26 —	2 9 16 23 30 —
Sa	1 8 15 22 29 —	6 13 20 27 —	3 10 17 24 —

	July	August	September
Su	— 2 9 16 23 30	— 6 13 20 27 —	— 3 10 17 24
M	— 3 10 17 24 31	— 7 14 21 **28** —	— 4 11 18 25
Tu	— 4 11 18 25 —	1 8 15 22 29 —	— 5 12 19 26
W	— 5 12 19 26 —	2 9 16 23 30 —	— 6 13 20 27 —
Th	— 6 13 20 27 —	3 10 17 24 31 —	— 7 14 21 28 —
F	— 7 14 21 28 —	4 11 18 25 —	1 8 15 22 29 —
Sa	1 8 15 22 29 —	5 12 19 26 —	2 9 16 23 30 —

	October	November	December
Su	1 8 15 22 29 —	— 5 12 19 26 —	— 3 10 17 24 31
M	— 2 9 16 23 30	— 6 13 20 27 —	— 4 11 18 **25** —
Tu	3 10 17 24 31 —	— 7 14 21 28 —	— 5 12 19 **26**
W	4 11 18 25 —	1 8 15 22 29 —	— 6 13 20 27 —
Th	5 12 19 26 —	2 9 16 23 30 —	— 7 14 21 28 —
F	6 13 20 27 —	3 10 17 24 —	1 8 15 22 29 —
Sa	7 14 21 28 —	4 11 18 25 —	2 9 16 23 30 —

Bold Figures indicate Bank Holidays

The calendar opposite is for a year in which the first day was on a Sunday.

EXERCISE

1 Write down the day for (a) 16th March (b) 13th July (c) 28th November.

2 How many days are there in a week?

3 How many months are there in a year?

4 How many days are there in a year?

Find how many days there are between these dates:

5 17th January and 8th February

6 15th April and 25th May

7 11th September and 9th October

8 20th March and 29th May

9 21st December and 13th January

10 19th November and 2nd February

These questions refer to a year different from that shown above. Find the answers to the following:

11 If 19th April was on a Saturday, on which day was
(a) 10th May (b) 31st March (c) 1st June?

12 If 30th November was on a Monday, on which day was
(a) 5th December (b) 8th November
(c) 1st January in the following year?

13 If 5th August was on a Wednesday, on which day was
(a) 1st September (b) 1st October (c) 10th July?

14 If 17th January was on a Thursday, on which day was
(a) 9th February (b) 1st January (c) 1st March?

15 If 28th March was on a Friday, on which day was
(a) 17th February (b) 5th May (c) 30th June?

24-hour clocks

In using 12-hour clocks we express time before noon (midday)
as a.m., and times after noon as p.m.

We would write this time
as 5.00 in figures,
'five o'clock' in words.

6.45 in figures,
'quarter to seven'
in words.

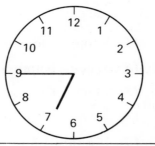

EXERCISE 1

Write these times (*a*) in figures   (*b*) in words.

1   **2**   **3**   **4**   **5**

Write these times in words.

6 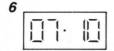   **7**   **8** 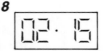   **9** 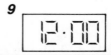   **10**

> 24-hour clocks avoid any possible confusion as to whether
> times such as 5.00 are taken as a.m. or p.m. The 24-hour
> clock shown indicates the time: 0500 if before noon,
> 1700 if after noon.

A time before noon such as 9.30 a.m. would be 0930 hours.
A time after noon such as 10.15 p.m. would be 2215 hours.

EXERCISE 2

Change these 12-hour clock times to 24-hour clock times.

1   9 a.m.   **2**   9.30 p.m.   **3**   11.15 a.m.

4   2.40 p.m.   **5**   5.20 p.m.

Change these 24-hour clock times to 12-hour clock times.

6   1425 hours   **7**   0810 hours   **8**   0015 hours   **9**   2355 hours   **10**   1816 hours

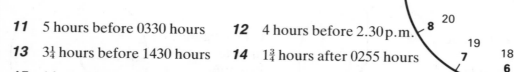

Give the time in either 12- or 24-hour time, as indicated by each question.

11 5 hours before 0330 hours   **12** 4 hours before 2.30 p.m.

13 $3\frac{1}{4}$ hours before 1430 hours   **14** $1\frac{3}{4}$ hours after 0255 hours

15 1 hour 20 min before 9 a.m.   **16** 3 hours 55 min after 10.30 a.m.

17 $3\frac{3}{4}$ hours before 0205 hours   **18** $5\frac{1}{2}$ hours after 2350 hours

19 18 hours before 5 a.m.   **20** 16 hours before 5 p.m.

Work out how long it is between each of these times.

21 9.50 a.m. to 10.15 a.m.   **22** 0730 to 0820

23 12.15 p.m. to 2.25 p.m.   **24** 1345 to 0015

25 10 p.m. Mon. to 7 a.m. Tue.   **26** 0917 to 1327

27 9.37 a.m. to 1.15 p.m.   **28** 0342 to 2214

29 8.30 a.m. Thu. to 11.15 a.m. Fri.   **30** 0915 Tue. to 0805 Wed.

Investigation A

The years 1980, 1984, and 1988 were all leap years. Can you find an easy test to check whether a particular year is a leap year? Find out which of the following years are leap years:

1935, 1942, 1947, 1952, 1958, 1960, 1970, 1975, 1990, 1996, 2006, 2012.

Investigation B

The rental on a television is £15 every 4 weeks. How much is this over a year? A man decides to pay £15 on the first day of every month, but is told at the end of the year that he has not paid enough. Comment on this.

Using time

Investigation A

Can you estimate time accurately?
Work in pairs. One of you begin by
counting to ten. The other times how
long it takes to count. Change over and
repeat. Can you count accurately to one
minute? Repeat the above activity for
counting to 60.

Make four estimates, and try to improve
your counting in seconds.

Counting	to ten
1	
2	
3	
4	

One	minute
1	
2	
3	
4	

ITV	
5.00am	ITN News
6.00	TV-am
9.25	Motormouth
11.30	America's Top 10
12noon	Trans World Sport
1.00pm	ITN News
1.05	Saint & Greavsie
1.35	Wrestling
2.15	Darts
4.15	The Snow Spider
4.45	Results Service
5.00	ITN News
5.05	Blockbusters
5.35	How to be Cool
6.35	Blind Date
7.20	Beadle's About
7.50	New Faces Final
9.05	ITN News
9.25	New Faces Results
9.40	Film: The Boys from Brazil
12m't	First Division Special
12.55am	The Hit Man and Her
2.00	Night Network
4.00	The Hit Man and Her

EXERCISE

1 Complete the table.

Flight number	Departure time	Arrival time	Flight time
AA152	0542	0914	
BA45	2220	0445	
TW492	1415		4h 40min
EA517	1002		4h 23min
AL419		0759	5h 37min
BL64	1917	0521	
TW910	0243		3h 51min
MA42		1217	2h 32min
EA105		0225	5h 29min
BA49	1539		6h 48min

Use the ITV schedule to answer the following questions.

2 How long was *Blockbusters*?

3 How long was *Blind Date*?

4 How long was *Beadle's About*?

5 What was the total duration time of the
two 'New Faces' programmes?

6 For how long does *ITN News* broadcast
during the day?

7 How long is the film?

8 How long is *Wrestling*?

9 How long is *Motormouth*?

Use the train route diagram to answer the following questions:

10 How long does it take to travel from Victoria to Atherton?

11 How long does it take to travel between Swinton and Hindley?

12 How long would a journey take from Kearsley to Wigan?

13 Jeremy is planning a trip from Swinton to Bolton. He will have to wait 12 minutes at Salford Crescent to change trains. How long would his total journey take?

14 Copy and complete the timetables:

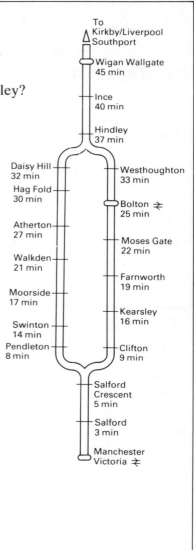

To Kirkby/Liverpool Southport

Wigan Wallgate 45 min

Ince 40 min

Hindley 37 min

Daisy Hill 32 min

Hag Fold 30 min

Atherton 27 min

Walkden 21 min

Moorside 17 min

Swinton 14 min

Pendleton 8 min

Westhoughton 33 min

Bolton 25 min

Moses Gate 22 min

Farnworth 19 min

Kearsley 16 min

Clifton 9 min

Salford Crescent 5 min

Salford 3 min

Manchester Victoria

Manchester Victoria	0905	1135
Salford		
Salford Crescent		
Pendleton		
Swinton		
Moorside		
Walkden		
Atherton		
Hag Fold		
Daisy Hill		
Hindley		
Ince		
Wigan Wallgate		

Wigan Wallgate	0830	1155
Ince		
Hindley		
Westhoughton		
Bolton		
Moses Gate		
Farnworth		
Kearsley		
Clifton		
Salford Crescent		
Salford		
Manchester Victoria		

ORDSALL—BURY via Pendleton, Lower Kersal, Prestwich and Unsworth

Saturdays

ORDSALL, Salford Quays				0730		0830		1830	1900	2000	2100	2200	2300
Trafford Road/Regent Road				0735		0835		1835	1905	2005	2105	2205	2305
Pendleton Precinct	arr.			0741		0841		1841					
Pendleton Precinct	dep.	0643	0713	0743	0813	0843	AND	1843	1910	2010	2110	2210	2310
Lower Kersal, Flats		0654	0724	0754	0824	0854	EVERY	1854	1919	2019	2119	2219	2319
Agecroft, Kersal Vale		0657	0727	0757	0827	0857	30	1857	1922	2022	2122	2222	2322
Carr Clough, Butterstile Lane/Sandy Lane		0704	0734	0804	0834	0904	MINS.	1904					
Prestwich, Tower Buildings		0710	0740	0810	0840	0910	UNTIL	1910					
Besses o'th' Barn Station		0714	0744	0814	0844	0914		1914					
Unsworth, Pole		0724	0754	0824	0854	0924		1924					
BURY, Interchange		0740	0810	0840	0910	0940		1940					

Answer the questions using the bus timetable above.

15 How long does the 0713 Pendleton bus take to get to Unsworth?

16 How long do buses wait at Pendleton?

17 At what time does the last bus arrive in Bury?

18 When is the first bus from Trafford Road?

19 How long does it take to travel from Agecroft to Besses o' th' Barn?

20 How long does it take to travel from Ordsall to Prestwich?

21 How many buses call at Trafford Road before 0900?

22 How many buses call at Carr Clough during the day?

23 How many buses call at Agecroft during the day?

24 Susan arrives at her bus stop at Prestwich at 7.50 a.m. How long must she wait for a bus?

25 David arrives at his bus stop in Trafford Road at 7.50 a.m. How long must he wait for a bus?

26 Umair lives 5 minutes away from his bus stop in Agecroft. What is the latest time he can leave his house to get to Bury by 9 a.m.?

Use the train route diagram to answer the following questions.

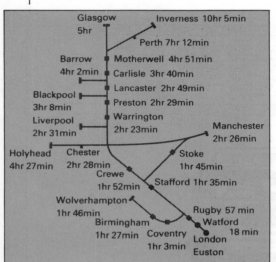

27 How long is the journey from London Euston to Carlisle?

28 How long would a trip be from Holyhead to Stafford?

29 How long is the journey time from Perth to Warrington?

30 What would be the total time for a journey from Chester to Inverness if a change of trains taking 45 minutes is necessary at Crewe?

31 What would be the total time for a journey from Blackpool to Glasgow if a change of trains taking 50 minutes is necessary at Preston?

32 Copy and complete these timetables.

Euston	0830	0955
Watford		
Rugby		
Stafford		
Crewe		
Warrington		
Preston		
Lancaster		
Carlisle		
Motherwell		
Glasgow		

Holyhead	0710	1430
Chester		
Crewe		
Stafford		
Rugby		
Watford		
Euston		

Wolverhampton	1005	1340
Birmingham		
Coventry		
Rugby		
Watford		
Euston		

Investigation B

British Rail is planning to run an hourly service to London from each of the terminus stations: Glasgow, Inverness, Barrow-In-Furness, Blackpool, Manchester, Liverpool, Holyhead, Wolverhampton, and Watford. Not less than 5 minutes is needed between trains arriving at Euston. Find out how many minutes past the hour you would start a train from each of the terminus stations.

Revision exercise

How many days are there between these dates.

1 10th March and 28th April   **2** 3rd August and 27th October

3 23rd May and 5th November   **4** 14th June and 10th September

5 28th March and 17th October   **6** 3rd January and 15th December in a leap year.

7 If 12th July was on a Saturday, on which day was (*a*) 5th August
(*b*) 10th November   (*c*) the previous 1st May?

8 If 3rd May was on a Wednesday, on which day was (*a*) 3rd August
(*b*) 28th November   (*c*) the previous 5th March?

9 If 1st August was on a Sunday, on which day was (*a*) 15th October
(*b*) the previous 1st June   (*c*) the previous 17th March?

10 Change these times into 24-hour clock times: (*a*) 7.50 a.m.
(*b*) 5.30 p.m.   (*c*) midnight.

Work out how long it is between these times.

11 0750 to 1340   **12** 0101 to 0252   **13** 0342 to 1510

14 1445 to 1942   **15** 0321 to 0555   **16** 1134 to 1632

17 1432 to 1840   **18** 1814 to 2330   **19** 2041 to 2301

20 1332 to 1814

Use the InterCity timetable to answer the following questions.

21 How long does it take to travel between Manchester and Stockport if the train takes 2 minutes to pick up passengers?

22 What is the journey time between Manchester and London on these trains: (*a*) 0600   (*b*) 0900
(*c*) 0847   (*d*) 1330?

23 Gordon needs to be in London on a Wednesday morning at 1130. What is the latest time he could arrive at Stockport station?

INTERCITY

Manchester and Stockport → London

Mondays to Saturdays

	Manchester Piccadilly depart	Stockport depart	London Euston arrive
�.	0030 mo	0044 mo	0441
🚂	0030 mx	0044 mx	0446
▲ ⊠	0600 sx	0608 sx	0837
▲ P	0705 sx	0713 sx	0930
IC	0705 so	0713 so	0930
IC	0718	0726	1059 k
▲ P	0735 sx	0743 sx	1000
IC	0735 so	0743 so	1000
▲ P	0800 sx	0808 sx	1037
IC	0900 so	0808 so	1037
G IC	0847 mo	0855	1135
✕	0900	0908	1140
✕	1030	1038	1316
IC	1200 so	1208 so	1444
P	1200 sx	1208 sx	1452
✕	1330	1338	1615
IC	1405 fo	1413 fo	1645
✕	1430	1438	1709
P	1530 sx	1538 sx	1811
P	1630 sx	1638 sx	1904
IC	1630 so	1638 so	1904
⊠	1730	1738	2008
✕	1830	1839	2106
IC	2015	2024	2255

Sundays

	Manchester Piccadilly depart	Stockport depart	London Euston arrive
A 🚂	0113	0123	0538
B C D 🚂	0113	0123	0548
IC	0806	0816	1214
D IC	0840	0850	1233
C IC	0840	0850	1238
A IC	0846	0856	1229
B IC	0846	0856	1238
C D IC	1020	1030	1419
A B IC	1026	1036	1419
D IC	1124	1134	1514
C IC	1124	1134	1516
A B IC	1126	1136	1514
C D IC	1248	1258	1646
A B IC	1254	1304	1646
C IC	1438	1448	1757
D IC	1438	1448	1824
A B IC	1451	1501	1757
IC	1555	1603	1842
IC	1625	1633	1918
IC	1725	1733	2017
G IC	1800	1808	2045
IC	1825	1833	2109
IC	2015	2023	2312

17. Volumes & nets

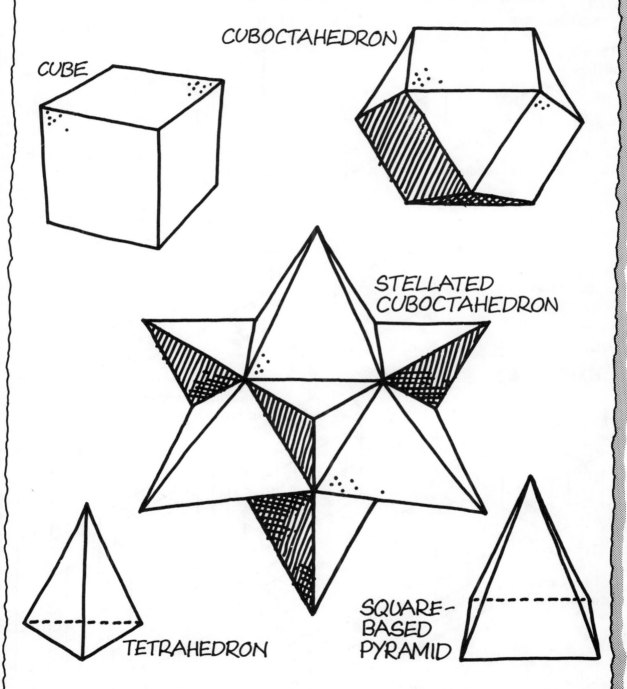

CUBE

CUBOCTAHEDRON

STELLATED CUBOCTAHEDRON

TETRAHEDRON

SQUARE-BASED PYRAMID

Volumes

CUBOIDS

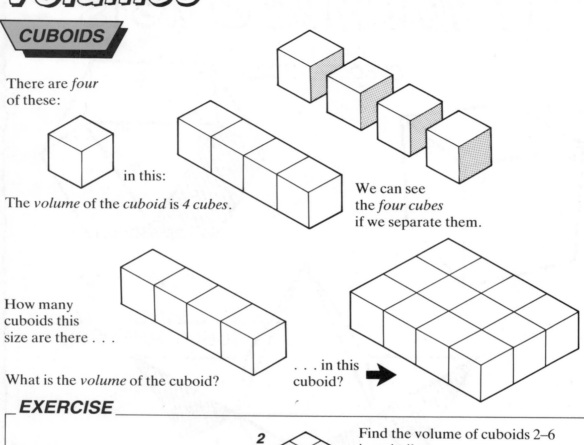

There are *four*
of these:

in this:

The *volume* of the *cuboid* is *4 cubes*.

We can see
the *four cubes*
if we separate them.

How many
cuboids this
size are there . . .

What is the *volume* of the cuboid?

. . . in this
cuboid?

EXERCISE

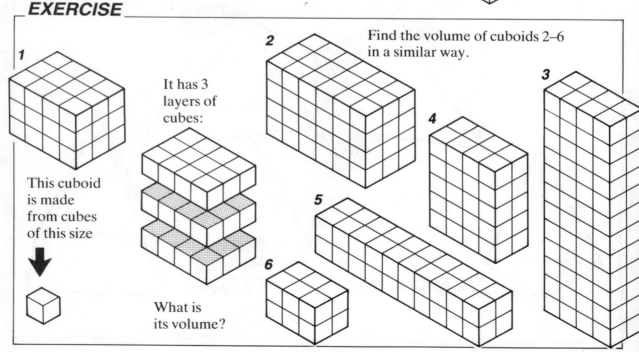

1

This cuboid
is made
from cubes
of this size

It has 3
layers of
cubes:

What is
its volume?

Find the volume of cuboids 2–6
in a similar way.

2

3

4

5

6

Investigation A — CUBOIDS

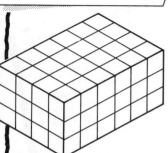

This cuboid has a volume of 72 cubes.
There are 4 rows of 6 cubes, so 24 cubes in each layer.
There are 3 layers of 24 cubes, so 72 cubes in total.

➤ Find and draw as many cuboids as possible with a volume of 72 cubes. Use 3-D paper (isometric).

Draw as many cuboids as possible with volumes of

12 cubes, 16 cubes, 24 cubes, 36 cubes, 48 cubes.

Record your results in a table similar to the one above.

Write your results in a table like this:

Length	Width	Height	Volume
6	4	3	72
			72
			72

Investigation B — CUBES

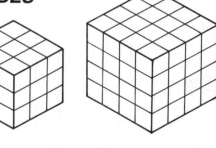

Each cube has the same number of single cubes in each row and column.

Copy this table and try to complete it.

Explain how you can work out the volume of a cube *without* counting the cubes.

Rows of cubes (Length)	Cubes in row (width)	Layers of cubes (height)	Volume
1	1	1	1
2	2	2	8
3			
4			
5			
6			
7			
8			
9			
10			
20			
n			

Formulas

You can see that we can find the volumes of cuboids without counting single cubes.

The **volume of a cuboid**
= **length** × **width** × **height**
= $l \times w \times h = lwh$

The **volume of a cube**
= $l \times l \times l = l^3$

UNITS   NOTE
1 cm cube   When measuring in centimetres the volume is measured in cubic centimetres or cm³
1 cm
1 cm   1 cm

EXERCISE

1 Find the volume, in cm, of each of these cuboids.

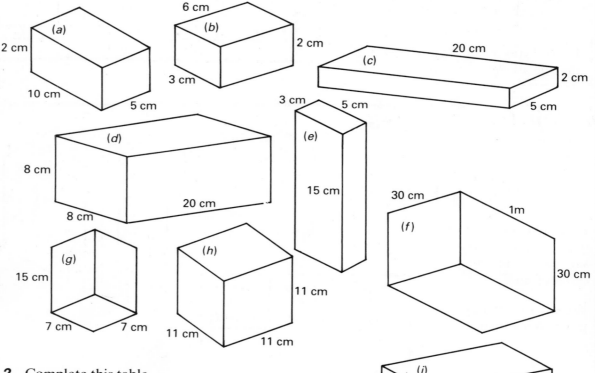

2 Complete this table

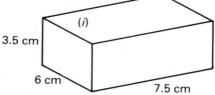

l	w	h	V
5		5	75
	8	12	960
16	5		360
2.5		8	10

All measurements are in cm³.

Packing

Look at this cuboid:
It has a volume of
6 cubes.

These diagrams show how
we could *pack* the cuboid A
into larger cuboids:

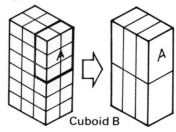

Cuboid B

B has a volume of
$3 \times 2 \times 6 = 36$ cubes.
We can see that cuboid A
will fit into cuboid B
6 times exactly.

We can check this: $\dfrac{\text{volume B}}{\text{volume A}}$

$= \dfrac{36 \text{ cubes}}{6 \text{ cubes}} = 6$

EXERCISE 1

1 Show all the different ways you can find of
packing cuboid A into cuboid B.

2 Find how many times cuboid A will fit into
each of the cuboids, C, D, E and F below
(C has been started). Draw at least one
3-D diagram to show how you have
'packed' the cuboids.

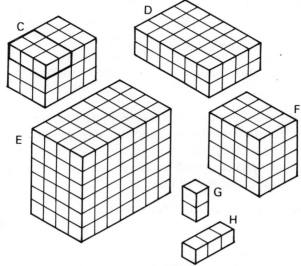

3 Find out how many times cuboids G and H
fit into cuboids A, B, C, D, E and F.

EXERCISE 2

1 Work out how many
of the small cuboids
will pack into the
larger cuboid
(a diagram might help).

7 cm 4 cm *(a)*
2 cm
2 cm 40 cm 70 cm

4 cm 3 cm *(b)*
8 cm
8 cm
30 cm 24 cm 12 cm

8 cm 8 cm *(c)*
8 cm
56 cm
64 cm 80 cm

2 Here are some actual packet sizes:

Cassette tape	7cm × 11cm × 1.5cm
Cornflakes	7cm × 22cm × 31cm
Crispbread	7cm × 18cm × 12.5cm
Tissues	7cm × 12cm × 25cm

(a) Find the volume of each 'cuboid'.

(b) Investigate what size cuboids are
needed to pack 4 dozen of each item.

(c) Can you explain why 7 cm is a common
size for one dimension of each item?

Nets

Investigation A / SOLID NETS

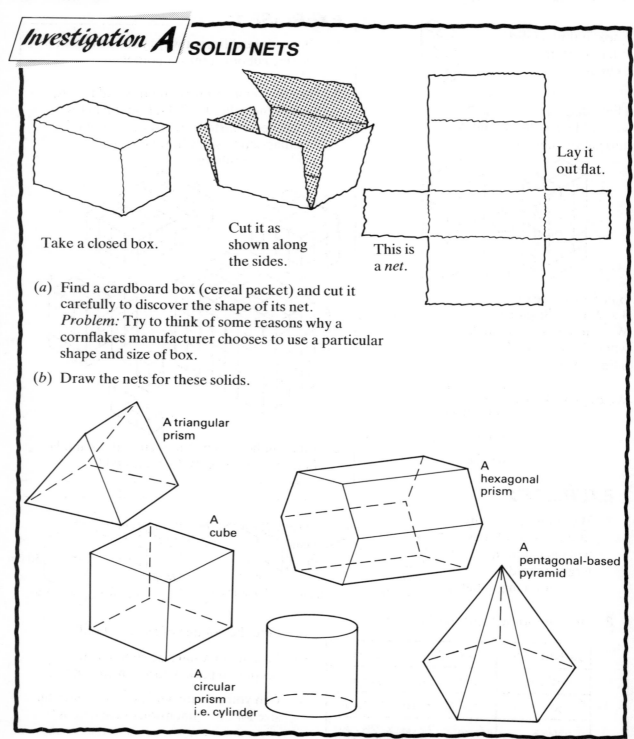

Take a closed box.

Cut it as shown along the sides.

This is a *net*.

Lay it out flat.

(*a*) Find a cardboard box (cereal packet) and cut it carefully to discover the shape of its net.
Problem: Try to think of some reasons why a cornflakes manufacturer chooses to use a particular shape and size of box.

(*b*) Draw the nets for these solids.

A triangular prism

A hexagonal prism

A cube

A pentagonal-based pyramid

A circular prism i.e. cylinder

Investigation B DICE

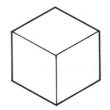

The net of a cube can be made in various ways:

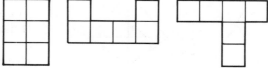

(a) Check that these will make cubes.

(b) Explain why these do *not* make cubes.

The net of a cube is called a **hexomino**.
How many other hexominoes make cubes?
(Draw as many as you can find.)

Dice are normally cubes.

They are numbered according to the system that

'the number of dots on opposite sides must total seven'.

(c) The dice show two dice views. Can you find the six other possible views?

(d) Make a small cube and number it like a single *die*.

(e) Which of these are *not* nets for dice? Explain your answers.

3	1	4
	5	
	6	
	2	

1	2		
	3	4	
		5	6

			6
2	4	3	5
1			

		5
	6	4
3	2	
1		

(f) Complete the numbering on these dice nets:

1			
5			4

6	2	
	3	

1		
2	3	

	3	
5	6	

EXERCISE 1

THE REGULAR SOLIDS

1 The **tetrahedron**

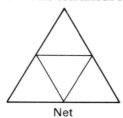

Net

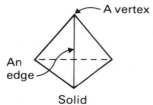

A vertex

An edge

Solid

The solid has **four** faces.
Each face is an **equilateral triangle**.
Three triangles meet at each **vertex**.
The solid has four **vertices**.
It has six **edges**.

Construct a regular tetrahedron with side 4 cm.

2 The **cube** has six *faces*.
Each face is a square.
How many *vertices* has a cube?
How many *edges* does it have?

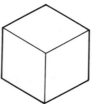

3

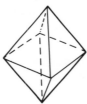

The **octahedron** consists of eight equilateral triangles.
How many (*a*) edges   (*b*) vertices does it have?
Which of these could be a net for an octahedron?
Construct an octahedron.

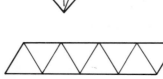
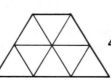
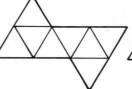
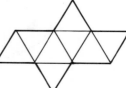

4 The **icosahedron** has 20 faces.
Construct one yourself.

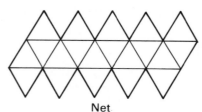

Net

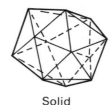

Solid

5

Net

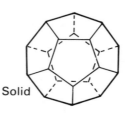

Solid

The **dodecahedron** has 12 faces.
Each face is a pentagon.
Make one yourself.

Note: You should have constructed the *five regular solids*. There are no more!

EXERCISE 2

OTHER SOLIDS

1 Look at these nets carefully and then *sketch* the solids they make.

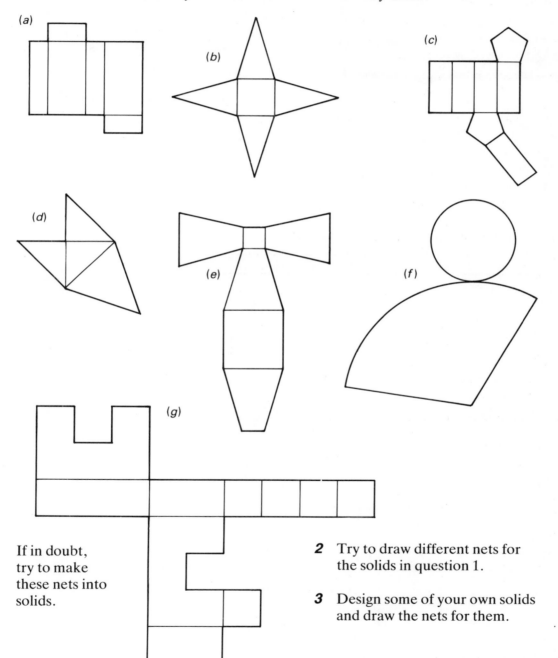

(a)

(b)

(c)

(d)

(e)

(f)

(g)

If in doubt,
try to make
these nets into
solids.

2 Try to draw different nets for
the solids in question 1.

3 Design some of your own solids
and draw the nets for them.

Leonard Euler (1707–1783) was a Swiss mathematician. He made contributions to every branch of mathematics and to physics, astronomy and music.
This section investigates the relationship which Euler discovered between the number of vertices, faces and edges of a solid.

Investigation C

EULER'S RELATION

You will need to have available either

    a set of solids

or the solids you have made

or a very good set of 3-D diagrams.

(a) For each of your solids, count the numbers of faces (*F*), vertices (*V*), and edges (*E*).

The regular solids

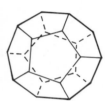 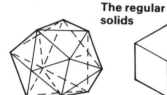 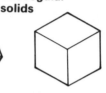

(b) Put your results into a table like this:

Name of Solid	Faces (F)	Vertices (V)	Edges (E)
Tetrahedron	4		
Cube			
Square Pyramid			
Triangular Prism			
Hexagonal Prism			
Octahedron			
Dodecahedron			
Icosahedron			

(c) Can you find a relationship between *F*, *E* and *V*? When you have worked out this relationship, it is known as **Euler's relation**.

(d) See if you can complete this table using your results.

F	V	E
7	7	
10	12	
	14	30
20		40
8		15

It may not be easy to draw *any* of these solids!

Packaging

SURFACE AREA

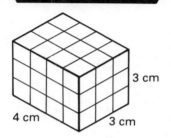

4 cm   3 cm   3 cm

Example:
This box is to be
constructed from card.
What area of card
is required to make it?
This is a possible net
for the box.
Check that you
agree with each
area shown.
The total **surface area**

3 cm	3 cm
9 cm²	12 cm²	9 cm²	3 cm
	12 cm²	3 cm
	12 cm²	3 cm
	12 cm²	3 cm

4 cm

$$= 9\,\text{cm}^2 + 12\,\text{cm}^2 + 9\,\text{cm}^2 + 12\,\text{cm}^2 + 12\,\text{cm}^2 + 12\,\text{cm}^2 = 66\,\text{cm}^2$$

EXERCISE

1   Find the surface areas of these cuboids.

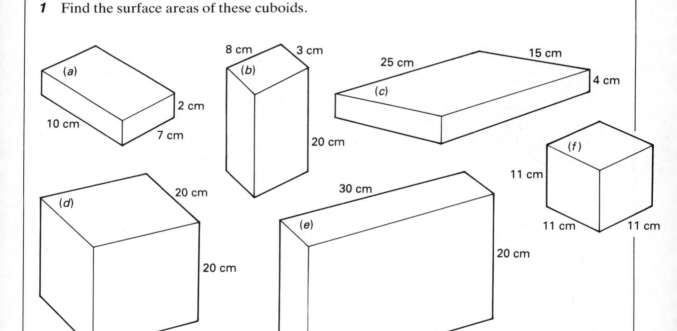

2   What is the smallest area of card required to make
a cuboid with volume 60 cm³?
(Investigate this carefully – show all your working.)

Revision exercise

1 Work out the volumes (in cubes) of each of these cuboids.

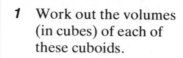

2 Calculate the volumes of these cuboids.

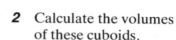

3

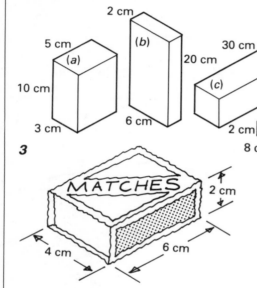

(a) How many boxes of matches (as shown) would fit into a box 30 cm by 20 cm by 20 cm?

(b) Investigate what shape boxes could be used to hold 48 boxes of matches.

(c) In part (b), what would be the *least* amount of card needed to hold 48 boxes of matches?

4 Draw nets for these solids.

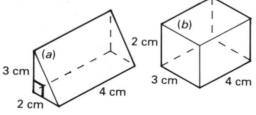 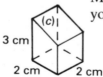

Name each solid, if possible. Measure accurately any lengths you have not been given.

5 (a) If $V = l^3$, find V when $l = 7\,\text{cm}$.

(b) If $V = lwh$, find V when $l = 6\,\text{cm}$, $w = 2\,\text{cm}$, $h = 3\,\text{cm}$.

(c) If $V = l^3$, find l when $V = 216\,\text{cm}^3$.

(d) If $V = lwh$, find l when $V = 60\,\text{cm}^3$, $w = 5\,\text{cm}$, $h = 3\,\text{cm}$.

6 If $V + F = E + 2$, find E when $V = 8$, $F = 12$.
(Can you sketch a solid for this question?)

18. EQUATIONS

Finding the unknown

EXERCISE 1

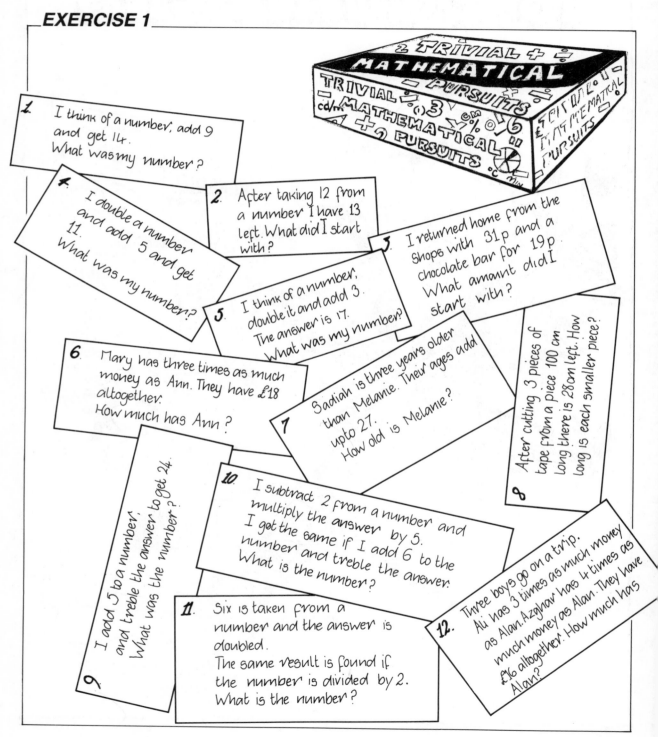

1. I think of a number, add 9 and get 14.
   What was my number?

2. After taking 12 from a number I have 13 left. What did I start with?

3. I returned home from the shops with 31p and a chocolate bar for 19p. What amount did I start with?

4. I double a number and add 5 and get 11.
   What was my number?

5. I think of a number, double it and add 3. The answer is 17.
   What was my number?

6. Mary has three times as much money as Ann. They have £18 altogether.
   How much has Ann?

7. Sadiah is three years older than Melanie. Their ages add up to 27.
   How old is Melanie?

8. After cutting 3 pieces of tape from a piece 100 cm long there is 28 cm left. How long is each smaller piece?

9. I add 5 to a number and treble the answer to get 24.
   What was the number?

10. I subtract 2 from a number and multiply the answer by 5. I get the same if I add 6 to the number and treble the answer.
    What is the number?

11. Six is taken from a number and the answer is doubled.
    The same result is found if the number is divided by 2.
    What is the number?

12. Three boys go on a trip. Ali has 3 times as much money as Alan. Azghar has 4 times as much money as Alan. They have £16 altogether. How much has Alan?

All these puzzles are examples of problems which involve us in finding an unknown number. Some seem quite difficult when they are written out in this way. Frequently it seems that the best way to solve them is by trial and improvement methods: try a number, and if it does not work try another number which seems more likely to work.

13. I have a number. When 2 is added to half of it the answer is 26. What is the number?

First guess: 10. Half of 10 is 5, so 2 + 5 = 7. This answer is not big enough. Try a bigger number.

Second guess: 30. Half of 30 is 15, so 2 + 15 = 17. Still not big enough! Try a bigger number.

Third guess: 50. Half of 50 is 25, so 2 + 25 = 27. Almost! But now just slightly too large.

Fourth guess: 48. Half of 48 is 24, so 2 + 24 = 26. Correct!

The number we want is therefore 48.

EXERCISE 2

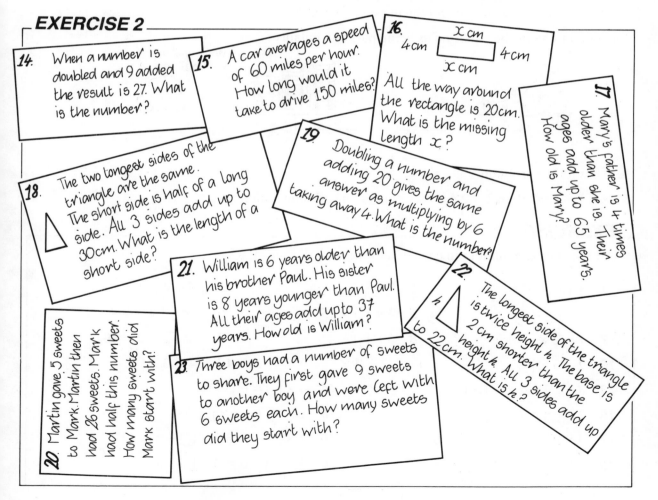

14. When a number is doubled and 9 added the result is 27. What is the number?

15. A car averages a speed of 60 miles per hour. How long would it take to drive 150 miles?

16. All the way around the rectangle is 20cm. What is the missing length x?

17. Mary's father is 4 times older than she is. Their ages add up to 65 years. How old is Mary?

18. The two longest sides of the triangle are the same. The short side is half of a long side. All 3 sides add up to 30cm. What is the length of a short side?

19. Doubling a number and adding 20 gives the same answer as multiplying by 6 taking away 4. What is the number?

20. Martin gave 5 sweets to Mark. Martin then had 26 sweets. Mark had half this number. How many sweets did Mark start with?

21. William is 6 years older than his brother Paul. His sister is 8 years younger than Paul. All their ages add up to 37 years. How old is William?

22. The longest side of the triangle is twice height h. The base is 2 cm shorter than the height h. All 3 sides add up to 22cm. What is h?

23. Three boys had a number of sweets to share. They first gave 9 sweets to another boy and were left with 6 sweets each. How many sweets did they start with?

Balancing equations

An equation is a type of mathematical balance:
the two sides of any equation are equal.

This card has two parts to it:

> 24. I have a number. When 2 is added to half of it the answer is 26.
> What is the number?

> 2 is added to half a number. $=$ 26

The card tells us these two parts are the same.
The two parts balance. They make an **equation**.
Problems such as this can be written in a shorter form:

$\frac{1}{2}\square + 2 = 26$ Can you find the missing number?

You could think of the equation as being part of a balance:

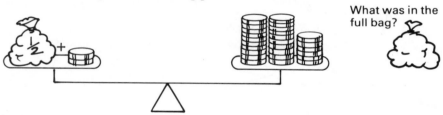

What was in the full bag?

Here is another problem.

If $2 \times \square + 3 = 7$ then $2 \times 2 + 3 = 7$, that is, the missing number is 2.

EXERCISE

Find the missing number in each equation.

1 $3 + \square = 10$ **2** $7 = \square + 6$ **3** $\square + 4 = 12$

4 $5 + \square = 13$ **5** $3 + \square = 15$ **6** $2 \times \square + 5 = 9$

7 $7 = 2 \times \square + 1$ **8** $3 \times \square + 2 = 11$ **9** $4 \times \square + 2 = 10$

10 $9 = 3 \times \square$ **11** $12 = 4 \times \square$ **12** $24 = 3 \times \square$

13 $8 \times \square = 5 \times \square + 6$ **14** $4 \times \square = \square + 15$

15 $2 \times \square = 7 + \square$ **16** $12 \times \square = 8 \times \square + 4$

17 $3 \times \square + 4 = 2 \times \square + 6$ **18** $2 \times \square + 7 = 3 \times \square + 5$

19 $5 \times \square + 2 = 3 \times \square + 8$ **20** $4 \times \square - 5 = 3 \times \square + 1$

Solving equations

In algebra we used letters for numbers we did not know.
Here again we can use letters for the missing numbers:

$\frac{1}{2}\square + 2 = 26$ we could write as $\frac{1}{2}x + 2 = 26$, and $x = 48$ is the answer.
$2 \times \square + 3 = 7$ we could write as $2x + 3 = 7$, and $x = 2$ is the answer.

This is called **solving** the equation.

EXERCISE

Solve these equations.

1 $x + 3 = 15$	**2** $12 = 4 + x$	**3** $10 = x + 2$
4 $7 + x = 16$	**5** $14 = x - 3$	**6** $4x + 1 = 13$
7 $x + 2\frac{1}{2} = 5\frac{1}{2}$	**8** $5 + x = 19$	**9** $8 = x - 4$
10 $9 - x = 7$	**11** $12 = x - 3$	**12** $14 = x + 2$
13 $x - 2 = 9$	**14** $x - 7 = 1$	**15** $9 = x - 5$
16 $x - \frac{1}{2} = 3$	**17** $2x = 12$	**18** $9x = 45$
19 $5x = 55$	**20** $2x + 4 = 12$	**21** $3x + 5 = 11$
22 $18 = 4x + 2$	**23** $10x + 7 = 67$	**24** $9 = 2x + 1$
25 $\frac{1}{2}x + 4 = 11$	**26** $2x - 4 = 12$	**27** $5 = 4x - 3$
28 $26 = 6x - 7$	**29** $9x + 4 = 24 + x$	**30** $5x + 3 = 4x + 7$

Investigation

Find the mass of each toy object given that the ball ●
has a mass of 40 grams.

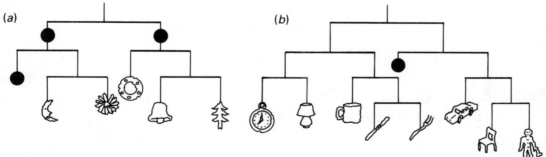

(a)

(b)

(c) Can you make up your own mobiles which balance?

Rearranging equations

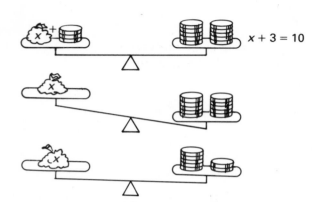

$$x + 3 = 10$$

$x + 3 = 10$

The practical way to solve the problem on the balance is to remove the three units on the left-hand side.
We have upset the balance. What will we need to do to restore the balance?
We will need to remove three units from the right-hand side also.
It is now easy to see that $x = 7$.

We can use letters and equations to write down what we have just done:

subtract 3 from
both sides $\longrightarrow$

$$x + 3 = 10$$
$$-3 \quad -3$$
$$\text{So } x = 7$$

Similarly if

$$2x + 7 = 13$$
$$-7 \quad -7$$

then

$$2x = 6 \quad \text{so } x = 3$$

EXERCISE 1

1	$3x + 2 = 14$	**2**	$4x + 5 = 21$
3	$5x + 4 = 29$	**4**	$2x + 7 = 17$
5	$3x + 2 = 20$	**6**	$6x + 9 = 27$
7	$4x + 10 = 34$	**8**	$5x + 8 = 28$
9	$2x + 7 = 23$	**10**	$6x + 6 = 30$
11	$5x + 1 = 26$	**12**	$4x + 15 = 47$

Other types of equation can be done in a similar way:

add 5 to both sides
to cancel the -5 $\longrightarrow$
then

$$2x - 5 = 17$$
$$+5 \quad +5$$
$$2x = 12 \quad \text{so } x = 6$$

Remember $-5 + 5 = 0$

EXERCISE 2

1	$2x - 4 = 14$	**2**	$3x - 6 = 0$	**3**	$5x - 5 = 30$	**4**	$4x - 2 = 30$
5	$3x - 10 = 5$	**6**	$6x - 8 = 28$	**7**	$8x - 12 = 36$	**8**	$9x - 4 = 59$
9	$2x - 4 = 20$	**10**	$4x - 18 = 6$	**11**	$7x - 8 = 20$	**12**	$5x - 20 = 0$

EXERCISE 3

Solve the equations.

1	$2x + 4 = 12$	**2**	$4x + 5 = 29$	**3**	$3x - 2 = 25$	**4**	$2x - 5 = 25$
5	$5x + 3 = 28$	**6**	$7x - 9 = 40$	**7**	$9x - 7 = 29$	**8**	$8x + 9 = 57$
9	$4x + 7 = 43$	**10**	$5x - 6 = 24$	**11**	$6x - 7 = 29$	**12**	$7x + 4 = 60$
13	$2x + 7 = 14$	**14**	$8x - 6 = 38$	**15**	$3x - 12 = 24$	**16**	$4x - 14 = 0$
17	$6x + 18 = 39$	**18**	$5x - 50 = 50$	**19**	$5x + 2 = 9\frac{1}{2}$	**20**	$4x + 150 = 250$

Sometimes equations need to be simplified before they can be solved:

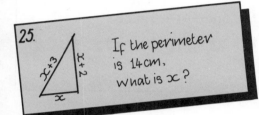

25. If the perimeter is 14 cm, what is x?

$$x + x{+}2 + x{+}3 = 14$$

First simplify: $3x + 5 \ = \ 14$
then solve: $-5 \ \ \ -5$
$$3x \ = \ 9$$
$$x \ = \ 3$$

EXERCISE 4

Solve the equations.

1	$x + 2x + 3 = 18$	**2**	$3x + 3x + 4 = 40$	**3**	$4x + 3x - 4 = 52$
4	$5x - 3x + 4 = 44$	**5**	$10x - 6x - 3 = 33$	**6**	$6x + 4x + 5 = 80 + 5$
7	$10x - 2x = 60 + 4$	**8**	$10x + 2x - 8 = 40$	**9**	$10x - 8x - 1 = 5 + 2 + 3$
10	$2x + x + x - 6 = 10$	**11**	$12x - 7x - 30 = 10 - 5$		
12	$12x - 9x - 9 = 9$	**13**	$9x - 5x + 10 = 20 + 20$		
14	$9x = 63$	**15**	$20x - 13x + 14 = 70 - 7$		
16	$7x - 4x = 30 - 6$	**17**	$2x + 4x + 3 = 25 + 5$		
18	$5x + 2 + 3 = 30$	**19**	$3x + 3x + 3x + 3 = 8 + 40$		
20	$20x - 10x = 30 - 5$	**21**	$12x + 10 = 30 + 15 + 25$		
22	$4x + 4x + 4 = 70 - 2$	**23**	$10x + x + 1 = 100$		
24	$10x - 4x + x + 5 = 40$	**25**	$10x - 4x + 4 = 20 + 5$		
26	$18x - 9x + 6 = 50 + 10$	**27**	$8x - 2 = 30$		
28	$6x + 2x + 4x = 72$	**29**	$x + x + 15 + 5 = 40 + 9$		
30	$9x - x + x = 40 + 10 - 5$				

Brackets

The same rules apply if the equation includes brackets.

$$
\begin{aligned}
\text{Solve} \qquad\qquad 6(x + 3) &= 48 \\
\text{Expand brackets: } 6x + 18 &= 48 \\
-18 &\;\; -18 \\
\text{then} \qquad\qquad 6x &= 30 \\
x &= 5
\end{aligned}
$$

EXERCISE 1

Solve the equations.

1 $3(x + 5) = 21$ **2** $4(y - 2) = 12$ **3** $4(c - 1) = 10$

4 $6(x - 3) = 18$ **5** $3(x + 4) = 15$ **6** $4(x + 2) = 16$

7 $7(x - 6) = 14$ **8** $9(x - 1) = 27$ **9** $11(x - 8) = 33$

10 $2x + 3(x + 1) = 13$ **11** $3y + 2(y - 1) = 18$ **12** $5(a - 4) + 6 = 21$

13 $3c + 2(c - 1) = 13$ **14** $4f + 3(f + 2) = 48$ **15** $2(g + 3) + 3(g + 1) = 24$

16 $4(3a - 5) + 2(5a + 11) - 14a - 21 = 5$

EXERCISE 2

Find the solution to each problem, using an equation, or otherwise.

1 I think of a number, divide it by 3, and add 10. The result is 16. What was the original number?

2 Tom has a number of records. Azhar has 4 more than Tom, while Colin has 3 less than Tom. If they have 22 altogether, how many has Tom?

3 John has 12 more stamps than Susie. Jane has 15 more than Susie. Altogether they have 63 stamps. How many stamps has Susie?

4 Bill has 4 more sums wrong than Janet. Wayne has 2 more wrong than Bill. If they have 16 wrong altogether, how many did Janet get wrong?

5 A number is multiplied by 7. From the result, 2 is taken away and 4 added. If the final answer is 37, what was the number?

6 Peter has a number of books. Kashif has 3 more than Peter. Sadiah has 4 less than Kashif. If they have 29 books altogether, how many has Peter?

X THE GREAT UNKNOWN

Getting the order right

It is very important when using algebra that we do things in the right order. There are many other times when we need to things are done. Flow charts can be used to help us plan the order.

Crossing the road:

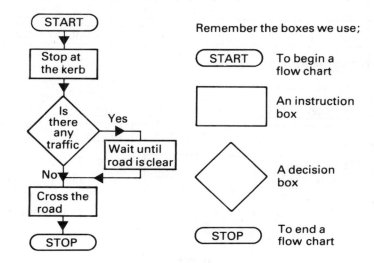

Remember the boxes we use;

| START | To begin a flow chart |

An instruction box

A decision box

| STOP | To end a flow chart |

EXERCISE 1

Work through these flow charts.

1

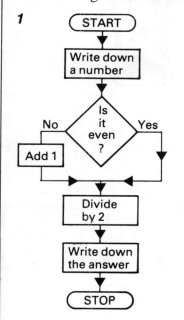

What does the flow chart do?

2

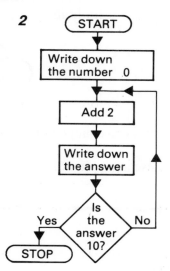

(*a*) What does the flow chart do?

(*b*) What happens if you change add 2 to add 3?

3

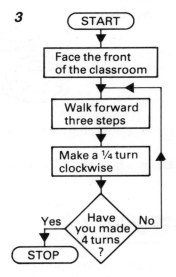

(*a*) What does the flow chart do?

(*b*) What happens if you change the decision box to:

Have you made 8 turns ?

EXERCISE 2

1 Arrange these instructions in a flow chart:

| Get out of bed | Put on shoes | Put on socks | Have a wash |

| Put on underwear | Put on shirt | Put on trousers | Go out |

| Have breakfast |

2 Arrange these instructions for taking a bath:

| Get in bath | Turn on taps | Get undressed | Put in plug | Get out |

| Pull out plug | Clean bath | Have wash | Get dressed |

3 Draw a flow chart to explain how to use the drinks machine.

INSERT COINS AND SELECT 2 x 10p

CHOCOLATE
WHITE COFFEE
BLACK COFFEE
TEA
SOUP

4 Draw a flow chart to explain how to use the petrol pump.

PRICE   LITRES   COST

TURN OFF ENGINES

5 Draw a flow chart for making a cup of tea.

6 Draw a flow chart for boiling eggs.

7 Draw a flow chart for a visit to the library to change library books.

8 Draw a flow chart to explain how to use a payphone.

START
↓
Write down 0
↓
Add 3
↓
Have you added 3 four times ?
No → / Yes ↓
Write down answer
↓
STOP

Investigation

Calculators and computers do multiplication and division by methods of addition and subtraction.

(a) For what multiplication sum is this flow chart used?

(b) Can you draw a flow chart for any other multiplication problem?

(c) Can you draw a flow chart which uses subtraction to do division problems?

Harder equations

It is not always necessary to use x as the unknown number.
For example,

$$8(2d - 3) = 3(4d - 7)$$

is a harder equation to solve, since it requires more steps to reach the solution.

First expand the brackets:

$$
\begin{aligned}
8(2d - 3) &= 3(4d - 7) \\
16d - 24 &= 12d - 21
\end{aligned}
$$

Move any letters to one side: $\quad -12d \qquad\qquad -12d$

to remove $12d$ from
this side

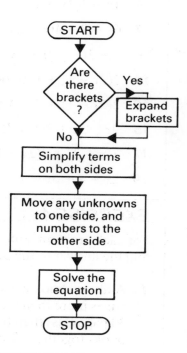

START

Are there brackets?   Yes

Expand brackets

No

Simplify terms on both sides

Move any unknowns to one side, and numbers to the other side

Solve the equation

STOP

Move any numbers to one side:
to remove the -24
from this side

$$
\begin{aligned}
4d - 24 &= -21 \\
+24 &\quad +24
\end{aligned}
$$

Solve the equation by dividing both sides
by 4 to cancel the 4 in front of the

$$4d = 3$$
$$\frac{4d}{4} = \frac{3}{4}$$
$$d = \frac{3}{4}$$

EXERCISE 1

1 $5x + 11 + 5x + 9 = 4x + 13 + 4x + 15$ **2** $5x + 2 - 4x = 6$

3 $12x - 7x + 2 = 7 + 2x$ **4** $9x + 6x - 2x - 7x = 14 + x + 11$

5 $15x - 10 + 2x - 4 = 7x - 10 + 6x$ **6** $7x + 2 + 3x + 12 = 4x + 3x + 12 + 11$

7 $8x + 3x - 6x + 11 = 6x + 17 - 4x$ **8** $12x - 36 = 8x - 12 - 6x + 6$

9 $7x + 6x - 2x - 5x = 17 + x + 8$ **10** $2x + 10 - 4x + 2x = 6x + 4 - 4x$

11 $8x - 24 - 6 + 2x = 2x + 4 - 25 + 5x$ **12** $6x - 5x + 30 = 2x + 10 + 5x - 20$

EXERCISE 2

1 $6(x - 3) = 18$ **2** $2(x + 5) = 10$ **3** $7(x - 6) = 14$

4 $9(x + 1) = 27$ **5** $3(x + 4) = 15$ **6** $3(2x + 5) = 27$

7 $2(3x - 2) = 20$ **8** $4(3x + 5) = 17x$ **9** $4(4x - 3) = 20$

10 $3(2x + 9) = 9x + 7$ **11** $3c = 2(c + 3)$ **12** $7(c + 1) = 5(c + 3)$

13 $5(a - 2) = 4(a - 1)$ **14** $5(x + 1) = 3(x + 3)$ **15** $7(2y + 3) = 5(2y + 9)$

16 $5(a + 5) = 3(4a + 7)$ **17** $4(3x - 4) = 11x - 3(x + 4)$

EXERCISE 3

1 $5(x + 2) = 3(2x - 5)$

2 $3(x + 4) = 5(x + 2) - 2$

3 $3x - 4(5 + x) = 7(5 - 2x) + 8$

4 $8(x - 3) - 3x = 3(x - 8) + 10$

5 $4x + 3(2x - 1) = 5(x - 1) + 2$

6 $5x + 3(x + 3) = 25$

7 $6x + 9 + 4(x - 2) = 51$

8 $5(3x - 1) + 2(x - 3) = 3(x - 7) + 10$

9 $5 + 2(x - 2) + 3x = 2(2x + 1)$

10 $15 + 5(x - 7) = x$

11 $2(2x + 1) + 10 = 6(3x - 5)$

12 $9(2x - 1) + 2(3x + 4) = 20x + 3$

13 $2(5x - 1) + 3 = 4(x - 3) + 16$

14 $3x + 3(x - 1) + 7 = 4x + 11$

15 $9x - 5x + 2(x - 7) = 17 - 2x + 5$

16 $6x + 2 - 5(x + 6) = 10$

17 $3(x + 2) + 4(2x + 1) = 6x + 20$

18 $2(4x - 5) = 3(x + 1) + 2$

19 $2x + 4 + 6x - x - 4 = 8x - 2 + 4x$

20 $4(x + 2) + 2(2x - 4) = 2(x + 3) + 10$

EXERCISE 4

For each problem write an equation, and solve it to find the answer to the problem.

For questions 6–12, find x.

1 A library book has x pages. Another has 125 pages more than the first, and a third book has 30 pages less than the first. Find x, if all three books together have 854 pages.

2 Thirty records are divided between Mark, Ann and Beejal. Ann has three times as many as Mark. Beejal has 6 records. How many records has Mark?

3 I have x £5 notes and twice as many £1 coins. Find the value of x, if I have £35 altogther.

4 Belinda is 3 years older than Kelly. Tania is 2 years younger than Kelly. All their ages together add up to 43 years. How old is Belinda?

5 I went for a walk today. Yesterday I spent twice as long walking. The day before I went for a walk which took 20 minutes longer than today's walk. Over the three days I have spent 3 hours walking. For how long did I walk today?

6

7

8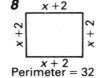
Perimeter = 32

9
Perimeter = 30

10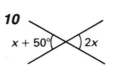

11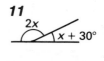

12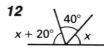

Revision exercise

Find the missing number.

1 $2 + \square = 10$ **2** $2 \times \square = 24$ **3** $4 \times \square + 4 = 36$ **4** $\square \div 4 = 28$

Solve these equations.

5 $x + 3 = 7$ **6** $x - 2 = 11$ **7** $14 - x = 9$

8 $19 = x - 3$ **9** $2x - 3 = 11$ **10** $3x + 4 = 16$

11 $2x + 1 = 3x - 5$ **12** $2\frac{1}{2} + 3x = 7$ **13** $20 - 2x = 8$

14 $5x + 1 = 26$ **15** $6x + 9 = 27$ **16** $10x - 2x - 8 + 2 = 38$

17 $2x + 6x + 4 = 34 + 34$ **18** $5x + 4 + 3 = 52$

19 $12x + 4x - 7x - 7 = 20 + 9$ **20** $4x - x + 3x - 4x + 4 = 8 + 4$

21 $3x + 15x - 9x = 63$ **22** $8x + 4 - 5x - 6 = 20 + 5$

23 $6(x + 3) = 39$ **24** $2(x + 4) = 14$

25 $2(2x - 7) = 4$ **26** $6(2x - 1) = 18$

27 $\frac{1}{2}(4x - 3) = 4\frac{1}{2}$ **28** $5(2x + 1) = 3(3x + 4)$

29 $8x + 2(x + 9) = 38$ **30** $7x + 8 = 2(3x + 5)$

31 $7 - x = x - 2$ **32** $2(3x + 7) - 3 = 20$

33 $6(2x + 3) + 9 = 9x + 30$ **34** $4(3x + 5) = 5(2x + 3)$

35 Paul has x toy cars. He buys 6 more, and then has twice as many. What is the value of x?

36 If the area is 35 cm^2, what is x?   **37** If the perimeter is 22 cm, what is x?

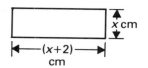

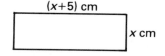

38 When I add 4 to a number I get the same result as halving the number and adding 10. What is the number?

39 Draw a flow chart to help you set up the timer on a video recorder to tape a film.

40 Draw a flow chart to show how you would go about cleaning a car.

19. TILES & TESSELLATIONS

LIZARDS

AFTER ✳
M.C. ESCHER

✳ **M.C. ESCHER** (1898-1972)

He was a Dutch artist. His skills are shown in his mastery of geometrical mathematics.

Tiles and tessellations

A tile or polygon will **tessellate** if several of them cover an area completely without any gaps.

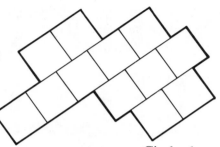

Squares tessellate.

Circles leave gaps.
So circles *do not* tessellate.

Investigation A — TILES

Investigate the polygons below to see if they tessellate. It will help to trace the shapes and cut them out of card so that you can draw round them.

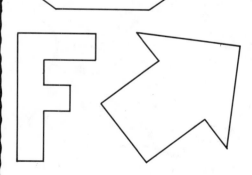

Investigation B — REGULAR POLYGONS

Do the regular polygons tessellate?
Try a *regular* (*a*) triangle (equilateral)
(*b*) quadrilateral (square)
(*c*) pentagon
(*d*) hexagon
(*e*) heptagon
(*f*) octagon

Investigation C — MAKING TILES

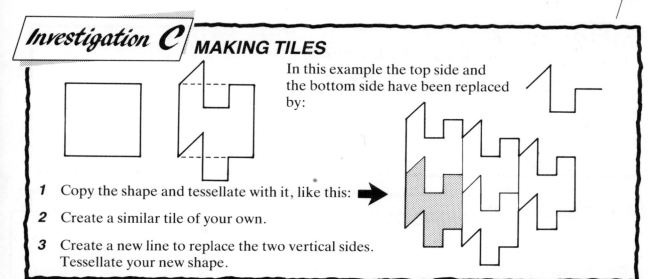

In this example the top side and the bottom side have been replaced by:

1 Copy the shape and tessellate with it, like this: ➡

2 Create a similar tile of your own.

3 Create a new line to replace the two vertical sides. Tessellate your new shape.

Investigation D — HEXAFACES

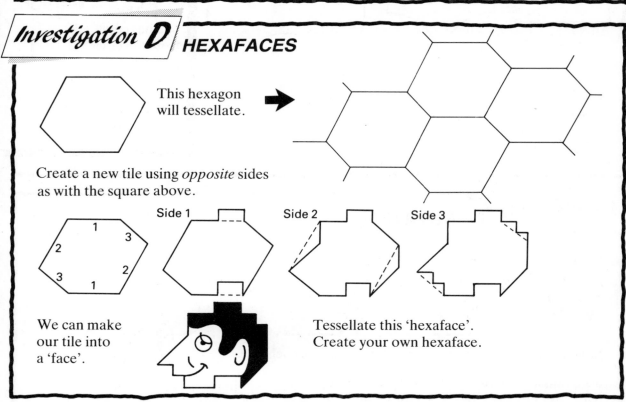

This hexagon will tessellate. ➡

Create a new tile using *opposite* sides as with the square above.

Side 1   Side 2   Side 3

We can make our tile into a 'face'.

Tessellate this 'hexaface'. Create your own hexaface.

PROBLEM

Find (*a*) an octagon (*b*) a nonagon (9-sided) which will tessellate.

Investigation E SQUARE-CURVES

A square
can become:

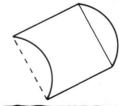

Show that this shape
will tessellate.
Create your own
'square-curve' tile.

Investigation F MORE CURVES

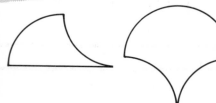

Note: This
one has come
from the circle
pattern at the
start of the chapter.
Can you see how?
Can you find another
tile from the same pattern?

Check that these
will tessellate.
Design your own tile.

Investigation G ROTATING

Some shapes will only tessellate if they are *rotated*.

  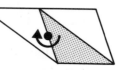 

Note: the triangle is rotated around the centre of each side.

(*a*) Is there a triangle which will not tessellate?
(*b*) Draw and tessellate a re-entrant quadrilateral like the one shown.
(*c*) Is there a quadrilateral which will not tessellate?
(*d*) Replace the longest side on the triangle above by:

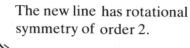

The new line has rotational
symmetry of order 2.

Tessellate the new shape.

EXERCISE

1 Determine whether the tiles in these tessellations have been translated, rotated, or translated and rotated.

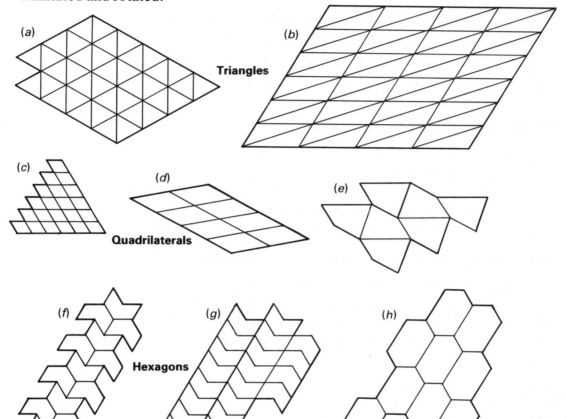

(a)

(b) **Triangles**

(c)

(d) **Quadrilaterals**

(e)

(f)

(g) **Hexagons**

(h)

2 Show how these shapes will tessellate (make a copy of each one):

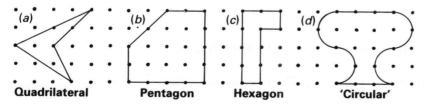

(a) **Quadrilateral**

(b) **Pentagon**

(c) **Hexagon**

(d) **'Circular'**

3 Some shapes leave gaps, so do not tessellate by themselves.

(a) Show how an octagon and a square might tessellate together.

(b) Find two other shapes which tessellate together.

Revision exercise

1 Show how each of these shapes will tessellate.

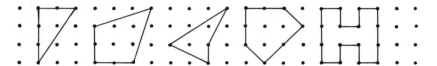

2 Which of these shapes will *not* tessellate.

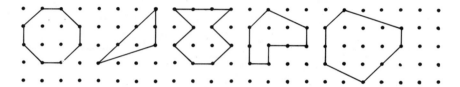

3 Find which regular shapes make up these tessellating tiles.

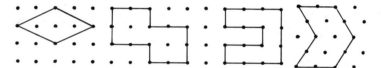

Tessellate each tile above.

4 Find *two* ways of tessellating this shape.

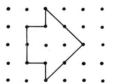

5 Find another tile which will tessellate in more ways than one.

6 Show how these two regular polygons will tessellate together.

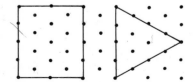